DATE DUE

COPYRIGHT DURATION:

Duration, Term Extension, The European Union and the Making of Copyright Policy

Robert L. Bard
Lewis Kurlantzick

COPYRIGHT DURATION:

Duration, Term Extension, The European Union and the Making of Copyright Policy

Robert L. Bard
Lewis Kurlantzick

Austin & Winfield, Publishers
San Francisco - London - Bethesda
1999

Library of Congress Cataloging-in-Publication Data

Bard, Robert L.
    Copyright duration/ Robert L. Bard. Lewis Kurlantzick.
      p. cm.
    Includes bibliographical references and index.
    ISBN 1-57292-131-5 (cloth : alk. paper).
    1. Copyright—Duration—United States. I. Kurlantzick. Lewis S., 1944
    II. Title
KF3010.B37   1999
 346.7304'82---dc21
                                  99-12060
                                      CIP

Editorial Inquiries:
Austin & Winfield, Publishers
7831 Woodmont Avenue, #345
Bethesda, MD 20814
(301) 654-7335
Website: www.interscholars.com
To Order: (800) 99-AUSTIN

For Ann and Jared
and for Rachel, Joshua, and Roberta

Table of Contents

Acknowledgements

We wish to thank Immanuel Wexler, Department of Economics, University of Connecticut, and Willajeanne McLean, School of Law, University of Connecticut, for their comments on drafts of the book. We are grateful to Dean Hugh Macgill for summer research support and to Janet Jendrzejewski for steadfast secretarial aid. For research assistance we also acknowledge the contributions of Patrick Cooney, Sarah Cox, Erin Galvin, Alan Giacomi, Andrea Joseph, Kevin Kuzia, Jonathan Lewis, Veronica Lee, Jacqueline Pennino, and Michael Tamarin

Chapter I. Introduction

In October 1993 the Council of the European Union issued a Directive establishing a uniform term of copyright protection among the Member States.[1] By July 1995 the laws of all EU countries were to provide copyright protection for the life of the author plus seventy years. For most EU countries this change represented a twenty year extension of their current copyright periods. This development prompted proposals that the United States amend its Copyright Act to extend the existing duration from life plus fifty years to match the European term.[1] Bills were introduced in both the House and the Senate to achieve this objective, and in 1998 the goal was accomplished with the enactment of the Copyright Term Extension Act.[2] This legislation received support not only from interested trade associations, in particular the American music and movie industries,[3] but also from some academic commentators.[4] The prime argument offered for the change was that in order for American copyright producers to receive the benefit of the extended European term the United States must match that term of protection; because the European countries need not apply the new, longer term to works originating in countries which provide a shorter protective term, American authors and publishers would not receive the advantages of extended protection abroad unless Congress increased the term in the United States to life plus seventy for European products. Some United States film and music producers, for example, might not enjoy the possibility of an additional twenty years of European royalties. Advocates of the change stressed the gains to American business, the desirable impact of enhanced foreign revenues on the United States trade balance, and the costlessness of extension. Perhaps not surprisingly, they presented the legislation as an opportunity to earn more revenue at the expense of foreigners, thereby gaining something for nothing.

The amendment of our law, however, is misguided, and the various justifications offered in support of change are deeply flawed. In asserting that the change would be virtually costless, the supporters ignore or understate the costs of copyright protection to American consumers, including its more subtle costs, and the fact that some of these costs increase as the term lengthens. In addition, they misstate the incidence of the burdens the change will produce. While American producers will benefit and some of their additional revenues will come from European consumers, the major burden will be borne by American consumers and users of intellectual and artistic products.

Moreover, the supporters of term extension take an exceedingly narrow view of the benefits which accompany expiration of copyright and the placement of a work in the public domain,[6] where it is free to be consumed by all or used, without inhibition, as a creative building block by other authors. To limit the ability of authors to make use of prior works by requiring them to seek permission or to subject their creative plans to the censorial veto of heirs of the original author is to unduly impede the initiation and execution of some intellectual and artistic works. That diminution in creative output due to copyright expense constitutes a serious cultural loss. Thus, it is socially desirable that, after some period of time sufficiently long to guarantee a reasonable return to the original producer of intellectual property, those planning a film of "Washington Square" not be shackled by the need to obtain the permission of the heirs of Henry James and the contemporary novelist looking to rework "Wuthering Heights" be free of any need to answer to Emily Bronte's assigns. And "Kiss Me Kate", Cole Porter's musical retelling of Shakespeare's "Taming of the Shrew" which takes great liberties with the text in setting it to music, represents but one example of the fact that imitation, borrowing, and copying are an inevitable part of creating informational and imaginative works, and the public domain constitutes the raw materials from which these activities draw.

In addition, predictions of the consequences of term expiration by proponents of change are empirically unsound and ignore microeconomic theory.[7] The assertions that termination of protection will neither reduce the price nor expand the availability of intellectual and artistic works can not be supported either factually or theoretically. (Some of their projections also misunderstand the meaning of inflation and its impact on investment decision-making.) To the extent they raise concerns which may be legitimate, for example about the quality of reproductions of public domain works, these concerns can be met without recourse to an extension of the term of protection; such a response, in fact, constitutes massive overkill. Finally, neither the value of international uniformity *per se*, *i.e.*, the interest in harmonization of copyright law independent of any particular length of term, nor predicted improvement in the United States' balance of payments justifies the change.

In the formation of copyright policy, the lack of empirical data and the inability to quantify important variables and to exactly calculate benefits and costs preclude precise evaluation of the impact of any significant changes in the degree of copyright protection. Though this imprecision renders it impossible to identify a single, obviously correct term of protection, it is possible, in addressing the issue of duration, to talk meaningfully about more or less protection. But the advocates of a major increase in the term have made no serious attempt to prove that the prior level of protection failed to provide sufficient incentives in terms of an optimum level of creation and dissemination of intellectual and artistic products. Rather they have limited the focus of their arguments to collateral benefits, such as the balance of payments, and to brazen misrepresentations that the change will be costless.

In this book we analyze the economic, equitable, and political considerations which bear on the wisdom of expansion of copyright protection. Though the issue of length of protection has important analytical aspects specific to it, it also provides a lens through which to view the more general question of the factors that should be brought to bear in the determination of an appropriate level of protection that meets the conflicting demands of producers and consumers. We will discuss the question of an increased term, then, both for its own sake and to contribute to the effort to provide a sound intellectual and public policy framework for analyzing copyright issues. This objective is particularly important because of the deep defects in the terms of public debate regarding copyright policy. These deficiencies are both analytical and political, and the two sets of defects interact, reinforcing each other. The analytical errors arise most often from a failure to grasp the peculiar economic characteristics of most intellectual and artistic goods and the corresponding core economic problem to which copyright is a response. The political problem lies in a legislative process which normally does not pay sufficient attention to these economic touchstones and the social interests served by limitations on copyright protection. That process is dominated by producers' interests with the inevitable consequence that the broader societal interests in limiting copyright protection are largely ignored.

Notes

1. *See, e.g.*, David Nimmer, *U.S. Should Extend Copyright Terms*, Billboard, April 16 1994, at 8.

2. Pub. L. No. 105-298, 112 Stat. 2827 (1998) (Sonny Bono Copyright Term Extension Act); S. 505, 105th Cong., 1st Sess. (1997); H.R. 604, 105th Cong., 1st Sess. (1997) (Copyright Term Extension Act of 1997); H.R. 989, 104th Cong., 1st Sess. (1995); S. 483, 104th Cong., 1st Sess. (1995) (Copyright Term Extension Act of 1995).

3. *See, e.g.*, Joint Comments of the Coalition of Creators and Copyright Owners, In the Matter of Duration of Copyright Term of Protection, Docket No. RM 93-8, September 22, 1993.

4. The most notable academic supporter is Professor Arthur Miller. *See* Arthur Miller, *Extending Copyrights Preserves U.S. Culture*, Billboard, January 14, 1995, at 4, reprinted in 141 Cong. Rec. S3394 (daily ed. March 2, 1995) (printed at request of Senator Feinstein, co-sponsor of S. 483, The Copyright Term Extension Act of 1995).

5. The "public domain" refers to the domain of unprotected works, which are freely available to any member of the public for unrestricted and uncompensated use.

6. The conflict with microeconomics is manifest in the failure to credit the value of efficiency, of production of desired goods at the lowest possible cost. *See* text at notes 118-130, 300-01, *infra*.

Chapter II. Legal Background

The history of copyright duration in the United States has been one of an ever-lengthening term of protection. With each comprehensive revision of the federal law, the term has increased.

The Statute of Anne of 1709[8]6 was the first modern copyright statute in Anglo-American law, and it served as a model for subsequent American legislation. The enactment located the origin of literary property in composition[9] and created a two term system of copyright duration. It provided protection for an original fourteen year term dating from publication and an optional fourteen year renewal term beginning upon expiration of the first fourteen years.[10] Our first federal[11] statute, enacted in 1790 soon after the ratification of the Constitution, adopted a similar scheme, recognizing an original term of fourteen years from the date of publication plus a second term of fourteen years if the author was living at the expiration of the first term.[12] In 1831 Congress extended the original term to twenty-eight years, producing a total possible period of protection of forty-two years.[13] In 1909 the renewal term was increased to twenty-eight years.[14] Thus, before the Copyright Revision Act of 1976 was enacted,[15] the scheme in place accorded protection for a period of twenty-eight years from publication with an additional twenty-eight year period in the event of proper renewal,[16] producing a maximum term of fifty-six years. The Revision Act dramatically departed from this traditional bifurcated scheme,[17] which had accorded protection for a fixed number of years. Instead the basic term of copyright protection was changed to the life of the author plus fifty years.[18]

At the time of passage of the 1976 Act, a large majority of countries, especially those countries where American works had a substantial market, afforded protection for that same life plus fifty term. The European Council Directive[19], then, altered this pattern of international uniformity, and put the Community at odds with the United States law. In the situation of a work whose country of origin is "a third country" and whose author is not a European Union national, for example a song by an American composer published in the United States, the Council Directive calls for application of "comparison of terms of protection".[20] This comparison of terms, in practice, yields what is known as the "rule of the lesser term" with the result that the American composer would have been protected in Europe for the shorter of the American and European terms, life plus fifty rather than life plus seventy.[21]

The Directive does provide, though, that its durational provisions are subject to the Members' international obligations, and that comparison of terms should not result in Member States being brought into conflict with those obligations.[22] The question, then, is posed as to whether a failure to apply the longer term to an American composer would have been inconsistent with the Berne Union, to which the United States and all countries of the European Union are parties. As a general principle the Berne Convention, the oldest and most comprehensive international copyright agreement, calls for national treatment--nationals from other Convention states are to be treated in the same way as a state's own nationals; no discrimination is allowed between foreign and domestic works. However, the treatment of duration under the Convention is complicated, and in the case of our American composer departs from the national treatment principle. The Convention grants a term of protection of life of the author plus fifty years.[23] This requirement constitutes a minimum period of protection. Member countries may choose to provide a longer term.[24] However, if a Member does accord longer protection and a foreign national claims the benefit of that greater protection,[25] the Convention explicitly states that the principle of comparison of terms or reciprocity applies rather than the general conventional principle of national treatment.[26] Under reciprocity a country treats a foreign national in the same fashion that its nationals are treated in the foreign country. Thus, EU nations, though Berne members, are free to condition extra-EU extension of the longer, life plus seventy term on demonstration of reciprocal protection by non-EU nations. The Convention does leave it open to generous countries to apply national treatment if they desire to do so, but the tone and language of the Council Directive evince no such generosity. The upshot is that, in the absence of term extension in the United States, the American composer would not receive the benefit of the additional twenty years in Europe, and that result would not violate the Berne Convention undertakings of the European countries.[27]

Notes

---

8. 8 Anne, c. 19 (1709).

9. The Statute of Anne, thus, was not only a signal occasion in legal history, but also an important event in the process by which the ideas of authorship and literary property were conceived and formulated. The institution of copyright law ratified the modern (re) definition of a literary work under which authors consider their works as a kind of property. It is, after all, not obvious that a single person should "own" a story. *See generally* John Brewer and Susan Staves, *Introduction, in* Early Modern Conceptions of Property 8-10 (John Brewer & Susan Staves eds., 1995) ("Literary property"). For a succinct account of the evolution and revision of the idea of "authorship" over the past three centuries, see James Boyle, Shamans, Software, and Spleens 51-60 (1996) ("Copyright and the Invention of Authorship").

For an instructive comparison that offers an historical account of the evolution of Chinese attitudes, which downplayed the idea of individual creation, the basis both for modern Western notions of authorship and for protection of intellectual property, see William Alford, To Steal a Book Is an Elegant Offense: Intellectual Property Law in Chinese Civilization (1995). In the lengthy period prior to contact with the West, China never developed an indigenous counterpart to intellectual property law.

10. 8 Anne, c. 19 (1709). The choice of fourteen years did not reflect a parliamentary judgment about the amount of economic incentive which had to be provided to induce the creation and dissemination of a socially desirable level of literary works. Rather the idea of a term measured in multiples of fourteen years was a vestige of the time when privileges were awarded as a means of encouraging printers. Fourteen years was just long enough to train two sets of apprentices in the new printing art. Herman Finkelstein, *The Copyright Law--A Reappraisal*, 104 U.

Pa. L. Rev. 1025, 1033-35, 1042 (1956). *See* Bruce W. Bugbee, Genesis of American Patent and Copyright Law 34 (1967); *see also* Economic Council of Canada, Report on Intellectual and Industrial Property, 73-74 (1971). For the suggestion of a related possibility as to the source of this chosen number of years, see Saul Cohen, *Duration*, 24 UCLA L. Rev. 1180, 1193 (1977) (multiples of common seven year term for grant of printing patent).

11. Prior to the federal legislation, the individual states had enacted copyright laws. After the American Revolution the Continental Congress recommended to the states that they each enact laws to protect authors and publishers. Under the Articles of Confederation all the states but Delaware had laws in place at the time of the first federal law, and the statutes all contained express term limits. Among these, seven accorded terms of fourteen years plus a renewal of fourteen years, and the others provided protection for a single term with periods ranging from fourteen to twenty-one years. *See* Copyright Office, Copyright Enactments 1-21 (Bull. No. 3 1973).

12. Act of May 31, 1790, ch. 15, 1 Stat. 124 (1790).

13. Act of February 3, 1931, ch. 16, sec. 1, 4 Stat. 436 (1831).

14. Act of March 4, 1909, ch. 320, sec. 23, 35 Stat. 1075 (1909). Under the 1909 Act the general rule was that copyright attached upon publication of a work with proper copyright notice. For certain limited classes of works, *e.g.*, a motion picture, protection could attach, and the term of protection commence, prior to publication, upon registration of a claim to copyright in the work prior to its publication.

15. Congressional attempts to alter the term of copyright protection between 1909 and 1976, and the reasons offered in support of and opposition to these proposals, are summarized in James J. Guinan, Duration of Copyright 9-19 (Copyright Office, General Revision of the Copyright Law Study No. 3, 1957); Cohen, *supra* note 10, at 1200-01.

12

16. If the copyright was not renewed before the expiration of the original term, protection would expire and the work would pass into the public domain.

17. The advantages and disadvantages of such a departure, *i.e.*, adoption of a life plus number of years term, are summarized in Guinan, *supra* note 15, at 24-25, 28.

18. 17 U.S.C. sec. 302(a) (1994). Thus, under the Revision Act for most works created on or after January 1, 1978, the term of copyright commenced with the work's creation and terminated fifty years after the death of the work's author. The Copyright Office estimated that protection of works for this new period of life plus fifty would result, on average, in a term of protection of seventy-six years. *See* Copyright Law Revision, Report of the Register of Copyrights on the General Revision of the U.S. Copyright Law, 87th Cong., 1st Sess. 50-51 (House Judiciary Comm. Print 1961). *But see* Guinan, *supra* note 15, at 28 (life plus fifty years, on average, will produce a term of more than seventy-six to eighty-six years). For the author who lives more than six years after a work's creation, the new arrangement provided lengthier protection than the 1909 Act's twenty-eight plus twenty-eight year scheme. If one compares a protective period of seventy-five years to that of fifty-six years, the result of the Revision Act's significant change of the length and structure of the copyright term was a 34 percent increase in the period of protection. Moreover, these numbers mean that a term of life plus seventy will often fix in place proprietary barriers to public access for a century or more.

The 1976 law, like its predecessors, contained specific durational provisions treating joint works, works made for hire, anonymous and pseudonymous works, as well as works created prior to January 1, 1978, the effective date of the Act, and works which were unpublished at that time. For example, in the case of a pseudonymous work, where uncertainty about date of death makes a term of fifty years after the death of the author speculative, protection endured for seventy-five years from the date of first publication or 100 years from creation, whichever expired first. 17 U.S.C. sec. 302(c) (1989); *see* H.R. Rep. No. 94-1476, 94th Cong., 2d Sess.

138 (1976) (this term intended to approximate an author's life plus fifty years). The details of this treatment do not bear on the core issue(s) we are addressing. Therefore we do not offer any in depth examination of these provisions or their ambiguities. Those which do bear on our basic analysis are addressed periodically throughout the book. *See, e.g.*, text at notes 185-88, 241-42 *infra* (works for hire).

In addition to changing the basic term, the 1976 Act made two other major changes in the nature of copyright duration. The separation of protection into two separate and consecutive terms was eliminated, and the structure of distinct original and renewal terms was replaced with a single unified term of protection. And, for most works, the point at which protection attached was changed, with fixation of the work in tangible form replacing publication and registration as the point of attachment.

At the time of passage of the 1976 Act, a large majority of countries, especially those countries where American works had a substantial market, afforded protection for a life plus fifty term.

19. This change was, in large part, a response to the *Patricia* case. That case involved a sound recording which enjoyed copyright protection in Germany but was out of copyright in Denmark. Copies were lawfully on the market in Denmark because the work was in the public domain there. The question presented was whether the importation of copies lawfully circulating in Denmark into Germany, where the work was still in copyright, could be prevented. The European Court of Justice answered the question affirmatively. The copyright in Germany, it held, could be enforced, and application of the national legislation was not precluded by the provisions of the EEC Treaty designed to insure the free movement of goods across borders. Case 341/87, EMI Electrola GmbH v. Patricia Im-Und Export, 1989 E.C.R. 79, 2 C.M.L.R. 413 (1989); *see also* Ysolde Gendreau, *An Intellectual Property Renaissance in European Community Law*, in International Trade and Intellectual Property: The Search for a Balanced System 41 (George R. Stewart et al.

eds., 1994) (historical context of *Patricia* case re conflict between national intellectual property rights and principle of free trade). The behavior at issue in *Patricia* is an example of so-called "parallel importation" or "gray marketing", the marketing of goods by importation through channels separate from the exclusive distribution channels authorized by the copyright (or trademark) holder for a particular jurisdiction. For an instance of this behavior and its legal status in an American setting, see Quality King Distributors, Inc. v. L'anza Research Int'l, Inc., 118 S. Ct. 1125 (1998). For a critical examination of the European Term Directive's history, justifications, and consequences, see W.R. Cornish, *Intellectual Property, in* 13 Yearbook Eur. L. 485 (1993).

The term enactment is part of a larger set of directives designed to harmonize copyright law within the European Union. Five directives have been adopted. *See* Council Directive 91/250, 1991 O.J. (L122) 42 (legal protection of computer programs); Council Directive 92/100, 1992 O.J. (L346) 61 (rental right and lending right and on certain rights related to copyright); Council Directive 93/83, 1993 O.J. (L248) 15 (coordination of certain rules concerning copyright and neighboring rights applicable to satellite broadcasting and cable retransmission); Council Directive 96/9, 1996 O.J. (L77) 20 (legal protection of electronic databases). For an informative summary of the contents and purposes of most of these directives, see Kevin Garnett et al., Copinger and Skone James on Copyright 9-17 (13th ed. Supp. 1994). There are at least two more directives, dealing with home audio and videorecording, and moral rights, at different stages of elaboration. Ysolde Gendreau, *Copyright Harmonisation in the European Union and in North America*, 10 Eur. Intell. Prop. Rev. 488 & nn. 6-7 (1995); Karl Ruping, *Copyright and an Integrated European Market: Conflicts with Free Movement of Goods, Competition Law, and National Discrimination*, 11 Temple Int'l & Comp. L.J. 1, 4 n.29 (1997).

20. *See* Directive at par. 22; art. 7(1). It has been suggested, though not forcefully, that the directive's provision for comparison of terms and limitation of benefits may

run afoul of article 4, the most-favored-nation clause, of the TRIPS Agreement, to which both the European countries and the United States have subscribed. *See Hearings on H.R. 989 Before the Subcomm. on Courts and Intellectual Property of the House Judiciary Comm.*, 104th Cong., 1st Sess. 355-56, 375-81 (1996) [hereinafter *House Hearings*]; J.H. Reichman, *Universal Minimum Standards of Intellectual Property Protection Under the TRIPS Component of the WTO Agreement*, 25 Int'l Law. 345 (1995).

21. *See* Directive at art. 7(1) ("Where the country of origin of a work...is a third country, and the author of the work is not a Community national, the term of protection granted by the Member States shall expire on the date of expiry of the protection granted in the country of origin...."); David Bradshaw, *The EC Copyright Directive: Its Main Highlights and Some of its Ramifications for Businesses in the UK Entertainment Industry*, 5 Ent. L. Rev. 171, 175 (1995).

22. *See* Directive at par. 24; art. 7(3).

23. *See* Berne Convention for the Protection of Literary and Artistic Works, art. 7(1) (Paris Revision 1971) [hereinafter Berne Convention].

24. *See id.* art. 7(6).

25. *See id.* art. 19.

26. *See id.* art. 7(8) ("[T]he term shall be governed by the legislation of the country whose protection is claimed; however, unless the legislation of that country otherwise provides, the term shall not exceed the term fixed in the country of origin of the work."); Sam Ricketson, The Berne Convention for the Protection of Literary and Artistic Works: 1886-1986 334-36, 350-51 (1987).

27. *See generally, National Treatment Under Berne Is Subject Of House Panel Hearing*, 46 Pat. Trademark & Copyright J. (BNA), at 116 (June 3, 1993); Paul

Edward Geller, *New Dynamics in International Copyright*, 16 Colum.-VLA J.L. & Arts 461, 465-66 (1992); Jane C. Ginsburg, *Reforms and Innovations Regarding Authors' and Performers' Rights in France: Commentary on the Law of July 3, 1985*, 10 Colum.-VLA J.L. & Arts 83, 111-12 (1985). Though the application of reciprocity by EU countries does not violate their Berne Convention obligations, the Directive's exception for existing treaty commitments has significant practical bite with respect to one of the most important European countries, Germany. Germany is bound by an existing bilateral agreement with the United States which commits it to national treatment. As a result American works are protected there for the full life plus seventy term regardless of whether term extension legislation was enacted in the United States. *See* note 281, *infra*. This provision significantly limits whatever negative effects might follow from an American decision against term extension.

Issued on October 29, 1993, the directive set out to make uniform the term of protection of copyright and certain related rights. Copyright in literary, dramatic, musical and artistic works will last for the life of the author and a further period of seventy (70) years calculated from January 1 of the year following his or her death. *Id.* at art. 1(1), 8. Protection for performances and phonograms, so called "related rights", will be fifty (50) years from creation or some other relevant date, such as publication. *Id.* at art. 3. Additional provisions of the directive deal specifically with the treatment of joint, anonymous, pseudonymous, and corporate works. *Id.* at art. 1(2-6).

The term chosen for uniform adoption, that of life plus seventy, was in force only in Germany and represented the longest duration provided by any Member State. Most European states accorded protection for life plus fifty years. This widely accepted term is often referred to as 50 years *pma* (*post mortem auctoris*).

The directive is not self-executing; it must be effectuated by domestic legislation in each member country. While the directive called for implementation by July 1, 1995, the historical pattern with prior directives suggests that it is likely that many member countries will take years after the 1995 date to actually effect implementation. And some Member States have, in fact, been slow to implement this directive. The United Kingdom, for example, did not have implementing legislation and regulations in force until January 1996. *See* Duration of Copyright and Rights in Performances Regulations 1995 sec. 1(1), (S.I. 1995 No. 3297); John N. Adams & Michael Edenborough, *The Duration of Copyright in the United Kingdom after the 1995 Regulations*, 11 Eur. Intell. Prop. Rev. 590 (1996); Lisa M. Brownlee, *Recent Changes in the Duration of Copyright in the United States and European Union: Procedure and Policy*, 6 Fordham Intell. Prop., Media & Ent. L.J. 579, 616 (1996).

Chapter III. The Problem(s) To Which Copyright Is A Response

The Constitution authorizes Congress "to Promote the Progress of Science and useful Arts, by securing for limited Times to Authors and Inventors the exclusive Right to their respective Writings and Discoveries."[28] Copyright, thus, is instrumental.[29] Aimed at the promotion of culture and learning, the formulation of copyright policy is designed to encourage the widest possible creation and dissemination of original works of art and the intellect. And copyright law assumes that, in the absence of public subsidy, authors and publishers[30] will not invest sufficient resources in creating and publishing original works--with the resultant social loss of the desired quality and quantity of works--unless they are promised rights that will permit them to control and profit from their works' commercial distribution.[31]

The economic justification case for legal intervention that would promise these rights lies in two related unusual (but not unique) characteristics of the process of production and dissemination of intellectual and artistic goods: 1) the peculiar cost structure of most such goods; and 2) the intangible, indivisible character of literary, musical, and artistic creations. The cost structure refers to the cost disadvantage that an original producer faces *vis a vis* later duplicators; more precisely, the initial producer incurs a significant, fixed cost that the duplicator avoids. In the case of a sound recording, for example, it would be the large cost of creating the master studio tape.[32] In the case of a book, it would include the costs of discovering and editing the author's work, of type composition, and of designing plates for printing.[33] Since the duplicator enjoys this substantial cost advantage[34] (and since there is no bar to a buyer becoming a rival to the original producer), he can usually undercut the original producer. Indeed, in a competitive setting price will move towards marginal cost, a result which is usually deemed socially beneficial as it promotes the efficiency value of production at the lowest possible cost. The P=MC scenario here, though, yields a problem for the initial producer in that most likely he will not be able to recover his initial sunk costs.[35] Unless the benefit of lead time,[36] *i.e.*, being first on the market with the product,[37] or other countervailing advantages[38] offset the duplicator's cost superiority[39] or unless there are alternative ways to appropriate the value of the work[40] other than direct sales to consumers[41] (or to prevent reproduction technologically)[42], authors and publishers, faced with this prospect of unrestricted duplication and price reduction, will limit or eliminate their investment in the creation and dissemination of intellectual and artistic works.[43] Because their expectation is that they can not easily recover enough money through market transactions to justify the expense of producing their works (or foregoing other profitable uses of their time and talent), the suboptimal result will be "too little" creative activity; original forms of expression will be underproduced and underdisseminated.[44]

The other signal, awkward property of intellectual and artistic works which differentiates them from standard goods is their indivisible, intangible character. Unlike the situation with tangible resources, once an intellectual creation comes into existence, an unlimited number of consumers can use the creation without depleting it; the good can be multiplied without accompanying decrease in size or quality.[45] It can be reproduced to the extent desired and can be usefully employed everywhere without causing deficiencies elsewhere.[46] This inexhaustible, "public goods" aspect[47] of such intangibles means that once a creation such as a musical performance has been produced, its use may benefit innumerable users without imposing any additional production cost on the producer.[48] The social benefits of indivisibility are clear and dramatic; access to intellectual and artistic works, with potential spillover effects, is facilitated, as reproduction and dissemination can be achieved at little or no additional cost.[49] These benefits must be kept in mind when confronting the question of whether there is a need for legal intervention to protect intellectual works, and in what form and detail, particularly as some of the arguments for creation and enforcement of property rights in tangible resources will be seen not to apply.

Due to its material properties, a tangible item is always the embodiment of a scarce resource. Most consumer goods, for example furniture or food, are tangible. Accordingly, a producer of these goods can rely on property protection in the tangible good to guarantee his investment in its production. His physical control and these property rights permit him to prevent people from consuming the goods without paying for them. As previously implied, intangible intellectual creations, in contrast, are characterized by difficulty of exclusion. It is costly to prevent non-paying beneficiaries ("free riders") from consuming the good. Thus, because it costs relatively little to replicate and transmit intellectual works, it is hard for one who has devoted resources to their production to appropriate their value through their sale.[50]

These differences between tangible and intangible resources indicate that one of the powerful arguments for the recognition of property rights in tangibles has no force with respect to intangible creations. Only one person or a limited number of people can use a tangible item, whether a pencil, chair or automobile, at any one time.[51] In order to prevent confusion, congestion, and strife, we therefore need some social mechanism to authoritatively allocate the resource, *i.e.*, to determine who may use the resource at any particular time.[52] However, since an indeterminate number of people may simultaneously make use of an intellectual or artistic creation, the "congestion externality" argument for creation of property rights has no application here.[53]

The case for legal protection of intellectual and artistic creations, then, rests principally on an economic incentive argument. That argument, which predicts suboptimal production and dissemination of new information with commercial or

22

artistic usefulness in the absence of protection, is rooted in the significant cost advantage enjoyed by duplicators and the peculiar public good characteristics of such works.[54] The argument itself, though, points to an important internal tension. The grant of protection creates an incentive for the creation (and distribution) of intellectual and artistic works by providing producers with the right to charge consumers for access to the work and thereby recover their investment. But if the rights established are too extensive, *i.e.*, greater than necessary to secure the desired quantity and quality of works, the outcome will be the imposition of costs on users without any compensating social benefits. Monopolists, after all, tend to discourage use of a good by overpricing it; as a result, some consumers will be unable to enjoy the work, leaving them worse off than they would have been in the absence of the legal protection.[55] On the other hand, if the rights established are too stingy, *i.e.*, less than necessary to support the investment, the result will be freer access by users but to a less than socially desirable number and quality of works.[56] As Professors Cooter and Ulen have succinctly framed the dilemma, "[W]ithout a legal monopoly not enough [intellectual and artistic works]...will be produced but with the legal monopoly too little of the [works]...will be used."[57]

The answer given by intellectual property law systems to the problems inherent in the commercial exploitation of intangible creations is to provide qualified creators with temporary grants of exclusive property rights.[58] The copyright monopoly, which prohibits unauthorized duplication[59], gives the proprietor the right to institute an action against nonpaying beneficiaries of the work[60] and therefore reduces the public goods problem involved with original intellectual and artistic creations.[61] Copyright, though,--perhaps inevitably--is an imperfect response,[62] as it must struggle with the tension[63] between its conflicting static (access) and dynamic (incentive) economic objectives.[64] Congress (and the federal courts) have pursued a desirable balance between these objectives by seeking a careful definition of the scope of protection.[65] Thus, the set of exclusive rights granted to copyright proprietors[66] to control reproduction and dissemination is subject to a series of specific[67] and general[68] statutory limitations and exemptions[69] as well as important judge-made limiting doctrines.[70] In setting the parameters of these rights, the term of protection is a key component of the overall design.[71] It is a central element in the delicate balance struck between the inducements that authors and publishers require to produce and distribute original works[72] and the latitude that they and others require to draw on earlier copyrighted works in their own productive and educational efforts.

24

Notes

28. U.S. Const. art. I, sec. 8, cl. 8.

29. Report of the Register of Copyrights on the General Revision of the United States Copyright Law, House Comm. on the Judiciary, 87th Cong., 1st Sess. 5 (Comm. Print 1961) (grant of exclusive rights for limited time is means to end of fostering growth of learning and culture for the public welfare).

> The point is not merely that the individual rights of authors must be *balanced* against the social good. The Constitution stipulates that authors' rights are created to serve the social good, so any balancing must be done *within* the overall context of the public good, i.e. between the specific aspect of the public good that is served by intellectual property ("the Progress of Science and useful Arts") and other aspects of the public good such as the progressive effects of the free circulation of ideas.

Jeremy Waldron, *From Authors to Copiers: Individual Rights and Social Values in Intellectual Property*, 68 Chi.-Kent L. Rev. 841, 848-49 (1993). *See* Tom G. Palmer, *Intellectual Property: A Non-Posnerian Law and Economics Approach*, 12 Hamline L. Rev. 261, 270 (1989)("As was made clear with the passage of the first Copyright Act,...the statutory rights granted involved no claim of *natural rights* by originators of ideal objects. The rationale presented was purely one of incentives to 'Promote the Progress of Science and Useful Arts'.")

30. We use the term "author" not in the popular sense of a writer of a literary work but in the broad constitutional sense of an original creator of an intellectual or artistic work. Burrow-Giles Lithographic Co. v. Sarony, 111 U.S. 53, 58 (author in copyright sense is "he to whom anything owes its origin; originator; maker...."); Feist

Publications v. Rural Tel. Serv. Co., 499 U.S. 340, 345 (1991) (originality, the "*sine qua non* of copyright....means only that the work was independently created by the author (as opposed to copied from other works)". Thus, "author" includes a composer of music, a playwright, a visual artist, and a computer programmer as well as a novelist. Similarly, "publisher" denotes the person or institution which selects the creative expression and funds and arranges the distribution of the physical embodiment of the intellectual or artistic creation. Thus, the term includes print and music publishers, film, television, and sound recording producers, and art gallery owners.

Under the 1976 Act the intellectual and artistic "works" subject to copyright include literary works; musical works; dramatic works; pantomimes and choreographic works; pictorial, graphic, and sculptural works; motion pictures and other audiovisual works; sound recordings; and architectural works. 17 U.S.C. sec. 102(a) (1994).

31. For criticism of these assumptions, see notes 32, 72 *infra*. The basic premise is that authors and publishers, like other people, will not invest in productive activities unless they expect to reap the rewards. If it is uncertain that the anticipated rewards can be appropriated, the value of expected returns will be adjusted downwards, and a lower or no investment made. Because creators and distributors would have lower expectations of recovering costs and of profiting by their efforts, there would be less creative activity. Without legal intervention, writers and artists, like inventors, risk the loss of control of their creation and, with it, the loss of financial returns; they face complete profit dissipation by free entry. The societal fear is that intellectual and artistic works that would be worth more to consumers than the expense of creating them will not be produced because the financial incentives for their production are inadequate. A legal regime which forbids reproduction or other use of a work without permission of the author or his assigns and thereby internalizes benefits to creators, *i.e.*, copyright, represents a response to this feared economic inefficiency.

32. While duplicators face only the marginal costs of reproducing the original, the initial publisher has to face the same variable costs plus the cost of creating the original master. *See* Douglas A. Smith, *Collective Administration of Copyright: An Economic Analysis, in* 8 Research in Law and Economics 137, 139-40 (John Palmer & Richard O. Zerbe, Jr., eds., 1986) (ex ante return to publishers negative in absence of copyright protection). The original record producer also incurs other costs, such as promotional and advertising expenses, which the duplicator avoids.

In addition, he likely pays a royalty to the performing artist. However, that cost is negotiable, and for a variety of reasons the record company might be able to reduce or eliminate it. Singers and musicians are motivated by a combination of economic and psychological factors. Undoubtedly, music is composed and performed for as great a variety of reasons as books are written. *See generally* Arnold Plant, *The Economic Aspects of Copyright in Books*, 1 Economica 167-69, 191 (new series 1934); Robert M. Hurt & Robert M. Schuchman, *The Economic Rationale of Copyright*, 56 Am. Econ. Rev. 421, 425-26 (1966); William W. Fisher III, *Reconstructing the Fair Use Doctrine*, 101 Harv. L. Rev. 1659, 1715 (1988); Denis Thomas, Copyright and the Creative Artist 21 (1967). *But see generally* Kenneth W. Dam, *Some Economic Considerations in the Intellectual Property Protection of Software*, 24 J. Leg. Stud. 321, 335 (1995) (nonmonetary incentives for writing of software trivial as compared with authorship of books); Rochelle Cooper Dreyfuss, *A Wiseguy's Approach to Information Products: Muscling Copyright and Patent into a Unitary Theory of Intellectual Property*, 1992 Sup. Ct. Rev. 195, 211 (pecuniary gain as major source of motivation varies among kinds of works; information products such as directories, for example, lack the intellectual challenges that produce psychic benefits). While the prospect of monetary gain certainly is a factor in stimulating creative effort, particularly in the popular arts, nonmonetary considerations may be of equal or greater importance. *See generally* Robert E. Lane, The Market Experience 364-371 (1991) (the concept of the intrinsic); Dreyfuss, *supra*, at 204 (authors write for various reasons many unrelated to finance: "They may wish to contribute to the cultural heritage, forge links to others, to satisfy their own aesthetic sense, to establish their reputation, or provoke others."); Ronald V. Bettig, Copyrighting Culture 104, 171 (1996); Richard A. Posner, Law and Literature: A Misunderstood Relation 339 (1988) (nonmonetary rewards from writing--"fame, prestige, the hope of immortality, therapy, inner satisfaction"); Andrew Reeve, Property 185-86 (1986) ("Labour under appropriate conditions may be fulfilling, not a disutility. Rewards other than property, like honour and fame, may be adequate to call forth exertion, even if labour is unpleasant."); Lloyd L. Weinreb, *Copyright For Functional Expression*, 111 Harv. L. Rev. 1149, 1226, 1232-33 (1998) (if some kinds of effort are so clearly not "fun" that they appear intrinsically to be labor, authorship is not among them; creative arts not heavily dependent on economic incentive); Thomas Bender & David Sampliner, *Poets, Pirates, and the Creation of American Literature*, 29 Int'l L. & Pol. 255, 269-70 (1996-97). Moreover, even economically motivated artistic efforts might continue without the assurance of legal protection for a defined period and the expectation of direct reward. The reason why recording artists may well continue their efforts at existing levels despite reduction in their record-derived income is that the efforts will pay off in other markets. Live performances by popular artists are quite profitable, and recording artists earn a significant proportion of their income from this source. But recordings and concert income are interdependent. Often it is difficult to obtain good bookings without a record, and preferably a recent record, to one's credit. As a result many performers, particularly the unknown artists who present the most risk to a record company, are initially willing to record for small compensation without regard to the money that might be earned from the recording.

Moreover, performers may well be willing to continue recording despite reductions in their record income simply because most artists do not have better economic alternatives. That is, there is a large gap between what they earn as performers and what they could earn in their next best employment choice. Like the successful professional athlete, the highly paid performer is being paid more than is necessary to coax out his effort. The excess of a gifted individual's income above the alternative wage he could earn elsewhere is termed a "pure rent". Between the two limits the individual's supply curve will be almost completely inelastic. Where a factor of production is inelastic in supply, its cost is price-determined rather than price-determining, and the return to it is called an "economic rent". Paul Samuelson & William Nordhaus, Economics 234, 248-49 (16th ed. 1998).

In fact, unqualified reference to the performer's royalty is misleading. In the typical contemporary artist-record company agreement, recording costs (*i.e.*, the costs of creating the master tape) are recouped from artist's royalties. In other words, until the royalties otherwise payable to the artist equal the recording costs no royalty is payable to the artist, and he is paid only on royalties earned thereafter. *See, e.g.*, Agreement Between Record Company and Recording Artist par. 4, in M. William Krasilovsky and Sidney Shemel, This Business of Music 663 (7th ed. 1995); *id.* at 12. The result of this standard recoupment arrangement is that many artists never get to the point where they earn royalties.

Finally, the original producer incurs another cost, a risk cost (or selection bias), which is difficult to quantify but would usually be avoided by the duplicator. The initial producer faces the uncertain odds of success; it bears the costs of both hits and misses. Unlike the duplicator, who may cherry-pick and limit himself to the reproduction of proven hits, the original record company runs the substantial risk of a record's failure. To survive economically, it must charge enough to cover all its costs, including the costs of unsuccessful releases. *See, e.g.* Lanier Saperstein, *Copyrights, Criminal Sanctions and Economic Rents: Applying the Rent Seeking Model to the Criminal Law Formulation Process*, J. Crim. L. & Criminology 1470, 1496-97 (1997). For an explanation of the great difficulty involved in assessing by how much the supply of intellectual and artistic effort will be reduced when the return to such effort is reduced, see Stanley M. Besen, New Technologies and Intellectual Property: An Economic Analysis 7-11 (1987).

Throughout this book we periodically refer to the music industry and sound recordings in order to illustrate points. Recordings are apt illustrations because they possess the distinctive economic characteristics of artistic goods we have noted and because their unauthorized duplication has been a prime focus of domestic and international attention over the past few decades. In addition, they, along with motion pictures, are among the principal American exports of copyrighted works.

"Sound recordings" are defined by the Copyright Act as "works that result from the fixation of a series of musical, spoken, or other sounds, but not including sounds accompanying a motion picture or other audiovisual work, regardless of the nature of the material objects, such as disks, tapes, or other phonorecords, in which they are embodied." 17 U.S.C. sec. 101 (1994). Sound recordings first received protection under federal copyright law in 1971. Pub. L. No. 92-140, 85 Stat. 391 (1971). Prior to that time any protection against their unauthorized duplication lay with state law.

For the important point that the producers of sound recordings would not be aided in Europe by enactment of the term extension bill, *see* text at notes 185-88 *infra*.

33. Stephen Breyer, *The Uneasy Case for Copyright: A Study of Copyright in Books, Photocopies, and Computer Programs*, 84 Harv. L. Rev. 281, 294-99 (1970). *See also* Meheroo Jussawalla, The Economics of Intellectual Property in a World Without Frontiers 29 (1992) (first-copy costs of knowledge-based journals). While literary authors, like recording artists, *see* note 32 *supra*, may be moved to creative activity for nonmonetary reasons, they generally depend on publishers to disseminate their work; and publishers must see at least the possibility of recovering their costs in selecting, editing, and marketing creative works. Thus, even if scholars may not need legal intervention to author scholarly works, publishers require that intervention to publish those works. *See* Bettig, *supra* note 32, at 171.

34. This differential reflects the basic fact that the value of the informational, literary, or artistic content of the work greatly exceeds the cost of the physical

30

product in which that content is stored. In the case of music, for example, once the initial recorded performance is created, any number of additional discs or tapes may be produced thereafter at a nominal additional cost per unit. *See* Bettig, *supra* note 32, at 93-94 (the economics of filmed entertainment; cost of producing an additional copy of the print of a feature-length film is "mere fraction of the cost of producing the original"). But the cost of producing the initial master copy does not change as the number of users changes.

35. *See* Yale M. Braunstein, Dietrich M. Fischer, Janusz A. Ordover & William J. Baumol, Economics of Property Rights as Applied to Computer Software and Data Bases II-1-2 (1977); Robert P. Benko, *Intellectual Property Rights and the Uruguay Round*, World Economy, June 1988, at 217, 218-19; A.A. Keyes & C. Brunet, Copyright in Canada: Proposals for a Revision of the Law 34 (1977) (inherent market defect).

36. In the centuries-old debate about the need for a patent system a key argument of those who oppose such a system has always been that the inventor's natural headstart--*i.e.*, the fact that imitators will need time to decipher his secret, to make plans, start construction, enter into production, and bring their products on the market--will generally permit him to recoup his development costs and more and thus will provide sufficient incentive to stimulate invention and innovation. *See* Fritz Machlup, An Economic Review of the Patent System, Study No. 15 for the Subcomm. on Patents, Trademarks, and Copyrights of the Senate Comm. on the Judiciary, 85th Cong., 2d Sess. 16, 24, 38-39, 59-60 (1958); *see also Patently Outdated: Changes in the Way Drugs Are Invented Are Making Patents Unworkable*, The Economist, July 18, 1987, at 17 (rewards of invention for drug firms will increasingly come from being first to market; the shorter the life cycle, the less the point in getting patents); Palmer, *supra* note 29, at 295 (substantial advantage to being "first to market" with product, especially with ideal objects); Richard C. Levin, et al., *Appropriating the Returns from Industrial Research and Development*, 3 Brookings Papers on Economic

Activity 783, 816 (1987) (survey confirms that lead time, which accrues naturally to innovator, and other non-legal means of appropriation are more important than patent system; importance of lead time as mechanism of appropriation varies substantially between industries); F.M. Scherer & David Ross, Industrial Market Structure and Economic Performance 626-30 (3d ed. 1990) (alternative protection from imitation) . *But see generally* Benedicte Callan, Pirates on the High Seas: The United States and Global Intellectual Property Rights 30 (1998) (lead time advantage reduced as product cycles have shrunk in most industries due to more targeted research approach). In the patent context the inventor has another advantage, an advantage which until recently has been largely overlooked in the patent literature and one which has no counterpart in a discussion of the need for copyright protection of artistic goods such as recorded performances. That advantage is the possible speculative profits available to the inventor from the pecuniary effects that will follow the release of information at his unique disposal. *See* Jack Hirshleifer, *The Private and Social Value of Information and the Reward to Inventive Activity*, 61 Am. Econ. Rev. 561 (1971).

37. The extent and import of lead time vary among different intellectual and artistic goods. In the case of recorded music, for example, the headstart that being first out gives is quite significant, for the bulk of record sales of popular music occurs within a short period of time after release, and record companies generally expect to recoup their investment and begin earning a profit within a few months of release. Priority in the market, then, should give the initial producer an important advantage in most cases, thereby limiting its loss of revenue due to duplication. Even where the demand for a particular release is sufficiently great to induce the duplicator to enter the market some time after the initial issue, the concentration of sales in the first few months should permit the initial producer to make a good return on the record despite duplication. *See generally*, Braunstein, *supra* note 35, at II-19 (length of copyright protection could be shortened if copyright holder can reap high returns in the initial

period of protection for his computer software package); Saperstein, *supra* note 32, at 1498 (lead time of particular import for products, such as software packages, with a relatively short market life. Digital technology, though, has the potential to limit or erase these lead time advantages, as it permits copiers--both free riding competitors and nonpurchasing consumers--to make and distribute high quality reproductions cheaply and quickly. Weinreb, *supra* note 32, at 1234-35. *See* Callan, *supra* note 36, at 30.

This lead time advantage, however, would apply primarily to artists whose work is not guaranteed success by the identity and reputation of the performer. A problem arises in the case of established successful performers, the demand for whose product is highly predictable. In the case of such performers, *e.g.*, the Beatles in their prime or R.E.M today, the initial producer's lead time would be severely reduced as the duplicator need not delay at all in entering the market; they are known quantities, and everyone is aware that their albums will be big sellers. Consequently, the duplicator is in a position to make serious inroads on the revenue earned from these products, and the return from these recordings accounts for a sizeable percentage of record company revenues. The result is that the initial producer will incur risk on what is really its most conservative investment. As a general matter, both lead time and predictability are factors cutting against a need for legal regulation. The point here, however, is that high predictability reduces the existence of lead time.

Analysis of lead time must take account of the possibility that consumers will delay their purchases of intellectual and artistic goods in the hope of buying a cheaper, "pirated" copy. Thus, record buyers might wait to purchase an attractive release. This possibility points to an interesting paradox. Duplicators usually will not move in until a release proves successful. (The duplicator, of course, could enter before a release's popularity is apparent. If he does so, though, he sacrifices ease of predictability and shares in the risk that the record will prove unpopular.) Thus, if sufficient potential buyers delay their purchases, it lessens the chance that the record will be copied. *See generally* Rudiger Pethig, *Copyright and Copying Costs: A New Price-Theoretic Approach*, 144 J. Institutional & Theoretical Econ. 462, 476-78 (1988). More importantly, the extremely short life of and the relatively inelastic demand for popular records strongly suggest that buyers value early access and are more anxious to acquire the release quickly than to save a few dollars awaiting a possible lower price copy. *See also* Alfred C. Yen, *The Legacy of Feist: Consequences of the Weak Connection Between Copyright and the Economics of Public Goods*, 52 Ohio St. L.J. 1343, 1371 n.128 (1991).

For an examination of the significance of lead time in the book publishing industry, see Breyer, *supra* note 33, at 299-302. For the position that the first-to-market argument against copyright protection for software is insubstantial, see Dam, *supra* note 32, at 333-34. Clearly, if a work's content is time-sensitive, being first will confer a significant advantage. *See* Yen, *supra*, at 1370-72 (factual compilations, lead time, time-sensitive information, and recoupment of development costs.)

38. The initial producer may have a superior distribution network, *see* Weinreb, *supra* note 32, at 1234-35, and he may be able to threaten retaliation by meeting the duplicator's price. However, it is questionable how credible a preemptive market saturation threat would be in an industry such as disc and tape reproduction where little capital investment and equipment are necessary to enter.

Another possible advantage of the initial producer is that he can promote his product as the original, authorized version. Some purchasers, either because they are distrustful of "copies" or due to psychological status considerations, may insist on patronizing the "original" product. Also the ability to advertise that his product is the only one authorized by the performer may be a valuable asset at least among those customers who strongly believe in the rights of a performer to the fruits of his creation. Finally, original producers may claim that their product is of higher quality. To the extent the original producer convinces buyers that the original possesses qualities not shared by the copy, he can exclude the copier from some portion of the release's total market. *See* Michael O'Hare, *Copyright: When Is Monopoly Efficient?*, 4 J. Pol'y Analysis & Mgmt. 407, 412-13 (1985). Historically, in the record industry, as a matter of technology, each step further removed from the master represented a decrease in quality, and duplicated products are at least two generations further removed than those of the initial producer. However, with the advent of digital technology, it is now possible to easily create copies which are of the same quality as the original. No special knowledge or manufacturing expertise is required to make additional discs or tapes indistinguishable from the original.

39. Disposition of the economic argument for legal regulation depends, in the end, on the resolution of a series of factual issues, and these questions and answers will vary among different intellectual and artistic goods. *See generally* Levin, *supra* note 36. In the case of recorded music, for example, what, in fact, is the duplicator's cost advantage? How large is the differential? Is it offset by advantages available only to the first producer? What is the extent and significance of the initial producer's headstart? Will this headstart in exploitation permit him to recoup his fixed costs and more before "freeloading" competitors enter into production? Are there means for minimizing his risks? In short, what would happen if there were unrestricted competition in the production and sale of individual record releases? Would record production be seriously threatened?

Recognition of the fact that the extent and significance of the original producer's countervailing advantages will vary among intellectual and artistic works means that the incremental effect of a proposed copyright policy change will depend on the protection that other alternative mechanisms provide. Accordingly, uniform adjustments of copyright law, such as an increase (or decrease) in the term of protection, may well affect some industries quite differently than others. For example, in a business setting where other mechanisms provide considerable appropriability, lengthening the life of copyrights (or patents) would likely have little incentive effects. Acceptance of the proposition that legal protection is neither the only nor necessarily the primary barrier that prevents general access to what would otherwise be public goods suggests that "institutions to protect intellectual property should be understood as social structures that *improve* the appropriability of returns from innovation." Levin, *supra* note 36, at 815-16.

40. *See* Besen, *supra* note 32, at v, 15-20 (production of intellectual property often supported by advertiser payments or "bundling" of property with sale of other private good for which exclusion is feasible). *See generally* Ejan Mackaay, *The Economics of Emergent Property Rights on the Internet, in* The Future of Copyright in a Digital Environment 13, 20-21 (P. Bernt Hugenholtz ed., 1996) (build your own fence). A key question in assessing the strength of the argument for copyright protection is whether, in the absence of that protection, other ways to sustain authors' and publishers' revenues would likely emerge. One possibility is that buyers interested in a product would organize to assure the publisher enough revenue to operate profitably and thereby assure production of the desired product. *See* Harold Demsetz, *Information and Efficiency: Another Viewpoint*, 12 J. Law & Econ. 1, 12-13 (1969). *See generally* Frank H. Easterbrook, *Intellectual Property Is Still Property*, 13 Harv. J.L. & Pub. Pol'y 108, 113-14 (1990) (intellectual property viewed as the result of voluntary undertakings). *See also* Paul Goldstein, *Copyright and Its Substitutes*, 1997 Wis. L. Rev. 865, 868 (technology may make feasible in the future contracts with sufficiently large numbers of subscribers to fund investment in new creative work and this approach may substitute effectively for copyright). This mechanism of organized buyers is most likely to prove feasible when the administrative costs of organization are low. Thus, when the number of buyers is relatively low and these buyers' preferences are set and known--for example, in states where elementary or high school textbooks are adopted on a state-wide basis--an advance arrangement with the publisher is a possibility. *See* Breyer, *supra* note 33, at 302-06. *See generally* Lance Rose, *The Emperor's Clothes Still Fit Just Fine Or, Copyright Is*

Dead. Long Live Copyright!, Wired, Feb. 1995, at 103 (Copyright aimed primarily at protecting mass-market works, not high-priced, small-circulation specialty products; small size of audience that makes copyright enforcement difficult also facilitates other legal protections such as distribution of narrowcasted materials under confidentiality restrictions). And in the history of the record industry advance subscriptions for the recording of symphonic and other classical music did exist in the 1930s and 1940s. Roland Gelatt, The Fabulous Phonograph 259-61 (1965) ("Society" projects--"idea was to form different societies for the purpose of recording the more recondite works of various composers and to obtain enough subscriptions in advance to defray the cost of the undertakings"). *See also* Comment, *Photocopying and Fair Use: An Examination of the Economic Factor in Fair Use*, 26 Emory L.J. 849, 866-69 (1977) (doubt that extensive photocopying will result in significant disincentive to authors and publishers as there are alternative revenue sources available to support copied publications). However, the organization of buyers would not be a feasible option with respect to popular music. In this market, not only are the buyers diffuse and their number very large but many of their purchases are made on impulse; more generally, these buyers tend not to make a purchase until they have first heard the recording. *See generally* Wendy J. Gordon, *On Owning Information: Intellectual Property and the Restitutionary Impulse*, 78 Va. L. Rev. 149, 236-38 (1992).

41. *See generally* Robert Cooter and Thomas Ulen, Law And Economics 113-15 (1988) (the market, unaided, may produce the optimal amount of information "because of the possibility of the original producer's indirectly appropriating enough revenue to justify incurring the costs of producing information").

42. *See generally* Palmer, *supra* note 29, at 287-300 ("markets for ideal objects in the absence of intellectual property rights"); Mary L. Mills, *New Technology and the Limitations of Copyright Law: An Argument for Finding Alternatives to Copyright Legislation in an Era of Rapid Technological Change*, 65 Chi-Kent L. Rev. 307, 311-

12 (1989) (tension between technologies of exclusion and access; exclusionary technologies often cumbersome to effectuate and soon penetrated).

43. *See* Keith E. Maskus, *Intellectual Property Rights and the Uruguay Round*, Federal Reserve Bank of Kansas City Economic Review, First Quarter 1993, at 11, 13-15 ("the economics of intellectual property rights"). The proposition is deliberately stated starkly here, though the conclusion is more nuanced particularly with respect to the effect on authors' motivation and behavior. See note 32 *supra* and note 72 *infra*.

Another perspective--one which points to possible situations where the publisher's revenues can be sustained without legal intervention--is to view such intervention as a response to a problem of coordination which the interested parties can not resolve themselves. Imagine an original record producer and a duplicator. Since the duplicator earns his living by reproducing works produced by the record company, he is dependent on the company's continued survival for his own commercial existence. In other words, the relationship is one of parasite and host. As it is in the interest of the parasite to assure enough return to the host so as to keep him in business. he should voluntarily limit the extent of his duplication so that the original producer earns a sufficient profit on the recording and is thus willing to continue to produce recordings. The workings of self-interest, then, without legal intervention would solve the problem. The problem with this scenario is that the relationship between initial producers and duplicators is not a "closed shop". No individual duplicator can afford to forego copying because he has no assurance that other duplicators will refrain. And in light of the large number of potential duplicators the costs of establishing an advance arrangement which would serve the collective interest of preserving the existence of original producers would be prohibitive. *See* Philip Heymann, *The Problem of Coordination: Bargaining and Rules*, 86 Harv. L. Rev. 797, 814-15, 831, 833 (1973). The size of the market and ease of entry are such that duopoly or oligopoly arrangements which would leave a profit for all producers are ruled out.

There is frequently a divergence between what people are individually motivated to do and what they might like to accomplish together. It is, for example, in each fisherman's self-interest to catch as many whales as he can before a competitor does, though each will regret the excessive depletion of the stock. *See generally* Thomas Schelling, *On the Ecology of Micromotives*, The Public Interest, Fall 1971, at 61, 65-88; Gunnar Breivik, *Cooperation Against Doping?*, *in* Rethinking College Athletics 183 (Judith Andre & David N. James, eds., 1991) (college athletes and use of performance-enhancing drugs; in some structures individual choices can not lead to individual satisfaction). In such a situation an outcome which no one wants is likely to be effected by the uncoordinated interaction of inputs; individually rational choices add up to a result which is inferior for everyone. *See* J. Donald Moon, Constructing Community: Moral Pluralism and Tragic Conflicts 195 (1993) ("the tyranny of small choices"--individual actions aggregate to yield outcomes no one wants). As Professor Heymann points out, *supra* at 415, this outcome may be expected or unexpected. For example, "it may have been entirely obvious to the buffalo hunters that their uncoordinated activities, motivated in part by each hunter's awareness of the lack of social restraints on the acquisitiveness of others, would deplete the herds at an uneconomical rate; yet this outcome of their individual decisions was unwanted and unplanned." The record duplicator's position in terms of lack of coordination is analogous to that of the buffalo hunter, the whaler, and the college football player contemplating the use of steroids to increase performance.

44. The problem is a divergence between individual and social benefits. As previously noted, an author may devote himself to creative activity for other than economic reasons. See note 32 *supra*. If those noneconomic benefits, such as aesthetic gratification and fame, are larger than his projected costs, he will labor to produce that new work. However, in the absence of profits from the sale of the work

(or economic payoff elsewhere), he will only produce new works if these direct personal benefits outweigh the costs. But the new intellectual or artistic work will likely be of value to many people other than the author, and the decision about the desirability of inducing new works should take account of that social utility as well. New works should be produced whenever the total benefits to everyone are larger than the costs to authors. Thus, the institutional design issue is to find a way to bring the benefits to others to bear on the author's motivation. *See generally* Richard T. Rapp & Richard P. Rozek, *Benefits and Costs of Intellectual Property Protection in Developing Countries*, 24 J. World Trade 75, 81, 84 (1990) (intellectual property protection as incentive for innovation); Dam, *supra* note 32, at 333 (intellectual property rights as response to appropriability problem, *i.e.*, the inability of authors, inventors, and publishers to appropriate the benefits of their investments).

The difficulty of denying access to intellectual and artistic works to people who have not paid for the right to benefit from them has been aggravated by the appearance of cheap and easy copying technologies.

45. Variations in terminology appear in describing this key characteristic of non-conflicting uses. *Compare* Patrick Croskery, *Institutional Utilitarianism and Intellectual Property*, 68 Chi.-Kent L. Rev. 631-32, 636-37, 641 (non-rival goods; least valuable use not conflict with most valuable) *with* Michael Laver, The Politics of Private Desires 29-32 (public or collective consumption goods v. private consumption goods). The core point is that the use by one person of a song or journal article does not decrease the availability of that good for use by others. Thus, intellectual and artistic works, unlike tangible resources, present no potential for a tragedy of the commons.

46. Michael Lehmann, *Property and Intellectual Property--Property Rights as Restrictions on Competition in Furtherance of Competition*, 20 Int'l Rev. Indus. Prop. & Copyright L. 1, 13-14 (1989). *See generally* James W. Child, *The Moral Foundations of Intangible Property*, 73 The Monist 578 (1990) (intangible personal

property is not subject to the zero-sum objection that accumulation leads to deprivation, *i.e.*, I can only get more by denying an equal amount to others).

47. Public goods generally involve two elements--nonrivalrous consumption and nonexcludability. Professor Paul Samuelson has defined a public good as one where "each individual's consumption of [the] good leads to no subtraction from any other individual's consumption of that good." Paul Samuelson, *The Pure Theory of Public Expenditure*, 36 Rev. of Econ. & Stat. 387 (1954). In fact, it is this lack of scarcity, the fact that once created the marginal cost of using a recorded performance is zero, that provides a key basis for the economic argument for protection of sound recordings. *See* Ludwig von Mises, Human Action: A Treatise on Economics 382-3 (1949).

48. Though our focus is on copyright and literary and artistic works, similar economic conflicts are present in the patent context. Thus, knowledge is not depleted with use. For example, no matter how often the formula for aspirin is used, it remains unchanged, and the marginal cost of using this knowledge (the formula) is zero. Not only can the same person make use of such knowledge repeatedly without danger of exhausting it through wear, but it can serve numerous users simultaneously, and as the number of users increases no one need be getting less of it because others are getting more. Wassily Leontief, *On Assignment of Patent Rights on Inventions Made Under Government Research Contracts*, 77 Harv. L. Rev. 492, 493 (1964). From a static perspective of economic efficiency, the knowledge should be made available to anyone interested since doing so does not reduce the stock of knowledge or reduce the number of times aspirin can be made. Over time, however, such a policy may well have unfortunate social consequences in its long-term effect on the extent of resources devoted to research and innovation. Patent law seeks to resolve this tension between incentives for innovation and widespread diffusion of benefits. *See* Scherer & Ross, *supra* note 36, at 621-24. For an account of differing conceptions of the patent system by economists over the past two centuries and an

assessment of their insights into property rights in invention, see Steven N.S. Cheung, *Property Rights and Invention, in* 8 Research in Law and Economics, *supra* note 32, at 5.

49. *See* Braunstein, *supra* note 35, at I-5.

50. As noted, text at notes 32-35 *supra*, as soon as the initial producer sells the embodiment of the artistic creation, *e.g.*, a musical performance captured on a compact disc, to a buyer, that buyer becomes a potential competitor in light of the low cost of reproducing and distributing the performance. *See generally* Richard P. Adelstein & Steven I. Peretz, *The Competition of Technologies in Markets for Ideas: Copyright and Fair Use in Evolutionary Perspective,* 5 Int'l Rev. L. & Econ. 209 (1985) (creators' ability to recover value of work from buyer depends on "impurity" of goods, *i.e.*, the extent to which users have trouble separating the intellectual goods from their "hosts", the physical entities in which they are carried; advances in technology generally increase purity and consumers of pure goods can become secondary producers, placing them in direct competition with the originators).

51. *See generally* Laver, *supra* note 45, at 29-31 (differential "crowdability" or "susceptibility to crowding" of goods).

52. In our socio-economic system this task is principally handled by a private property arrangement in which the institutions of property and contract designate an "owner" of the resource who may then enter agreements with others about its use and transfer. Of course, the scarcity problem does not necessarily dictate this private property response. Other mechanisms, including governmental decision, could be utilized to respond to the allocation questions.

We are, of course, not suggesting that the confusion-congestion-strife argument is the only persuasive underpinning for recognition of property rights. For example, it has often been argued that establishment of individual property rights in tangible resources is justified by reference to an interest in efficiency. *See, e.g.,* Lehmann *supra* note 46, at 13. *See generally* Frank Michelman, *Property, Utility, and Fairness: Comments on the Ethical Foundations of "Just Compensation" Law,* 80 Harv. L. Rev. 1165, 1202-1213 (1967)("Some Theories of Property").

53. *See* Lehmann, *supra* note 46, at 14 ("[I]n the area of intellectual and industrial property, the economic nature of the protected objects does not compel permanent exclusive allocation and specification of the property rights, but such allocation and specification is rather determined by the needs of the respective economic-social situation.") *See generally* Brewer & Staves, *supra* note 9, at 10 ("Unlike property in such material things as land or animals, literary property and other species of intellectual property depend on reification, that is, on regarding an abstraction...as a thing. According to copyright law doctrines, the owner of textual property owns neither the manuscript nor the physical book in which his or her text has been printed, nor the ideas it expresses; instead, the owner owns the particular sequence of words he or she has 'created' to express those ideas."); Jeremy Waldron, The Right to Private Property 30 (1988).

54. Sound recordings, recorded performances of music, provide a good example of these advantages and characteristics. They are peculiar economic goods. Like books, almost all the costs of producing the product are expended on the first record, which requires large inputs of labor and some capital by composers, performers, producers and recording engineers. Thereafter, any number of additional records may be produced at a nominal additional per unit cost. In view of the high cost of the first record, record companies cannot price their records anywhere near that cost. Rather, they must hope to sell a large number of records at substantially lower prices and to recoup their initial costs through a large volume of sales. However, the large proportion of fixed versus marginal costs involved in record production--the fact that most of the costs of record production are incurred before the first record is produced--and the cheapness of increasing the supply of records means that

duplicators can easily undersell the original producer. Moreover, if duplicators only reproduce successful records, they would enjoy a double advantage over the original producer. They need not make the expenditures to produce the first recording, and they need not recoup losses from failures. If duplication were unrestricted, the extremely low capital costs of duplicators would attract sufficient entrants to drive record prices down to the level of production costs. This price would be well below that required to maintain the solvency of an original record producer. Thus, the incentive to produce would be destroyed by the prospect of widespread reproduction by "freeloaders". A scheme of unrestricted copying would lead to a situation where artists and record companies could not recover the cost of their recording and production done in the hope of financial reward would cease. In the absence of legal protection, uncompensated duplication and sale of recorded performances would lower the rate of return and weaken the economic incentives for artists and record producers to the point where consumers will be deprived of the variety of musical experience they desire (and now enjoy).

55. The manner in which rational pricing (above marginal cost) by an author who has been granted an exclusive property right in his creation will result in reduced access to that creation is spelled out both graphically and in more detail employing the terminology of economics in Fisher, *supra* note 32, at 1700-02. As we previously noted, the characteristic of indivisibility means that once an intellectual or artistic work has been produced, its use by a consumer may benefit him while imposing no additional cost on the producer.

A grant of rights which are too extensive, whether in terms of the items which fall within the protection, the scope of that protection or its duration, may impose a significant social cost in addition to the limitation of access to resulting works by consumers and later authors. Such overprotection also raises the prospect of inefficiency across industrial sectors. That is, it would lead to overinvestment in and overproduction of goods in the copyright-based sectors of the economy, drawing

44

resources into the production of additional copyrightable works when those resources would otherwise have been more valuably used elsewhere in the economy. Copyrighted works, after all, compete not only with other copyrighted writings but also with all other products that might be produced with the same resources. Glynn S. Lunney, Jr., *Reexamining Copyright's Incentives-Access Paradigm*, 49 Vand. L. Rev. 483 (1996).

56. 1 Paul Goldstein, Copyright: Principles, Law and Practice, sec. 1.1, at 6-7 (1989). A complex assessment is involved in the reference to a socially optimal output, as the manner in which we allocate rights in "ideas" may affect the kinds of intellectual and artistic works that are produced as well as their quantity, quality, and dissemination.

57. Cooter & Ulen, *supra* note 41, at 135. *Cf.* W. Kip Viscusi et al., Economics of Regulation and Antitrust 831-33 (2d ed. 1995) (economics of invention and patents).

58. These rights represent a social attempt to achieve a balance in the fundamental tension between providers and users of information. The economic function of the financial returns generated through the copyright system is to give the author of a creative work the opportunity to receive from consumers a return commensurate with the value the consumers place on his creation. This return is designed to provide potential creators with the incentive to produce works the public values. Copyrights allow creative interests to extract a return to their investments in exchange for making available new intellectual and artistic efforts. Society, thus, realizes the twin ends of promoting new creation and having it disseminated by transferring some portion of consumer surplus to producers. In principle, both consumers and producers benefit from this protection. *See* Weinreb, *supra* note 32, at 1237.

This answer is not the only possible public response to the problem that the unregulated market will produce suboptimal amounts of creative works. Copyright represents one way of resolving the conflict between the need for revenues high enough to secure production and prices low enough not to inhibit widespread dissemination of what is produced. Alternatively, we might, through grants and prizes from general government revenues, directly subsidize the creation and distribution of intellectual and artistic works. We do, in fact, employ some such subsidies, but their use is not extensive. Such a mechanism has decided theoretical advantages, for when the government pays for a work's creation and subsidizes its distribution, a copyright fee is not needed to assure production. Thus, this scheme can secure production without restricting a work's dissemination. *See* Braunstein, *supra* note 35, at IV-37-39; Timothy J. Brennan, Taxing Home Audio Taping 3 (1986); *see generally* Roger A. McCain, *Information as Property and as a Public Good: Perspectives from the Economic Theory of Property Rights*, 58 Libr. Q. 265, 273 n.13 (1988) (free public provision of computer software possibly justified on transaction cost grounds); John M. Hartwick, Aspects of the Economics of Book Publishing 7 (1984). However, it is doubtful that an administratively feasible government financing system could be developed on a wide scale so as to substitute for copyright protection without diluting much of these theoretical benefits. Operationally, such a system would require regular bureaucratic estimates of the value of a work to every user of each copy. It is doubtful that such estimates can be made with reasonable accuracy, *id.*; and making production decisions turn on such rough governmental estimates of social value would invite corruption. Put differently, in the absence of market signals, government may well encounter considerable difficulty in deciding whether to support particular types of production and the amount of support to offer. *See generally* Croskery, *supra* note 45, at 636-37 (relative incapacity of government in effectively gathering information about preferences and in being innovative). Any system which places primary reliance on a scheme of government subsidies to production encounters not only the difficult administrative problems of estimating how much of the good should be produced but also our lack of analytic models of the behavioral rules which guide the decisions and actions of governmental agencies. *See* Otto A. Davis and Andrew B. Whinston, *On the Distinction Between Public and Private Goods*, 57 Am. Econ. Rev., May 1967, at 360, 367-68; *see generally* Rapp & Rozek, *supra* note 44, at 89-90 (inadequacy of prize system and R&D activity). In addition, increased reliance on the government for financing would raise the risk of censorship; our present arrangements, which reject comprehensive public subsidies to the arts, reflect a judgment that the market provides a better guarantee of varied expression than public patronage. *See* Breyer, *supra* note 33, at 306-08; Hartwick, *supra*, at 21 (airing of unorthodox ideas most likely in environment of decentralized, competitive publishing). *See generally* Tyler Cowen, In Praise of Commercial Culture (1998). (Correspondingly, substitution of a public prize system for patents would likely be attended by similar problems of uncertainty, arbitrariness, and special interest rent-seeking. *See* Roger E. Meiners & Robert J. Staaf, *Patents, Copyrights, and Trademarks: Property or Monopoly?*, 13 Harv. J.L. & Pub. Pol'y 911, 921, 940 (1990).) Attention to the potential vice of censorship indicates that adoption of a copyright system represents more than a choice on technical grounds among a set of equally desirable alternative public responses. One of copyright's functions is structural in that it supports a sector of creative and communicative action that is relatively free from reliance on government subsidy and corporate patronage; and that support serves to enhance the democratic character of civil society. *See* Neil Weinstock Netanel, *Copyright and a Democratic Civil Society*, 106 Yale L.J. 283 (1996). *But see* Weinreb, *supra* note 32, at 1233 n.340.

Anglo-American copyright law originated as a child of print technology and state censorship. In a fortunate historical irony it so divorced itself from its second ancestor that it became a system of incentives to idea-processing involving singularly little day-to-day intervention by the state and thus minimal opportunities and temptations to censor.

A legitimate reluctance to place primary reliance on a subsidy scheme, though, does not preclude judicious use of government or foundation support for artistic and literary endeavors. *See generally* Besen, *supra* note 32, at vii, 24-25, 66-

67; Weinreb, *supra* note 32, at 1233-34 (role of universities in stimulating scholarly research and writing; academic culture offers significant rewards to successful scholars and these stimulate the production of new knowledge without conferring exclusive rights on authors in the way that copyright does). Recognition of the faults and drawbacks of copyright should not only influence one's construction of the detailed terms of protection but should also inform one's analysis about the necessity and desirability of supplementary support. *See* text at notes 218-26 *infra.* Those who introduced the copyright clause itself never viewed copyright as the exclusive means for promotion of learning. James Madison spoke in terms of power "[t]o secure to literary authors their copyrights for a limited time. To establish a university. [and] To encourage, by premiums and provisions, the advancement of useful knowledge and discoveries." Charles Pinckney recommended power "[t]o establish seminaries for the promotion of literature, and the arts and sciences....To grant patents for useful inventions [and] To secure to authors exclusive rights for a limited time." 5 Debates on the Adoption of the Federal Constitution 440 (Jonathan Elliot, ed. 1974).

59. As we have indicated, the long-run social problem occurs when the cost of reproducing a work is less than that of purchasing it. The aim of copyright protection is to raise the cost of reproduction, including the likelihood and penalties associated with being caught, to the point where the expected returns to those considering unauthorized reproduction will be so low that they will not engage in that behavior.

60. Copyright thus responds to the problem outlined in note 40 *supra* of creating a mechanism to bring to bear the benefits to others on the author's individual decision to invest time and effort in producing new works. Since no one can use the work except on terms agreed to by the copyright proprietor, he can charge a price for use and thereby benefit to the extent that others in the marketplace expect to benefit from his work. Thus, the expected utility of the contemplated product to everyone will be taken account of in his decision. Optimally, then, the rational self-interest of authors will yield effort up to the point at which the social costs of new works equal their

social benefits.

Granting limited legal protection by means of copyright attempts to alleviate distortions arising from the partial inability of authors to exclude all nonpayers from obtaining their writings. As previously noted, without such protection this inability of creators to fully appropriate returns from their writings would result in underproduction of new works.

61. Copyrights, then, like patents, depart from the norms of free competition by establishing a form of monopoly control that solves the appropriability problem and thereby establishes economic incentives to create and publicly distribute literary and artistic works. In fact the purpose of copyright protection is to transform a competitive situation into a temporary noncompetitive one in order to increase the supply of intellectual and artistic works. Ideally, the increased returns to producers will yield the benefit to consumers of a larger quantity and wider variety of outputs. By creating quasi-rents copyright (and patent) protection substitute the current "market failure" of restricted supply in order to surmount the future market failure of inadequate innovation. The current welfare losses from protecting intellectual property, thus, can be seen as a social investment in the promotion of creative activities; in this compromise some static misallocation in the use of a given cultural and knowledge base is accepted as the cost of preserving dynamic incentives for the generation of new information. And the overall policy goal is to maximize the differential between the additional benefits induced by the grant of intellectual property rights and the costs of protection.

Judging copyright markets solely from an efficiency perspective, the relevant objective is to bring the marginal social return to investments in producing copyrighted works and raising their quality closer to the marginal costs of those investments. In the case of music, for example, the copyright system ideally should provide composers the incentive to compose music for which listeners collectively would be willing to cover the expense. And the better that system works the closer the correspondence between the value listeners place on copyrighted music and the cost of writing music. Timothy J. Brennan, *An Economic Look at Taxing Home Audio Taping*, 32 J. Broadcasting & Electronic Media 89, 99 (1988).

It should be made clear that the rationale here has nothing to do with fairness or the moral desert of author or publisher. Though the argument is sometimes spoken of as equitable and that this equity requires that the publisher obtain a return on his investment, *see, e.g.*, Zechariah Chafee, Jr. *Reflections on Copyright Law: I*, 45 Colum. L. Rev. 503, 509 ("it is only equitable that the publisher should obtain a return on his investment.") copyright, under the rationale stated in the text, is not, in fact, aimed at guaranteeing a fair return to publishers; the publisher, like other investors, takes a risk and is not entitled to a profit under our market system. That is, copyright protection has never been intended to provide a guarantee of reward, but simply the prospect of obtaining such a reward. *See generally*, Edmund W. Kitch, *The Nature and Function of the Patent System*, 20 J.L. & Econ. 265 (1978). The grounds underlying the argument in the text, and a judgment of its validity or invalidity, are those of economic efficiency. The intervention is a response to an inherent problem with how a given market is structured; it is not supported on grounds of fairness to cover investors' costs. The contentions that intellectual and artistic works will not be forthcoming or that businessmen will not assume the risks associated with the introduction of something new unless the possibility of monopoly "rewards" is tendered to them are totally different arguments "from that which insists on the moral obligation of society to pay a reward, the appropriateness of which is measured by the monopoly profit obtained." Edith T. Penrose, The Economics of the International Patent System 30 (1951). For related treatment of these points, see text at notes 195-217 *infra*.

62. *See generally* Joan Robinson, The Accumulation of Capital 87 (1958) (the paradox of patents):

A patent is a device to prevent the diffusion of new methods before the original investor has recovered profit adequate to induce the requisite investment. The justification of the patent system is that by slowing down the diffusion of technical progress it ensures that there will be more progress to diffuse. The patent system...leads to many anomalies. Since it is rooted in a contradiction, there can be no such thing as an ideally beneficial patent system, and it is bound to produce negative results in particular instances, impeding progress unnecessarily even if its general effect is favorable on balance.

63. Netanel, *supra* note 58, at 285:

Copyright law strikes a precarious balance. To encourage authors to create and disseminate original expression, it accords them a bundle of proprietary rights in their works. But to promote public education and creative exchange, it invites audiences and subsequent authors to use existing works in every conceivable manner that falls outside the province of the copyright owner's exclusive rights. Copyright law's perennial dilemma is to determine where exclusive rights should end and unrestrained public access should begin.

The task is the definition of rights to private use so as to balance the need to permit building on previous knowledge against the need to encourage creativity in the first place. *See* Besen, *supra* note 32, at 44. *See generally* David Schmidtz, *The Institution of Property, in* Property Rights 42, 60-61 (Ellen F. Paul et al. eds., 1994) (open access versus maximum access). In light of the tension between the short and long term economic effects of both authorship and copying, the determination of what balance of access and incentives will produce the highest net value is no easy task. *See generally* Frank H. Easterbrook, *Foreword: The Court and the Economic System*, 98 Harv. L. Rev. 4, 22 n.23 (1984) (there may be no satisfactory solution to the creation-use conundrum even in theory).

64. The principal efficiency question in the economics of copyright involves balancing the incentives to induce the production of intellectual and artistic works with the cost to society of creating deadweight loss from supracompetitive pricing (the lost value of the output restricted by the single producer). And in judging copyright laws, the social value effected by the creation of additional intellectual works must be contrasted with the decreased output of embodiments of those works which would have been produced without any remuneration to the creator of the work. S.J. Liebowitz, *Copyright Law, Photocopying, and Price Discrimination, in* 8 Research in Law and Economics, *supra* note 32, at 181, 183-86. Accordingly, unless proposed stronger rights enhance the incentive to author new works, the result of their adoption would be just to increase the costs to the public and to deprive that public of unrestricted access to works that would have been created in the absence of these stronger rights.

65. The decision to employ copyright as a response is supported not only by its relative ease of administration and by a general reluctance to expand the area of government (subsidy) activity in the absence of a clear need but also by the recognition that copyright need not be an all-or-nothing device. Through a combination of grants and reservations the possibility exists of adjusting the rights granted so as to allow maximal access while still permitting the exclusion needed for private rewards. Copyright protection can be circumscribed so as to minimize its costs while retaining its benefits. One appropriate and useful focus for this tailoring is the definition of the term of protection. *See generally* Braunstein, *supra* note 35 (trade-off between scope of protection and length of time for which protection lasts); Paul Klemperer, *How Broad Should the Scope of Patent Protection Be?*, 21 RAND J. Econ. 113 (1990) (trade-off between a patent's length, *i.e.*, its lifetime, and its width, *i.e.*, its scope of coverage). The term chosen, the line drawn on the relevant temporal continuum, may be conceived as a compromise in a number of different

senses--practical, epistemic, and political. *See* Dale A. Nance, *Foreword: Owning Ideas*, 13 Harv. J.L. & Pub. Pol'y 757, 759-60 & n.18 (1990).

The "monkey-see, monkey-do" kinds of arguments advanced in favor of change, *i.e.*," The Europeans have done X, therefore we should do X", tend to ignore the overall structure of copyright law as a considered design and the place of the durational term as an element in the balances struck.

66. 17 U.S.C. sec. 106 (1994) ("Exclusive rights in copyrighted works").

67. 17 U.S.C. sec. 108-120 (1994).

68. 17 U.S.C. sec. 107 (1994) ("Limitations on exclusive rights: Fair use").

69. In practice, in addition to these statutory limitations, limitations are also imposed by the market environment in which the copyright is exploited. If there are close substitutes for the work, for example, power conferred by the exclusive rights may be severely limited. On the other hand, if there are no close substitutes, the right will provide greater bargaining leverage. The strength of the monopoly for any individual work will depend on both the legal and market constraints.

70. Among these basic doctrines that limit the breadth of copyright's reach are those of originality, the idea/expression dichotomy and the related notion of merger, and the noncopyrightability of the design of useful articles. They largely define the existence and scope of copyright in a work. Originality affords the basic requirement for copyrightability; it provides that only "original works of authorship" are eligible for protection. 17 U.S.C. sec. 102(a) (1994). Thus, copyright does not protect works which lack minimal creativity or are only copies of other pre-existing works. However, the fact that a work is entitled to protection because "original" does not mean that copyright prohibits all taking from that work. Under the judicially created "idea-expression" dichotomy, ideas are not protected, only the manner of their expression. This dichotomy permits some borrowing from every copyrighted work

by excluding ideas from protection; a future author is free to borrow the ideas embodied in the book though the book's expression may not be copied. More generally, the law bars protection to any idea, process, procedure, system, principle, concept or method of operation. 17 U.S.C. sec. 102(b) (1994). Copyright, then, is limited both in time and in the facets of the work that are protected. Adoption of the idea-expression dichotomy represents a judgment that the free use of "ideas" results in more works from subsequent authors than the society loses by failing to protect ideas. *See generally* Julie E. Cohen, *Reverse Engineering and the Rise of Electronic Vigilantism: Intellectual Property Implications of "Lock-Out Programs*, 68 S. Cal. L. Rev. 1091, 1122, 1133, 1136 & n.227 (1995); Wendy J. Gordon & Sam Postbrief, *On Commodifying Intangibles* 10 Yale J.L. & Human. 135, 154, 156 (1998) (book review). The dichotomy affirms that "some portion of the value of intellectual creativity is best sustained only if it is withheld from the market and not made the subject of exchange." Weinreb, *supra* note 32, at 1240-41 (social, cultural, and economic value of open, unimpeded exchange of ideas supported by dichotomy thought to exceed benefit of any hypothetical allocative effect of protecting ideas). When the expression of an idea is inseparable from the idea itself, *i.e.*, the idea can be expressed in only one way or a very limited number of ways, the doctrine of merger applies, and copying the expression is permitted to avoid conferring a monopoly on the idea. So the expression will not be protected where there are so few ways of expressing the idea that protecting the expression would effectively protect the underlying idea itself. *See* Dam, *supra* note 32, at 337 (merger doctrine tends to reduce economic rent and rent-seeking). These central precepts have given rise to bewildering difficulties of interpretation as to whether copying has been of protected expression or of the unprotected underlying ideas. For a thoughtful recent example of judicial application of the idea-expression and merger doctrines, see CCC Information Services, Inc. v. Maclean Hunter Market Reports. Inc., 44 F.3d 61 (2d Cir. 1994).

The limitation of protection to the form of expression rather than the ideas expressed means that copyright's main incentive goes much more to the processing of knowledge into widely accessible form than to the creation of new knowledge, although it sometimes may contribute a measure of subsidiary stimulation to the latter. Economic Council of Canada, *supra* note 10, at 130.

Copyright's low originality standard for protection bears centrally on any argument for increased protection rooted in recognition of intellectual and artistic excellence. *See* text at notes 218-26 *infra*. The elusiveness of the line between idea and expression pervades the application of copyright law. The malleability and indefiniteness of the dichotomy are well-recognized. *See, e.g.*, Nichols v. Universal Pictures Corp., 45 F.2d 119, 121 (2d Cir. 1930) ("Nobody has ever been able to fix that boundary, and nobody ever can.") (L. Hand, J.). *See generally* Peter Drahos, *Decentring Communication: the Dark Side of Intellectual Property, in* Freedom of Communication 249, 257 (Tom Campbell et al. eds., 1994) (dichotomy restates rather than resolves problem of distinguishing protectable from non-protectable expression). The pervasive difficulties for authors, counsellors, and judges in applying the idea-expression dichotomy (and related doctrines such as fair use) to determine how much use, if any, can be made of a copyrighted work point to an often-overlooked cost of the system and to one of the benefits of the expiration of protection and the entrance of a work into the public domain. *See* Alfred C. Yen, *The Interdisciplinary Future of Copyright Theory*, 10 Cardozo Arts & Ent. L.J. 423, 437n.37 (1992); text at notes 159-82 *infra*.

For the point that Congress and the judiciary have made little effort to limit the universe of copyrightable subject matter to those areas in which incentives are likely to affect the level of creative activity, see Stewart E. Sterk, *Rhetoric and Reality in Copyright Law*, 94 Mich. L. Rev. 1197, 1213-15, 1220-22, 1225-26 (1996) (creation of photographs and commercial advertisements not dependent on copyright incentive).

71. *Cf.* Fisher, *supra* note 32, at 1719 n.265. The term determines how long users

must accept the restrictions and fees a copyright proprietor may impose on the use of the work. The temporal dimension is essential for the question of financial value; how long protection will last is often the major factor in determining the market value of a copyright.

72. In an insightful, stimulating article Jessica Litman points to a disjunction between the creative process of authorship and the incentive-based notions underlying the Copyright Act and much of the secondary copyright literature. In particular, she pokes holes in the common assumption present in the literature that authors are in fact aware of copyright law. *See* Jessica Litman, *Copyright As Myth*, 53 U. Pitt. L. Rev. 235 (1991); *see generally* Jessica Litman, *The Exclusive Right To Read*, 13 Cardozo Arts & Ent. L. J. 29, 46-48 (1994) (proposition that production and dissemination of works is directly related to degree of protection available too simplistic); Cohen, *supra* note 10, at 1181 (1977) (skepticism that amount and quality of writer's output significantly correlates with period of copyright); Bender & Sampliner, *supra* note 32, at 269-70 (relationship between commerce and cultural creativity); Linda J. Lacey, *Of Bread and Roses and Copyrights*, 1989 Duke L.J. 1532, 1571-80. However, no matter what one's model of authorship, as long as economic return is the central consideration for publishers, *i.e.*, those who invest in dissemination, the copyright law's terms and their effects on investment return will be of prime importance to decisions to engage in publication or not. *See* Jessica Litman, *Copyright Noncompliance (Or Why We Can't "Just Say Yes" To Licensing*, 29 Int'l L. & Pol. 237, 249 (1996-97). That law is designed to permit recoupment for both the initiative in creating material and the investment risked in producing and marketing it.

As noted previously, note 32 *supra*, noneconomic motivations may stimulate authors to create. And even if moved by the prospect of economic return, an author may labor to produce a work even though there is no expectation of direct financial reward, as the effort may pay off financially in another market. In actuality, authors of different kinds of works undoubtedly respond to economic and noneconomic inducements in considerably differing degrees, and the threats to their livelihoods presented by different sorts of unauthorized uses of their works differ significantly by context.

The point here is not that authors and performers should go uncompensated, but that the traditional rhetoric of copyright apologetics should be taken with a grain of salt.

Chapter IV. The Costs of Protection
and the Asserted Costlessness
of an Increase in Duration

Copyright protection imposes several kinds of costs. These exactions include higher prices for those goods which are produced, transaction costs necessitated by the requirement to obtain permission to use a work, and administrative and enforcement costs. While the scope of protection conferred by copyright is less extensive than that granted by patent,[73] the exclusive right to control reproduction of the work empowers the proprietor to charge a price higher than would obtain if there were active competition in its production and marketing.[74] As a result, fewer people will have access to the work[75] with a corresponding cost to consumers (and authors) in underutilization of the product. We noted previously that the indivisibility characteristic of intellectual and artistic goods means that once the good is produced its beneficial use by a consumer may occur without imposing any additional cost on the producer. However, under a copyright regime where the owner may charge for access to the work, an individual who values the work at more than the cost of making a copy but less than the price will opt not to buy it.[76] This inefficient scenario, under which users surrender benefits that exceed the cost of their use, produces a deadweight loss.[77] And the interest in access and the corresponding social gain from the widespread dissemination of the ideas and information embodied in intellectual works are compromised.[78]

A second set of costs copyright exacts is the transaction costs incurred in obtaining permission to use or reproduce a work. These costs include identifying and contacting the copyright holder, bargaining with him, and arranging compensation.[79]

The rules for use of existing matter significantly influence the creation of new works, and the high cost of licensing and transacting with the copyright holder may prevent an author from using material from an earlier copyrighted work in his own work.[80] Put generally, the prohibition on unauthorized duplication and the attendant transaction costs operate to raise the cost of producing new creations.[81] The ban on borrowing from existing works constricts the sources on which the author may build, and this constriction of the public domain from which future authors may draw for inspiration and education makes it harder for them to create new works.[82] The restriction precludes or raises the costs of other authors' efforts. If sufficiently high, these costs hold the potential to subvert the copyright regime's objective of achieving an appropriate stream of original authorship over time.[83]

A third category of costs is the administrative costs of operating the protective system.[84] These costs are primarily the input of legal and clerical resources in government, the affected industries, and law offices.[85] As a general matter, public expenditures for court and administrative expenses are minor for a copyright system as compared with those for a patent system.[86] Since copyright protects the form of expression rather than the idea expressed, the person entitled to copyright is generally easy to identify.[87] Copyright's low originality standard for protection, *i.e.*, to qualify for protection the work need only demonstrate a dot of creativity and not be copied from another source, eliminates the need for any administrative screening of works for merit or imagination.[88] On the other hand, it is more costly to enforce systems of rights in copyrighted works than it is for most kinds of tangible resources. The difficulty of defining what is to be protected and who owns it in a copyrighted work raises these enforcement costs. One can fence a piece of real estate to indicate boundaries and prevent trespass. Fencing a copyrighted work is harder because the dividing line between what the author created and what he took from the public domain and other authors is often indistinct.[89]

The costs that copyright imposes are likely to increase as the period of protection lengthens. Transaction costs, for example, will expand with extension of the durational term. As time goes by, people who are interested in duplicating or using old copyrighted works will find it progressively more difficult to identify and locate the owner of the reproduction right and to obtain his permission.[90] Tracing the remote heirs of the author or other claimants of the copyright will be onerous,[91] and the uncertainty as to ownership attendant on these practical difficulties may well affect investment decisions.[92] Facilitation of the copying of old works, such as literary writings or recordings, is particularly important, though, for an old work which someone wishes to duplicate is likely to be of unique merit or to be needed for research or education, socially valuable activities.[93]

A realistic example will bring some of these generalizations to life. Over the past few decades there has been increased interest in preserving the work of early blues and jazz artists. A number of companies, particularly some small, specialty concerns, have labored to put together and reissue recordings of these artists.[94] These projects have a clear historical, cultural, and educational value. Under a protective scheme those involved in such a project not only have to locate decent-quality recordings of these artists--a very time-consuming job in itself--but they also have to identify, locate, and obtain the permission of those who control the rights to reproduction of each of the recordings. This task could prove a formidable obstacle to a project's fruition,[95] and a producer may well prefer to forego the activity rather than pursue permissions. A twenty year extension of the copyright term will simply expand the practical hurdles faced by the producer of such a project. Although the transaction cost problem can be mitigated by a registry arrangement[96], these costs can not be eliminated, and the passage of time only exacerbates them.[97]

While the costs of copyright protection rise significantly with the passage of time, the benefits do not. In markets where business decisions are moved by relatively short term considerations, extension of the term is unlikely to have decided incentive effects. Will the prospect of a possible sale more than seventy-five years from now significantly affect a record company's decision to produce a sound recording? Similarly, it is highly unlikely that a musical artist or composer would be deterred from performing or composing by the recognition that his royalties will cease fifty years, rather than seventy years, after his death.[98] Moreover, once the value of future income is discounted, the present value of a future copyright advantage is quite small. At a 10 percent discount rate, for example, a dollar to be received seventy-five years from now is worth a small fraction of one cent![99] Common sense aligns with economics, then, in concluding that the additional creation incentives provided by a twenty year increase in the copyright term will be minute. On the other hand, films or recordings which last seventy-five years or more may be uniquely valuable ("classics"); and extension of the copyright term may make it more likely that proprietors of these works can raise their prices above the competitive level, while it is progressively less likely that any such power will have influenced the decision to perform or produce.[100] Indeed, contrary to what is often asserted or assumed,[101] the fact that a particular work enjoys lasting popularity is not a reason to extend the term of copyright but rather a reason to limit it.[102] Its continued value heightens the interest in widespread dissemination and underlines the contribution to national culture and learning which follows from its entrance into the public domain where it can function as a building block of intellectual and imaginative activity.[103] Thus, at a time when the markets for copyrighted works are increasing and businessmen are rarely moved by any but quick-return considerations, proposals for the prolongation of copyright seem out-of-place.[104]

Professor Landes and Judge Posner properly observe that in analyzing the wisdom of an extension of the copyright term, not only must the additional revenues to be earned by authors and publishers from the extra twenty years be discounted to present value, but so also should the added costs to authors of new works due to the increase in time before source works will enter the public domain.[105] Such parallel treatment, dictating entries on both sides of the ledger, is called for if the increase in the term is prospective--that is, if the addition of twenty years applies only to those works which are created and fixed after the effective date of the legislation. However, such prospectivity characterizes neither the proposals which were urged on Congress nor the extension legislation which was, in fact, enacted in response. Under the Term Extension Act the term increase of twenty years applies to existing copyrights as well.[106] Indeed, that was a prime objective of some of the interest groups lobbying for the change.[107] The unbalanced result is that while benefits in terms of incentives to creation or publication will be negligible, if not non-existent (due to the time value of money), the increase in the cost of expression due to constriction of the public domain will be immediate and significant as the legislative change applies to borrowing from all works, both those in existence and those not yet produced.[108]

Professor Miller, however, claims that the discount calculations which underlie the proposition that the present value of a future copyright advantage is insignificant are in error because they fail to take proper account of inflation. He puts his criticism as follows:

> [Professor Kurlantzick] fails to see that the dollar value placed on future copyright advantages will increase more or less in proportion with the inflation rate. That is to say, if the dollar loses 90% of its value over the next 75 years, then the cost of goods and services will be roughly 90% higher in 75 years than it is today.[109]

This criticism betrays a misunderstanding of both the meaning of inflation and of its policy implications.

From the point of view of impact on incentives, the critical perspective is that of the person deciding whether or not to invest in the production and distribution of an intellectual or artistic work. Assume that in making that decision the potential producer estimates the long term return on his investment and, as a component of that estimate, he determines that he will earn $100 in today's prices in seventy-five years. To complete the calculation he will discount that $100 to its present value by applying an appropriate interest rate. This discounting process reflects the time value of money, the fact that he will have to wait to receive the income and that earlier availability is worth more to him than later availability.[110] Assuming a positive rate of interest, the more distant the deferred income the lower its present price. And this discounting of future income has nothing to do with inflation.

It is true that inflation--a rise in the general level of prices of goods and services--will likely affect the nominal price at which his goods are sold in the future and therefore his dollar receipts. However, as long as everything else costs more, the additional dollars he receives will not be worth more in terms of purchasing power.[111] Thus, while inflation may increase the nominal number of dollars received, it will also decrease the purchasing power of those dollars. The result is a wash. Apparently what Professor Miller has done is to factor in a relevant element on one side of an equation but not on the other. Or as a noted political columnist observed in a different setting, "It is like arguing that anyone should be able to walk from California to New York in a few hours, since the Earth's rotation is hurtling us all eastward at a rapid pace. Never mind that California and New York are also hurtling eastward at the same speed."[112]

In terms of a domestic calculus alone, then, an analysis of the probable costs and creation-inducing benefits of a twenty year increase in the copyright term does not support such a change.[113] The costs of this increase include both the wealth transfer payments to copyright owners during the period of the extension from consumers and producers who would otherwise have unrestricted use of works and also the loss to the community of works that are not authored because of the diminished public domain. Advocates of the change, though, commonly deny, minimize, or ignore these costs. The National Music Publishers Association (NMPA), the principal trade group for American music publishers, for example, contends that extending the term can be done "without causing harm to the interest of any person or entity."[114] A coalition of theatrical, music, and artistic trade groups concurs, declaring "that we can obtain 20 years of protection in the EC at virtually *no cost to ourselves.*"[115] And Professor Miller asserts:

> [W]orks of art become less available to the public when they enter the public domain--at least in a form that does credit to the original. This is because few businesses will invest the money necessary to reproduce and distribute products that have lost their copyright protection and can therefore be reproduced by anyone. The only products that do tend to become available after a copyright expires are "down and dirty" reproductions of such poor quality that they degrade the original copyrighted work.[116]

Similarly, the NMPA claims that the public availability of works is often diminished, rather than increased, when they enter the public domain with the result that there is a lack of quality copies of many works after their term has expired.[117]

Two prime concerns appear in these statements.[118] The first emphasis is a contention that the price of public domain works is frequently not lower than that of works under protection so that the value of wider availability is not served by a decision not to increase the term. The second concern is that public domain reproductions will be of inferior quality. The first contention is unpersuasive as it contradicts accepted microeconomics and some powerful contemporary empirical evidence, though it is worth noting why in a particular situation the price of a work might not decline. As for the quality of reproductions, it is not clear that this reference points to any problem worthy of social concern; *i.e.*, differences of quality in goods are typically handled by the economic system without legal intervention. However, even if a legitimate interest worthy of legal concern may be involved, an increase in the term of copyright protection is most definitely not an appropriate response.

64

Term Expiration and the Availability of Works

The first contention of the lesser availability of works after the expiration of copyright is of suspect credibility[119] because it is at odds with the tenets of accepted microeconomics.[120] Application of those tenets here indicates that all things being equal, expiration of copyright protection can only push in one direction, the direction of lower price, *i.e.*, price lower than would exist if copyright had not expired. Entrance of the work into the public domain means the elimination of one of the costs of production. The prospective publisher need no longer identify, bargain with, or pay a fee to the copyright proprietor. The effect of this reduction in the cost of a factor of production is a willingness of the producer to supply more of the good at each possible price. Expressed graphically, the change produces a shift of the supply curve to the right and downward. Assuming that demand is constant, the equilibrium or market-clearing price will drop; an increase in supply has a price-decreasing and quantity-increasing effect.[121] Another way to put the point is that under competitive conditions, price moves towards marginal cost, and the expiration of copyright removes one of the marginal costs of production. That process serves the interest in availability and exemplifies what has been termed "the competitive mandate"[122]--the social commitment to cheap and plentiful satisfaction of wants via a norm to produce goods as cheaply as we can unless reason to depart from the competitive process is shown. The opportunity for competitive, and therefore cheaper, dissemination of intellectual and artistic works is the means by which the betterment of the general public is achieved.

More concretely, with the lapse of copyright new, more varied, and better editions of great novels can be offered.[123] Orchestras can begin playing music that requires a great deal of rehearsal because they no longer have to pay large royalties. Derivative works such as musical plays and films based on literary creations[124] can be produced without risk. And the authoritarian estates of certain authors can no longer censor interpretations of an author's work with which they disagree or prevent critical biographers from quoting works freely.[125] In short, whenever copyright expires on a work, the public's access is almost always improved.[126]

The microeconomic propositions, though, do not mean that whenever a work's protection expires, a new cheaper edition of the work will appear. For example, even with the cost reduction, there may not be enough demand to justify putting out a new edition. The obstacle here--the lack of demand to call forth a new edition--does not exist because the expiration of copyright is irrelevant, and therefore this situation does not support the conclusion that copyright expiration is irrelevant to production. Similarly, there may be "stickiness" in the process by which the cost reduction gets translated into decisions. Again, such a situation would not support the proposition that expiration of copyright has no relevance for publication of works. Indeed, the publication of a new edition at a higher price would not necessarily be inconsistent with our economic propositions, as the work might not have been published at all in the presence of the copyright cost. The proponents of an increase in the copyright term seem to assume that the only proof that copyright expiration is relevant is a reduced price; and if a new edition appears without a price reduction, copyright expiration is therefore irrelevant. But as we have indicated, neither the assumption nor the conclusion is valid. The absence of copyright can manifest itself in a variety of ways leading to wider availability of works.

There is also strong contemporary evidence which tends to refute the advocates' contention of diminished availability of public domain works. American producers of entertainment products and computer software have been in the forefront of those complaining about and urging action against the unauthorized reproduction of American goods in foreign countries. The lack of effective protection abroad permits local manufacturers to reproduce a work without concern for copyright payments, and to sell the duplicates at prices below those charged by the original American producer. In other words, in environments where reproduction is unrestricted as a matter of law or fact, instances of *de jure* or *de facto* public domain, the result is widespread availability of the goods at reduced prices.[127] The irony is apparent--the same industries which point to widely available, lower priced "public domain" reproductions when seeking tougher national and international action against duplicators deny the existence of these same reproductions when seeking an increase in the copyright term. In any case, for policy makers to take their contention more seriously, proponents need to offer considerably more evidence of the situations they have in mind, evidence beyond anecdote and assertion. Until then, the proposition to be accepted is that expiration of the copyright term is relevant and pushes in the direction of lower price.[128]

A related confusion is expressed by other proponents of change who claim that without the market exclusivity that copyright offers, there is no incentive to distribute public domain works.[129] One of the errors in this line of thinking is the assumption that the same policy imperative that applies at the time of initial creation and dissemination also applies at later times. Exclusive rights and the prospect of supernormal profits are held out in order to solve the unique problem flowing from the initial producer's cost disadvantage and the distinctive economic characteristics of intellectual and artistic works. However, once the work has been created and a time sufficient to recoup investment has passed, there is no more reason to assume a call for monopoly profits or subsidy here than with any other product. At that point the artistic good is no different from any other, and the same incentive for distribution applies. As with other goods, distribution will occur if the distributor can cover the costs of distribution plus a normal profit.[130]

Inferior Reproductions and Misrepresentation of Source

The other theme which runs through the advocacy of those who support an increase in the term of protection is that reproductions of public domain works are generally of inferior quality.[131] The term "inferior" is somewhat ambiguous. It could refer to at least two kinds of qualitative attributes of the reproduction. The first sense of "inferior" is illustrated by the reproduction which is made with materials that are of lesser quality than those used by other manufacturers. This kind of inferiority might be well exemplified by sound recordings. For example, a prerecorded tape recording might be made of tape which will not last as long as another available ingredient. Similarly, the raw material used may not convey the musical performance with the same fidelity as another kind of tape; that is, its ability to accurately recreate the original sound signal is less.[132] In this kind of situation the copy is "inferior" in the descriptive sense of being less durable or of lower fidelity.

Surely the production of goods which are inferior in this sense can be imagined. Indeed, the manufacture and sale of such goods occur every day. The homeowner intent on improvements is faced with a variety of roofing shingles, some more expensive than others, some longer lasting than others; he confronts a similar array when looking at paints. In making his decisions he presumably weighs considerations of price, safety, durability, and aesthetics; and he is generally pleased to have the choices. The question, then, is why should the production and sale of these "inferior" goods be seen as a problem deserving of legal attention. Rather than worthy of regulation or prohibition, the availability of these transactions is socially desirable. And, of course, every producer has the incentive to make an acceptable product in order to sell it and to make subsequent sales.

Certainly, intellectual and artistic goods, like any others, may be marketed in a way that is misleading. Attributes may not be truthfully stated. For example, a record duplicator may not only copy the recording, but also reproduce the label and the album jacket which contains the original producer's name and trademark.[133] This kind of behavior introduces an element of deceptive merchandising into the transaction, thereby violating the consumer's and the economic system's interest in providing accurate information to purchasers as to the source and other salient characteristics of the product being purchased. The consumer, who wants to get the same thing he got before, is injured in our record example in that he is unable to pinpoint responsibility for defects and to assign praise or blame to the true source of the product. The original producer is injured by losing trade and by possible loss of reputation. The economic system is harmed in that misrepresentation results in misallocation of resources by leading purchasers to buy products that do not match their wants; the misled consumer buys a product which he would not have purchased if he had been accurately informed. When a consumer makes a purchase on the basis of inaccurate information, his demand is not satisfied, skepticism about the information received from producers is increased, and effective functioning of the market system is frustrated.

This kind of behavior may also be seen as socially harmful from a somewhat different angle which has particular bearing with respect to intellectual and artistic works. The ability to insure accurate attribution reduces the transaction costs involved in dissemination of the ideas of a society's most talented members. And it is principally by knowing to whom to attribute work, superior and inferior, that society moves creators to do their best.[134]

In light of the lack of any net social benefit in the practice of misrepresentation, it is not surprising that this behavior violates a whole host of legal proscriptions, both federal and state, civil and criminal, judge-made[135] and legislatively[136] and administratively[137]-defined.[138] Moreover, to facilitate consumer understanding the original producer is able to advertise his product's virtues and point out the differences in quality. Thus, both public and private responses to the problem of misrepresentation are available.

One can clearly and unqualifiedly condemn the practice of misrepresentation without disapproving of the non-deceptive duplicator. The behavior that is justifiably condemned goes to the marketing of a product and not to the manufacture of the good itself. Accordingly, as long as one has attended to the problem of consumer deception, no need exists for the extension of a general prohibition on duplication. To respond to the possibility of occasional deceptive practices in the sale of public domain works by lengthening the term of copyright, with all its attendant costs, would be to use a megaton explosive to kill an ant.

Degrading Reproductions and the Interest in Integrity

The second sense of "inferior"[139] is illustrated by the reproduction which alters or deforms the work being copied. Thus Professor Miller refers to a "degradation" which does not do credit to the original work.[140] The reference here is to the author's personal interest[141] in insuring respect for the integrity of his composition and in preventing alteration and deformation of the work, what is often termed the right of integrity.[142] In the case of a sound recording, the fear would be an unauthorized duplication which distorts the performance and does not fairly represent the artistic and technical standards of the recording artist.[143] However, even if one has sympathy for this integrity interest, it does not support an extension of the copyright term.[144]

Several bases, pecuniary and nonpecuniary, underlie the protection of integrity. The principal root appears to be a concern for the author's reputation. Thus the standard formulation speaks of the author's right "to object to any distortion, mutilation or other modification of...the said work, which would be prejudicial to his honour or reputation."[145] But that reputational interest is weakened if not extinguished by the author's death. Under our law we generally recognize no action for defamation of the dead; one who defames a deceased person is not liable to either the person's estate or to his descendants or relatives.[146] And under the 1976 Act's scheme the author is not only deceased, he has been dead for fifty years when the copyright term expires. Thus, it is difficult to see how one can seriously argue for a twenty year extension of the period in terms of concern for the author's reputation.[147]

Similarly, if the basis for the integrity concern is the view that an intellectual or artistic work should be regarded as an extension of the author's personality, again it does not provide a grounding for extension of the copyright term. Under this conception an unauthorized alteration of the work is deemed akin to a physical or psychic assault on the artist's persona; he experiences personal anguish and damage to his self-conception from seeing his work abused.[148] But in our hypothetical situation the author or artist has already been dead for fifty years. So this approach affords no more support for change than the reputational one.

Another possible basis for insuring respect for integrity is the social interest in cultural preservation. This interest is at its strongest in the case of "one-of-a-kind" works, *i.e.*, works which are embodied in only one original representation (*e.g.*, a painting) or a limited edition (*e.g.*, an etching).[149] And, not surprisingly, in the United States both federal and state legislative responses to the integrity claim have centered on such works of the plastic and visual arts.[150] Of course, most of the works which have historically been protected by the copyright system, including music and recorded performances, are not characterized by this singularity. They are reproducible in numerous copies, the presence of a "distorted" copy does not foreclose access to the original,[151] and it is these kinds of works which are regularly reproduced abroad with and without permission. Moreover, a concern for cultural preservation would be better served by some kind of landmark-like approach which focuses on the safeguarding of designated individual works of historical or cultural importance rather than a copyright device which forbids the use and reproduction of all works.[152] So again the cited concern does not support the change enacted.

The conclusion is inescapable that a concern about distorted copies and the low quality of reproductions provides no support for an extension of the copyright term. Indeed, the fact is that even if interference with integrity is viewed as a serious problem, and the author's interest as creator in maintaining the integrity of his work and his reputation in connection with it not only survives his death but endures for (more than) an additional five decades,[153] the interest can be satisfied without recourse to a copyright scheme with all of its attendant costs. That a duplicator may sometimes interfere with the integrity interest does not indicate that he will frequently or always do so. A general prohibition on duplication is not necessary to vindicate the integrity interest.[154] It can be protected directly, and less restrictively, either by means of explicit statutory recognition, as is done in many civil law countries,[155] or by the development of judge-made tort law.[156] While the evolution of applicable tort law will involve difficult questions of fact and law--for example, as to what constitutes "distortion"[157]--the interest in simplicity of litigation is hardly weighty enough to justify the extension of a general prohibition against duplication.[158]

In sum, the contentions put forth by proponents of change about the price and quality effects of the expiration of copyright are unconvincing and do not justify an extension of the term of protection. The assertions about the cost and price of public domain works are implausible, as they conflict both with accepted microeconomic theory and historical evidence. The claims about quality are ambiguous. Under one meaning of inferiority, no problem requiring legal attention is presented. Under the other meaning, it is questionable that the integrity interest is sufficiently weighty fifty years after the death of the author to support legal intervention; but if such intervention is called for, it can be accomplished by a less restrictive and costly means than via a copyright scheme.

Term Extension and the Subtle Costs of Copyright Protection

The emphasis of proponents of change on the lack of benefit from copyright expiration, in particular the misguided contentions that public domain works will be of inferior quality and no cheaper, focuses attention on the reproduction of entire works. This focus on reproduction in whole of works tends to deflect thought from the more subtle costs that copyright protection imposes and other related considerations of importance in thinking about duration. These costs include the opportunity for censorial use of the copyright power by the copyright proprietor, whether by the suppression of material which he deems to reflect poorly on himself or an ancestor[159] or by the imposition of restrictive conditions on the interpretive performance of the work so as to produce artistic frustration and sterility.[160] These inhibiting effects are not limited to explicit acts of censorship but encompass, as well, self-censorship by authors and publishers fearful of litigation.[161], particularly with respect to the use of unpublished materials. In addition, those effects are heightened by the vagueness and accompanying unpredictability of copyright's limiting doctrines, such as fair use[162] and the idea-expression[163] and fact-expression dichotomies.[164]

Consider, then, the impact on and reaction of historians to a well-known, recent set of cases decided by the Supreme Court and the Second Circuit Court of Appeals which, in interpreting the bounds of fair use, significantly limited a writer's ability to quote from or paraphrase unpublished materials, in particular unpublished letters, composed by an historical or biographical subject.[165] The decisions, which apparently enjoined anything other than minimal use of unpublished documents, elicited a strong, critical response. Historians and biographers contended that compliance with the rulings' strictures would seriously crimp historians, run against the canons of historical scholarship, and produce historical writing which lacks texture and accuracy.[166] They claimed that the professional commandment to go to the original sources and effective pursuit of their craft to forward knowledge require the ability to quote from unpublished sources such as letters, diaries, memos, and rough drafts. As the distinguished author, Taylor Branch, put it, "The quotation, in modest and appropriate amounts, of source materials is crucial to providing intimacy, immediacy, ambience, and re-creation of motives and values that history requires and readers need."[167]

Even if one regards as hysterical the tone of some of these critiques proclaiming the end of history and journalism and the serious impairment of the ability to produce professional biography, one still needs to acknowledge that the author and publisher planning to quote from unpublished sources ran (and still run) a serious risk.[168] The use of letters[169] and similar materials to shed light on character or style or to support arguments had been considered a standard academic research practice. Yet this practice and other historical uses of archival manuscript materials were now attended by deep uneasiness.[170] One result, reflecting both the case outcomes and the lack of clarity of the line between permissible limited quotation or paraphrase (fair use) and infringement, was considerable, and troubling, self-censorship by authors and book publishers.[171]

These disconcerting effects have both an individual and a social dimension. The costs exacted are individual in the sense that the liberty of the historian is constrained, his freedom as an intellectual limited. The reference to the liberty of the potential defendant shifts the spotlight away from the more usual emphasis on the perspective of the putative property owner to that of the predicament of the frustrated copier.[172] That individual's freedom of expression and use of cultural materials are curtailed when that expression is central to his self-constitution and the ideal of personal autonomy.[173] The exacted costs are public in the sense that the historian has a social role in the promotion of learning. And the execution of that role in the achievement, articulation and dissemination of historical knowledge is impeded.[174] To the extent that the spread of knowledge bolsters democratic institutions, the social harm resulting from the silencing of the author goes well beyond the loss to consumers who would have paid to read his work.[175]

To extend the copyright term is to increase and perpetuate these costs at the expense of, among others, literary critics, biographers, and especially contemporary historians,[176] without the receipt of any obvious productive gain in exchange.[177] On the other hand, entrance of works into the public domain removes these costs. Public domain status permits historians and other creators to avoid not only the dilemmas and risks posed by fair use but also the uncertainties presented by other difficult-to-apply copyright doctrines[178] when they face the question of whether and how much use they can make of a work. As the work is now freely accessible without the need to obtain consent or pay royalties, any concern about censorship disappears. Similarly, the possibility of self-censorship, which discourages the creation of new works, should fade. Scholarly publication of archival documents can be made without discomfort; and textual and historical criticism of the work can be freely engaged in.[179] The historian need no longer balance the risk of copyright liability against what he regards as professionally sound treatment.[180] Though often neglected, the public domain--a type of intellectual commons in which all have rights to entry--is a central element in the copyright schema,[181] as it serves the social value in easy access to works which educate, enlighten, inform or entertain. More generally, authorship is possible only when future authors are able to borrow from those who have composed before them, and one way to insure access to the building blocks so as to avoid a decrease in production of creative works is to restrict the term and therefore the need to pay a price to borrow.[182]

The constitutional policies, expressed in the Copyright Clause, of promotion of learning and protection of the public domain are disserved by extension of the copyright term. As a step which shapes the kind of intellectual life we are each able to lead, it is mistaken. The creation-inducing effects of the proposal will be negligible or non-existent. On the other hand, the costs of protection will expand, and the restriction of the public domain, with consequent harm to users and future authors, is clear.[183] That restriction will be significantly exacerbated by a retroactive element, as the Term Extension Act does not limit the grant of an additional twenty years of protection to works fixed after the date of the legislation but confer that increase on existing works as well.[184] Adoption of copyright extension will produce a permanent twenty year loss to the public domain with no public benefit and significant potential harm to the healthy advance of science and culture.

Remarkably, what has gone unnoticed in the debate about term extension is that one of the principal American exporters of artistic works, the record industry, will not, in fact, benefit in Europe from enactment of the extension legislation. Sound recordings are generally regarded as works for hire under American law, and the record company is therefore deemed to be the "author" and initial copyright owner of the recorded performance. Under the 1976 Act works made for hire were protected for a term of seventy-five years from publication or one hundred years from creation, whichever expires first.[185] Holders of rights in such works received a term of protection twenty-five years longer than that provided by the European Union system, which is fifty years from first publication or communication to the public.[186] Since the maximum term of protection for producers of sound recordings in Europe is fifty years, increasing the work for hire term in the United States by twenty years to ninety-five years will have no effect on the term that American companies are granted in the European system.[187] In other words, for these works--which constitute a sizeable percentage of American popular cultural exports--enactment of change will result in domestic burdens with no offsetting foreign gains![188]

Without doubt Congress has considerable latitude in deciding how to comply with the Constitution's injunction that protection be for "limited times". At some point, though, an ever-lengthening term crosses a line beyond which the constitutional provision's prescription about "limited times" and its underlying purposes are mocked as the term becomes limited in form and name only.[189] A term of 200 years from publication, for example, would presumably render hollow the constitutional notion of limitation.[190] An exceedingly long term also raises First Amendment concerns as the time limit is one key way in which copyright law accommodates to the First Amendment interest in people being able to hear and read as well as express themselves freely.[191] In view of the costs and benefits we have identified, the enacted twenty year increase, which will produce a representative term just short of a century, comes close to crossing that line if it does not, in fact, do so.[192]

Reference to the First Amendment underlines the proposition that the durational limit serves important public interests in addition to economic ones; and the case against lengthening the term is rooted in the values of robust debate, citizen education, and expressive diversity as well as that of economic efficiency. Copyright law governs entree to the culture of our society. Professor Netanel has ably argued that copyright plays a central role in democratic self-governance and underwrites political competence.[193] Under this view, copyright promotes the democratic character of public discourse by serving two democracy-enhancing functions. In service to its production function copyright offers an incentive for creative expression on a wide array of issues, thereby supporting the discursive foundation for democratic culture and civic association. Its second function is structural. Here copyright, by according a proprietary entitlement, sustains a sector of creative activity that is free from reliance on government subsidy and elite patronage. The democratic paradigm requires that protection be strong enough to insure support for copyright's production and structural functions; but at the same time it would grant authors a limited entitlement so as to make room for and to encourage transformative and educational uses of existing works. Copyright, then, is a limited grant fashioned to foster the expressive diversity and citizen autonomy needed for democratic governance, and its term of protection should be determined with that objective in mind. Viewing the term issue through this democratic lens and therefore accepting that copyright should offer protection beyond that necessary to provide a possibility of return to induce the creation and distribution of new works, the conclusion remains that a lengthening of the term with the attendant impairment of public access and expressive diversity is undesirable. The democratic paradigm supports a rich public domain in order to maintain an acceptable degree of transformative expression and discursive exchange; to expand the public domain is to further the interest of maximizing the capacity of people to express themselves effectively. In light of the existence of an independent and diverse sector of authors and publishers under prior law, the damage to cultural development and expressive diversity which an increase in the term will produce is a cost that can not be justified.[194]

Notes

---

73. *E.g.*, Paul Goldstein, Copyright's Highway 19-20 (1994). The patentee's right to forbid all others to make, use, or sell his invention is the most exclusive right in intellectual property law. While copyright law protects only the author's "expression" and does not extend to any idea, process or system described, patent law protects the process against exploitation by others. In addition, independent invention is not a defense to a claim of patent infringement. Thus, if a second inventor created his process or product without ever having any contact with the patentee's work, his "innocence" and original creation would not be defenses. In copyright law, on the other hand, coincidental independent creation of a similar work is not an infringement. Infringement requires proof that the defendant actually copied the protected work and that his product was not the result of his original effort. Sheldon v. Metro-Goldwyn Pictures Corp. 81 F.2d 49, 54 (2d Cir. 1936) (L. Hand, J.) ("[I]f by some magic a man who had never known it were to compose anew Keats's Ode on a Grecian Urn, he would be an 'author,' and, if he copyrighted it, others might not copy that poem, thought they might of course copy Keats's.... But though a copyright is for this reason less vulnerable than a patent, the owner's protection is more limited, for just as he is not less an 'author' because others have preceded him, so another who follows him, is not a tort-feasor unless he pirates his work"). As a practical matter, though, it is difficult to succeed with the defense of independent creation, particularly given the doctrine of unconscious copying. *See* Bright Tunes Music Corp. v. Harrisongs Music, Ltd., 420 F. Supp. 177 (S.D.N.Y. 1976, *aff'd sub nom.*, ABKCO Music, Inc. v. Harrisongs Music, Ltd., 722 F.2d 988 (2d Cir. 1983).

Professor Kasdan suggests that one result of these differences in the scope of protection, which make it more likely that a patent holder will enjoy significant market power, is that the misallocative effects of copyright are less than those of patent. And he speculates that the lesser misallocation effects may explain why the topic of duration has not received as much attention in copyright discussion as the equivalent topic in the patent literature. John Kasdan, The Economics Of Copyright With Applications To Licensing 7-8 (1986). *See generally* Frank H. Easterbrook, *Intellectual Property Is Still Property*, 13 Harv. J. L. & Pub. Pol'y 108, 111n.7 (1990); Lotus Dev. Corp. v. Borland Int'l, Inc., 49 F.3d 807, 819 (1st Cir. 1995) (Boudin, J. concurring)("no accident that patent protection has preconditions that copyright protection does not--notably, the requirements of novelty and non-obviousness--and that patents are granted for a shorter period than copyrights"). *But see* Mark A. Lemley, *The Economics of Improvement in Intellectual Property Law*, 75 Texas L. Rev. 989, 1013-14, 1038-40 (1997) (for some types of works scope of copyright owner's rights may be broader than that afforded by patent). Perhaps ironically, Fritz Machlup complained some thirty years ago of the absence of study of the length of the patent term, Fritz Machlup, *Some Economic Aspects of the United States Patent System*, in Ad Hoc Committee on the Role of Patents in Research, Nat'l Research Council, Pub. No. 980-B, The Role of Patents in Research: Proceedings of a Symposium of the National Academy of Sciences 63 (1962)("[T]here has not been a single study made why 17 years may not be too long or too short, or whether it is just right. Seventeen years is accepted because this has been the historical term. No one has yet found any good reasons."); and there have been a number of recent sophisticated analyses of the optimum duration of copyright protection. *See* William M. Landes & Richard A. Posner, *An Economic Analysis of Copyright Law*, 18 J. Legal Stud. 325, 361-63 (1989); Braunstein, *supra* note 35, at IV-1-IV-58.

74. *See* McCain, *supra* note 58, at 270-72. In the music industry, for example, one probable result of lack of copyright protection would be a reduction in price of recordings, particularly high-volume popular recordings. While it is impossible to determine precisely the extent to which lower prices would result, there is every reason to believe that without protection the price of many popular records would drop due to active competition in their production and marketing. The first producer will either charge less initially for a successful album, the demand for which is not

in serous doubt, in order to reduce the pirate's price advantage or he will reduce his price when the pirate enters. The other probable result would be a reduction in new releases. Protection encourages the assumption of greater risks; the odds facing the producer are increased and winners may prove highly remunerative. In the absence of protection these odds are decreased, and the receipts on successful products are reduced due to competition. Thus, one possible consequence of permitting duplication would be fewer new releases with lower prices and therefore wider dissemination of many of those popular records which are released. The question of legal protection, then, might involve a choice between more new releases at higher prices or fewer releases with wider circulation at lower prices. Economic theory, unfortunately, offers us no answer to the question of which of these alternatives will maximize net satisfactions.

A reduction in price of some goods may produce secondary benefits beyond the benefit to the immediate consumer. For example, a reduction in textbook prices, Breyer has noted, would have significant social value. *See* Breyer, *supra* note 33, at 315-16; Hartwick, *supra* note 58, at 23-24 (externalities in publishing). Increased circulation of a textbook or scholarly work can produce benefits whose value far exceeds the cost of the extra books. Placing texts in the hands of more students means more intellectual stimulation, greater productivity, and increased research. Moreover, funds for education are always and inevitably in short supply; by leaving students, colleges, and school boards with more money to spend, lower textbook prices can lead to the beneficial result of more expenditure on research and education. Thus price reductions in the case of textbooks would be quite valuable socially. Similar statements can not be made with respect to recordings; comparable spillover benefits would not accompany record price reductions. Records generally are not "intermediate" products--like a reference book, for example--from which other works flow, but rather a "consumption" item. Thus the effect of lower record prices in transferring wealth from performer or producer to consumer is likely to be more important than its effect on record distribution.

75. *E.g.*, Wendy Gordon, *Assertive Modesty: An Economics of Intangibles*, 94 Colum. L. Rev. 2579, 2590-91 (1994). Put differently, copyright imposes a "tax" on consumers, audiences, and later authors. The more expansive the definition of rights the larger the increase in the cost of watching, reading, and listening to an author's expression. The result is that in some cases and for some people access to the work will become too expensive. The extent of the "tax" imposed by copyright, *i.e.*, the extent to which it raises significant obstacles to listener, viewer, or reader access, depends on a number of factors including the degree of the owner's market power (due to product differentiation) over any given consumer use of his particular work. Netanel, *supra* note 58, at 294-96 & n.39. *See also* Lunney, *supra* note 55 (efficiency cost from overprotection in addition to reduced access).

The proposition that intellectual and artistic works would be underproduced in a market without copyright protection rests on the assumption that one work is not a complete substitute for another and therefore that, with protection, an author does enjoy market power to some degree. Recognition of the fact that substitutability will vary among works, see note 77 *infra*, leads to the conclusion that copyright gives each creator at least some monopoly power, and it gives greater power to some authors than to others. Sterk, *supra* note 70, at 1205 & n.45.

76. *See* Braunstein, *supra* note 35, at II-2, II-13, IV-1. Thus, the benefit to the copyright proprietor is secured at the expense of those who would have purchased the work at the lower price if there were no copyright protection but who are unable or unwilling to purchase it at the price set by the copyright owner. One effect of copyright protection, then, is to force some consumers to satisfy their demands by switching to goods that cost society more to produce than the copyrighted work. That added cost is a social waste.

Assuming some market power--*i.e.*, consumers view other works as imperfect substitutes--the copyright holder's pricing policy will also have another economic effect: dollars that would have remained in consumers' wallets, had the work been priced at the point where the marginal cost of producing it equalled the demand for it, will now go to the copyright holder. This wealth transfer from consumers to producers, though, is generally viewed as having no predictable impact on allocative efficiency. *See* Fisher, *supra* note 32, at 1701 & n.204.

77. In the terminology of economists, the deadweight or social loss refers to a gauge of how much worse off people are paying the monopoly price than paying the competitive price. It measures the value of lost output, *i.e.*, the output which would have been produced had competitive pricing existed. Its two components are 1) the extent of lost satisfaction experienced by each consumer who can not buy the product because of its monopolistic price and 2) the number of consumers who experience such loss. Deadweight loss reflects the fact that consumers who value the product at more than its marginal cost but less than its monopoly price will not buy it; instead they will shift to what they view as less satisfactory substitutes or do without that sort of intellectual product altogether. As long as these consumers regard other artistic and intellectual products as imperfect substitutes for a particular copyrighted work, the right-holder's pricing will leave them buying a less-valued work. Technically, the deadweight loss in allocative efficiency comprises the total of the consumer surplus that would have been reaped by the denied consumers and the producer surplus that would have been garnered by the copyright proprietor had he sold the work to them. *E.g.*, Hal R. Varian, Intermediate Microeconomics 404-06 (2d ed. 1990). Adjustment of the duration of protection is one way that a copyright system may reduce deadweight losses without deterring authors from creating new works.

These efficiency losses vary significantly between types of copyrighted works depending on the degree of market power enjoyed by the copyright holder. At one extreme are singular works for which there are no substitutes in the eyes of the consumer. At the other extreme are works for which nearly perfect substitutes exist; here if the holder raises the price, the quantity of copies bought will drop sharply. Most copyrighted material lies between these extremes. (Also, the degree of market power held by a particular copyright holder may differ dramatically as between different types of consumers, *i.e.*, within different markets.) Any thoughtful analysis of the copyright system must recognize the existence of this spectrum.

78. Put more generally, copyright impedes the ease with which information and goods are exchanged between members of the society. Keyes & Brunet, *supra* note 35, at 38.

79. Related costs are those involved in the initial decision as to whether there is a need to seek permission. The author and his lawyer, for example, might have to determine the scope of protection for the copyrighted work in order to assess whether the proposed use would likely constitute an infringement.

80. With recent developments in digital technologies, multimedia works often take small parts of existing works and transform them into dramatically different combinations of sounds and images for entertainment and educational purposes. A life plus fifty period of protection may well impede the creation of valuable multimedia works because of the transaction costs involved in bargaining for the number of licenses required. Extending the term of protection can only aggravate this problem. *See generally* Michael A. Heller & Rebecca S. Eisenberg, *Can Patents Deter Innovation? The Anticommons in Biomedical Research*, 280 Science 698 (1998) ("tragedy of the anticommons"--complex obstacles that arise when downstream user needs access to multiple patented inputs to create a single useful product; paradoxical consequence of biomedical privatization is possible underuse of resources when government gives too many people rights to exclude others).

81. An important point to note is that the potential users are not simply parasites. These users, copyists, and adapters may be creators themselves; they "may reach markets different than those reached by the original creators, or they may bring new perspective, reduced cost, special expertise, deeper insights, or innovative technology

to the exploitation and adaptation of established works." Transaction costs, though, may discourage or prevent these desirable creative efforts and results. Gordon, *supra* note 40, at 157-58, 250.

82. Landes & Posner, *supra* note 73, at 332 (copyright protection beyond some level may be counterproductive; raising the cost of expression to future creators may lower the number of works created); Posner, *supra* note 32, at 339 (absence of copyright protection reduces cost of writing by enabling author to take freely from his predecessors); Dreyfuss, *supra* note 32, at 217-20 (limit to how much increase in protection will raise output since cost of producing new works rises as level of property rights granted existing material is raised; optimal protection seeks to balance benefit of improving incentives upstream against burden of raising costs to downstream users). Determination of the comparative strength of producers' interest in lowering the cost of production and idea originators' interest in recouping their investment, and fine-tuning translation of that determination into copyright doctrine may be more complicated than initially appears. For exploration of that complexity and criticism of Landes and Posner's claims that non-protection of ideas (the "idea-expression" dichotomy) and the greater strength of producers' interests can be deduced from their model, see Croskery, *supra* note 45, at 641-45. Croskery admits that a different ground, the high costs of fencing, supports non-protection of ideas.

With respect to the term extension enactment, the implication is that the more we tie up old works in ownership rights that do not produce a public benefit in the form of greater creation incentives for new works, the more we limit the ability of current authors to add to the common fund of knowledge, culture, and entertainment by building on and enlarging the cultural heritage passed on by their predecessors. The probable net impact will be a reduction in the authorship of new works, as a term extension must to some extent discourage the production of new works derivative of those for which protection has been extended and which would otherwise be in the public domain. Thus, transaction costs and the attendant diminution of the public domain impose a social detriment in the form of works that are not produced. Little attention is paid by extension supporters to the loss represented by the absence of valuable new works that are not authored because underlying works, domestic and foreign, that would have served as a foundation remain under copyright protection. While the magnitude of this loss can not be known, it is nonetheless real. *See generally* White v. Samsung Electronics America, Inc., 989 F.2d 1512 (9th Cir. 1993) (Kozinski, J., dissenting); Steve Zeitlin, *Strangling Culture with a Copyright Law*, N.Y. Times, April 25, 1998, at A15.

83. *See* Kenneth W. Dam, Intellectual Property in an Age of Software and Biotechnology 3-4 (1995); Dam, *supra* note 32, at 337-38 (care needed to avoid undue favor of innovation today at expense of innovation tomorrow; objective of copyright law policy should be achievement of appropriate balance of innovation over time); Richard A. Posner, Economic Analysis of Law 47 (5th ed. 1998). The important general point is that negative effects result from too-extensive protection; such protection can actually impede artistic innovation, reduce the opportunities for creativity, decrease the availability of new products and of our cultural heritage, delay scientific progress, and restrict public debate. At some point the provision of additional copyright protection will yield a reduction in the supply of new works because the number of marginal authors dissuaded from creation by the high cost of source material will exceed the number stimulated to create by the increased value of a work tied to the marginal increase in protection. *See generally* Justin Hughes, *The Philosophy of Intellectual Property*, 77 Geo. L.J. 287, 323-25 (1988). For an account of the information society which underlines the blindness of an author-centered legal regime to the importance of the public domain (and the corresponding undervaluation of the interests of audiences for information) and its destructive economic consequences, both allocative and distributional, in denying future creators--novelists, scientists, computer programmers--the raw material they need to fashion new products, see Boyle, *supra* note 9. Professor Boyle is especially, and

appropriately, critical of the analysis and recommendations of the Clinton administration's 1995 Commerce Department White Paper, "Intellectual Property and the National Information Infrastructure: The Report of the Working Group on Intellectual Property Rights."

84. *See generally* Jussawalla, *supra* note 33, at 25. The reference to administrative costs bespeaks a tacit assumption that the legal and technical expertise needed to argue and assess competing claims is present in the society. Internationally, the quest by technology-exporting countries for a strongly protective intellectual property agreement, one with high standards and adequate enforcement, fails to recognize that this expertise is lacking in many technology-importing countries whose legal systems probably can not be readily modified to handle the more technical cases of alleged copyright and patent infringement. See Keith E. Maskus, *Intellectual Property, in* Jeffrey J. Schott, ed., Completing the Uruguay Round: A Results-Oriented Approach to the GATT Trade Negotiations 164, 172-73 (1990).

85. In addition to administrative costs one must consider the possible "transcendent costs" of protection. "Transcendent costs" refer to restrictions upon production as a result of monopoly power strengthened through copyright positions. *See* Machlup, *supra* note 36, at 63-64; Machlup, *supra* note 73, at 61. Professor, (now Justice), Breyer speculated in the context of college textbook publishing that the power to accumulate copyrights may produce such costs with the result that not only is competition in the same title eliminated but competition between titles also is reduced, a result which can find no support in the rationale of copyright, Breyer, *supra* note 33, at 318-19. While his reasoning on this point is not completely persuasive, it is sufficient to note here that in light of the apparent ease of entry into most copyright-related industries, the record business for example, significant transcendent costs are unlikely.

As a general matter, the power to accumulate patents is likely to prove more detrimental to actual and potential competition than the power to accumulate copyrights, for the scope of protection afforded patents is significantly greater. *See* note 73 *supra*; Ejan Mackaay, *Economic Incentives in Markets for Information and Innovation*, 13 Harv. J.L. & Pub. Pol'y 867, 904-05 (1990). *See generally* Phillip Areeda & Louis Kaplow, Antitrust Analysis 557-562 (4th ed. 1988); Dam, *supra* note 32, at 336. While copyright protection only extends to an author's "expression", a patent protects the use of an inventor's "idea"; the patent blocks related processes based on the patented principle. This protection limits the production of competing products which might keep down the price of the patented product. In contrast, under the copyright system protected works generally have many competitors as exclusive rights are granted only to each form of expression. Thus, the potential monopoly power of individual copyright holders whose works must compete with each other is usually likely to be insubstantial. *See* Douglas A. Smith, *Recent Proposals for Copyright Revision: An Evaluation*, 14 Canadian Pub. Pol'y 175, 178 (1988) ("Copyright by its nature confers some degree of monopoly power but since copyright works compete directly with each other, the degree of monopoly will be limited in many cases"). *See also* Gordon, *supra* note 75, at 2580 n.8.

86. Where the copyright system calls for registration, the administrative cost of operating it is greater than in systems where the benefit of copyright protection is conferred automatically. But that cost is still small relative to the costs of a patent (or trademark) registry because the element of examination is missing.

During fiscal year 1992 gross expenditures by the Copyright Office amounted to $26 million. The comparable figure for the Patent and Trademark Office was $421 Million. Office of Budget and Management, Budget of the United States Government, Fiscal Year 1994 Appendix-39, 65 (1993). *See also* John P. Palmer, *Copyright and Computer Software*, *in* 8 Research in Law and Economics, supra note 32, at 205, 217-18.

87. B.V. Hindley, The Economic Theory of Patents, Copyrights, and Registered Industrial Designs 38 (1971).

88. In comparison the patent system mandates a time-consuming, demanding, and expensive process under which a patent applicant must prove that his invention meets the stringent statutory requirements of novelty, utility, and nonobviousness. *See* 35 U.S.C. secs. 101-03, 111 (1994). To receive a patent, an invention must be previously unknown, include a nonobvious step, and be industrially useful. *See generally*, Ralph S. Brown, *Eligibility for Copyright Protection: A Search for Principled Standards*, 70 Minn. L. Rev. 579, 588-89 (1985) ("The right to control use of a work, although granted to inventors, has never been part of copyright except as performance may be considered 'use.' Indeed, the absence of a 'use right' helps justify the relatively casual approach to granting copyright as opposed to the more searching tests for patentability.")

89. William M. Landes, *Copyright Protection of Letters, Diaries, and Other Unpublished Works: An Economic Approach*, 21 J. Legal Stud. 79, 83 (1992); Posner, *supra* note 32, at 342 (particularly costly to enforce copyrights because infringed and infringing works lack the ready observability of conflicting uses of tangible resources; easier to observe the trespasser standing on one's land than to spot and prove a plagiarism). Also, the public goods characteristic of intellectual and artistic works increases enforcement costs because detection of "theft" is rendered more difficult. A duplicator may be able to copy a copyrighted work without the author knowing of it. One cannot steal an automobile without the owner discovering it. *Id. See generally* Carol M. Rose, Property and Persuasion: Essays on the History, Theory, and Rhetoric of Ownership 17 (1994):

Some objects of property claims indeed seem to resist clear demarcation altogether--ideas, for example. To establish property rights in such disembodied items, we may be reduced to translating the property claims into sets of secondary symbols that are cognizable in our culture. In patent and copyright systems, for example, one establishes an entitlement to an idea's expression by translating the idea into a written document and going through a registration process--though from the unending litigation over ownership of these expressions and over which notions can or cannot be subject to patent or copyright, we might conclude that these secondary symbolic systems do not always yield universally understood "markings."

See also Peter Drahos, A Philosophy of Intellectual Property 153-155 (1996) (abstract objects, legal judgments of identity, and drawing of boundaries). Professor Gordon suggests that legal prohibitions on copying impose noneconomic costs, at least as compared with private methods of fencing-off, "such as creating in the user population a perception of governmental compulsion which could give rise to a species of resentment." Wendy J. Gordon, *Asymmetric Market Failure and Prisoner's Dilemma in Intellectual Property*, 17 U. Dayton L. Rev. 853, 856 n.13 (1992).

90. *See, e.g.*, Michael Holroyd, *How Do We Block The Drain? The Problems of Locating and Retaining Literary Papers*, Times Literary Supplement, June 23, 1995, at 24. *See also* Ayn Rand, *Patents and Copyrights, in* Capitalism: The Unknown Ideal 125, 127 (1966):

If [intellectual property] were held in perpetuity, ... it would lead, not to the earned reward of achievement, but to the unearned support of parasitism. It would become a cumulative lien on the production of unborn generations, which would ultimately paralyze them. Consider what would happen if, in producing an automobile, we had to pay royalties to the descendants of all the inventors involved, starting with the inventor of the wheel and on up. Apart from the impossibility of keeping such records, consider the accidental status of such descendants and the unreality of their unearned claims.

See generally Gordon & Postbrief, *supra* note 70 at 151-52 (full property rights in common culture may alter self-conceptions in damaging ways).

91. Passage of time and multiple dealings with the copyright in a work produce

difficulty in identifying who is entitled to particular rights and with whom negotiations for permission must be conducted.

> [A]fter only a few hereditary successions owing to the often complex laws of succession and the increasing legal fragmentation, the certain determination of the legal owners which is necessary for legal transactions would no longer be at all possible or only with great difficulty.

Preamble to West German Copyright Law of 1965, quoted in Adolf Dietz, Copyright Law in the European Community 161 (1978). Tracing costs are likely to be substantial when a creative work is old not only because of the obvious succession puzzle but because the author may well have entered into many contracts for the work's use. *See also* E.P. Skone James, et al., Copinger and Skone James on Copyright 137-38 (13th ed. 1991) (practical difficulty of tracing title after long period to kind of property of which there can be no physical possession; unreasonable to give protection to author's remote successors); Cohen, *supra* note 10, at 1185:

> Because copyright ownership is...disembodied, and because exclusive ownership of the various rights under a copyright is possible, the task of tracing ownership many years after an author's death certainly presents both practical and theoretical problems not present with ordinary real or personal property.

These practical problems are accentuated by the approach used, at one time, in some countries of making the term of protection depend on the life of the surviving spouse or children. *See* Finkelstein, *supra* note 10, at 1048. Under these schemes a potential user of a work would have to know not only the date of the author's death but also the identity and dates of death of his spouse and various children. *See* Cohen, *supra* note 10, at 1191-92; *see also id.* at 1218 (joint authorship exacerbates difficulties; much more difficult to determine date of death of last member of large musical recording group than to find date of death of author of a novel).

While collective licensing and computerized tracking systems hold out the promise of significant reduction of these transaction costs, the complexities of ownership guarantee that these costs will persist and that the passage of time will aggravate them.

92. Concern about these tracing costs formed a significant part of the reasons for the Copyright Office's opposition to a copyright term measured by the death of the author in the Office's initial comments on the revision process leading to passage of the 1976 Act. The Register of Copyrights' 1961 Report recommended that the term of protection be computed, instead, from the time of first public dissemination. That recommendation derived from an overriding commitment to the value of the ability of the public to determine the date of the event triggering the measurement period. Thus, for someone wishing to reproduce a work, "the death date of authors who are not well known would often be difficult to ascertain." Report of the Register of Copyrights, *supra* note 29, at 47-49.

93. The presence of spillover benefits will vary among kinds of writings and their settings. Thus, a reduction in textbook prices, Breyer has noted, supra note 33, at 315-16, would likely have significant social value. Increased circulation of a textbook or scholarly work can produce benefits whose value far exceeds the cost of the extra books. Placing texts in the hand of more students means more intellectual stimulation, greater productivity, and increased research. Moreover, funds for education are always and inevitably in short supply; by leaving students, colleges, and school boards with more money to spend, lower textbook prices can lead to the beneficial result of more expenditure on research and education. Price reductions in the case of textbooks, then, would be quite valuable socially. Similar statements can not be made with respect to sound recordings. Comparable spillover benefits would not accompany record price reductions. It is true that record purchases by libraries

and educational institutions are on the rise, but these represent a trivial part of the market. Records generally are not "intermediate" products--like a reference book, for example--from which other works flow but rather a consumption item. Thus the effect of lower prices in transferring wealth from performer or producer to consumer is likely to be more important than its effect on record distribution. And to the extent that the question of protection becomes one of simply shifting income between buyers and sellers, one is more likely to be neutral or to favor sellers when the buyers are just listeners of popular records than when they are students, colleges, or school districts.

94. *See, e.g.,* John S. Wilson, *Time Remembered--Blues, Jazz and Swing*, N.Y. Times, Nov. 28, 1971, sec. 2, at 32; Phil Elwood, *Record Archives in Sorry Shape, Magazine Series Laments State of Historic Material*, San Francisco Examiner, July 18, 1997, at D6. *See generally* Bill Holland, *Upgrading Labels' Vaults No Easy Archival Task*, Billboard, July 19, 1997, at A1.

95. Several years ago the president of one of the small concerns specializing in reissues of early black artists stressed in his conversations with one of the authors the lengthy, difficult, often unreasonable negotiations for permission to reproduce as a major obstacle to his efforts.

96. Congressional awareness of this problem led to the inclusion in the 1976 Act of provisions directing the Copyright Office to maintain records containing information about the death of authors and designed to provide key data to prospective users of authors' works. 17 U.S.C. sec. 302(d)-(e) (1994). In a life plus system, the year of an author's death is a critical date in computing the length of copyright. Section 302(d) permits anyone having an interest in a copyright to file a statement of the date of the author's death or a statement that the author is alive as of a particular date. Section 302(e), as amended, provides those with an interest in a copyrighted work with a financial incentive to file information that the author remains alive or that less

than seventy years have passed since his death. Users of a work who, after a prescribed interval, rely on the absence of such recorded information in the Copyright Office files, are given the benefit of a presumption that the author has been dead for at least seventy years. This "good faith" reliance on the Copyright Office's report, stating that its records contain no indication that the author is still living or died less than seventy years before, operates as a complete defense to an infringement action.

Some countries with lengthy terms of protection have tried to minimize the costs imposed through a variety of measures. Canada, for example, formerly provided that any person can reproduce a copyrighted work during the last twenty-five years of the copyright term upon payment of a 10 percent royalty to the copyright proprietor. *See* Copyright Statute of Canada sec. 7, 1 UNESCO Copyright Laws and Treaties of the World (1992). Other countries attempt to alleviate the difficulty of contacting proprietors of old copyrights by providing that a person may reproduce a copyrighted work after he has made a reasonable, but unsuccessful, effort to contact the copyright owner. *See e.g.*, Copyright Act, R.S.C., ch. C-42, sec. 77 (1985) (Can.) (owner who cannot be located); Copyright Act of Czech and Slovak Republics sec. 18(1), 1 UNESCO, Copyright Laws & Treaties of the World (1992); Francis J. Kase, *Copyright in Czechoslovakia--The New Copyright Statute of 1965*, 14 Bull. C. Soc'y 28, 45 (1966). Another country requires payment in order to prolong copyright beyond an initial brief term. *See* Honduras, Copyright Provisions in Patents Statute, art. 4, 8-9, 2 UNESCO Copyright Laws and Treaties of the World (1992). Such measures are probably unnecessary if the term of protection is short. However, in the case of a lengthy term of protection, such mitigating measures merit serious attention, and no extension of protection can justifiably be enacted without incorporation of some such devices.

Presumably in response, in part, to the concerns articulated here, the 1998 Copyright Term Extension Act departed from predecessor bill versions by providing that libraries, archives, and nonprofit educational institutions may reproduce and distribute copies of works for preservation, scholarship, teaching and research during the added twenty years of copyright protection, if the work is not being commercially exploited and can not be obtained at a reasonable price. *See* Copyright Term Extension Act, *supra* note 3, at sec. 104; S. Rep. No. 315, 104th Cong., 2d Sess. 6, 18 (1996). It is questionable, though, that this provision offers any more than is already permissible under a proper application of the principle of fair use. *See* Statement of Copyright and Intellectual Property Law Professors in Opposition to H.R. 604 and S. 505 "The Copyright Term Extension Act of 1997" 6 n.6 (June 16, 1997).

97. *Cf.* Richard Gilbert & Carl Shapiro, *Optimal Patent Length and Breadth*, 21 RAND J. Econ. 106, 112 n.3 (1990) ("simply the costs incurred by a future would-be inventor to determine whether an invention infringes any existing patents are likely to increase markedly with the statutory patent lifetime. The costs of searching previous patent records, and the uncertainties imposed on inventors, could be large indeed if an inventor were exposed to the risk of being found to infringe a hundred-year old patent").

98. *See* Stephen R. Barnett & Dennis S. Karjala, *Copyrighted From Now Till Practically Forever*, Washington Post, July 14, 1995, at A21 (de minimis incentive effect; "What author is going to decide not to write another book because copyright royalties will flow only for 50 years, not 70 years, after her death?"); Thomas, *supra* note 32, at 21 (questionable that ever-lengthening term enters calculations of prospective writers, artists, or composers); Cornish, supra note 19, at 489-90 (decisions to create and exploit works made by reference to much shorter time scales); Sterk, *supra* note 70, at 1207-08, 1223-24 (number of works produced not directly proportional to level of copyright protection; present term unnecessary to stimulate creative activity). *See generally* Arnold Plant, The New Commerce in Ideas and Intellectual Property 11-12 (1953). Is it really believable that authors' and publishers' decisions in 1999 will be influenced by rights that their successors will have in 2074 and thereafter? In this context, worthy of note is the observation of the

Second Circuit in the case challenging the constitutionality of New York's Son of Sam law under which revenues owed to authors from books relating their criminal activities are to be held in escrow to satisfy the claims of creditors and victims and released to authors only after five years: "The possibility of a payday five years or more down the road...can hardly be seen as providing an adequate incentive." Simon & Schuster v. Fischetti, 916 F.2d 777, 781 (2d Cir. 1990).

The Copyright Act's termination of transfer provisions complicate the analysis of the creation-inducing effects of an increased term, but they do not alter the conclusion that the incentives for creation and publication will at most be minimally affected by a change. The 1976 Act continues the policy of allowing authors or their heirs to avoid copyright transfers after a certain number of years. Section 203 creates a right to terminate transfers or licenses, whether exclusive or non-exclusive, of a copyright or any right under a copyright executed by the author after January 1, 1978. Generally, this termination may be effected at the end of thirty-five years from the execution of the grant. *See* 17 U.S.C. sec. 203 (1994). However, accepting that it is very difficult to predict at the time of creation which works will have long term survival value, the existence of inalienable termination rights exercisable thirty-five years after any transfer by an author means that an additional twenty years on the ultimate duration of the copyright can not add value to initial transfers of the copyright by the author and thus, can not serve as a further economic stimulus to creative production. In other words, no natural person will receive anything more in exchange for terminable rights in his work under a life + 70 system than under the life + 50 term. The reason is that a purchaser of the right to exploit the work will pay nothing for the extra twenty years because those putative additional years can be freely terminated, along with whatever remains of the current period, before they ever begin. *See* Sterk, *supra* note 70, at 1217-20.

Admittedly, at the time termination rights accrue, the holder of the termination right, who will be the author or his descendant, may have a better estimate of the work's survival value than was possible at the point of creation.

Therefore, an additional twenty years of duration at that time may increase the work's value to the rightholder. However, if the holder of the right is in fact the author, the additional twenty years will hold minimal value since by hypothesis the term has at least fifty years to run. Given the riskiness of any investment in a copyright, even one with continued value after thirty-five years, the present value of a life plus seventy copyright will not be significantly greater than that for a life plus fifty one. If, on the other hand, the author has been dead thirty years when the termination right accrues, the forty year duration of the descendant's post-termination rights under a life plus seventy scheme may well render those rights more valuable than if the remaining period were only twenty years. Thus, the enacted system will give some differential economic benefit to some authors' descendants that is not present under the life + 50 system, namely those who make use of termination rights long after the author's death. What is not clear, though, is whether there is evidence to demonstrate that providing such an uncertain benefit to these heirs would stimulate authors to greater production. Comment of Copyright Law Professors on Copyright Office Term of Protection Study, Oct. 27, 1993, at 7-8.

99. Jerome N. Epping, Jr., *Harmonizing The United States and European Community Copyright Terms: Needed Adjustment or Money for Nothing?*, 65 U. Cin. L. Rev. 183, 214-15 n.192 (1996); Posner, *supra* note 83, at 46-47 ("as a result of discounting to present value...the knowledge that you may be entitled to a royalty on your book 50 to 100 years after you publish it is unlikely to affect your behavior today"). A 10% rate yields a result of $.00078. Significant risk attends the production and sale of many intellectual and artistic goods, *see* Hartwick, *supra* note 58, at 3 (enterprise of book publishing is largely one-shot), and riskiness elevates the discount rate. At 15% the result would be $.000028. The formula used to make this computation is $1/(1+i)n$ where i is the interest rate and n is the period of time. *See, e.g.*, Meir Kohn, Money Banking and Financial Markets 113 (2d ed. 1993).

If the term of protection were lengthened so that we would be speaking of the case of a dollar due twenty years later, *i.e.*, ninety-five years from today, the present value would be even more minute. At a 10% discount rate, the result would be $.000117; and at 15% $.000002. *See generally* Braunstein, *supra* note 35, at IV-18 (if discount rate increases, then optimal period of protection decreases); F.M. Scherer, *Nordhaus' Theory of Optimal Patent Life: A Geometric Reinterpretation*, 62 Am. Econ. Rev. 422, 424 1972) (determination of socially optimal patent life must take account of diminishing return effect arising from fact that later years' monopoly rents are discounted more heavily than those in early years). Put more generally, as a motivator of behavior distant benefits tend to be considerably less persuasive than relatively immediate advantage.

The point about de minimis incentive effect is made in strong, non-mathematical terms in 1 Thomas B. Macaulay, Miscellanies 241 (1901) (parliamentary speech of Feb. 5, 1841).

100.   Lord Macaulay eloquently made this point some 150 years ago in a parliamentary speech delivered in opposition to a bill to extend the copyright term to 60 years *pma*. In reference to Dr. Johnson, who had been dead for half a century at the time of his speech, he noted:

> Now, would the knowledge that this copyright would exist in 1841 have been a source of gratification to Johnson? Would it have stimulated his exertions? Would it have once drawn him out of his bed before noon? Would it have once cheered him under a fit of the spleen? Would it have induced him to give us one more allegory, one more life of a poet, one more imitation of Juvenal? I firmly believe not. I firmly believe that a hundred years ago, when he was writing our debates for the Gentleman's Magazine, he would very much rather have had twopence to buy a plate of shin of beef at a cook's shop underground. Considered as a reward to him, the difference between a twenty years' term and a sixty years' term of posthumous copyright would

have been nothing or next to nothing. But is the difference nothing to us? I can buy Rasselas for sixpence; I might have had to give five shillings for it. I can buy the Dictionary, the entire genuine Dictionary, for two guineas, perhaps for less; I might have had to give five or six guineas for it. Do I grudge this to a man like Dr. Johnson? Not at all. Show me that the prospect of this boon roused him to any vigorous effort, or sustained his spirits under depressing circumstances, and I am quite willing to pay the price of such an object, heavy as that price is. But what I do complain of is that my circumstances are to be worse, and Johnson's none the better; that I am to give five pounds for what to him was not worth a farthing.

1 Thomas B. Macaulay, Miscellanies 242-43 (1901) (speech of Feb. 5, 1841).

101. *See, e.g.*, Statement of Sen. Orrin G. Hatch Before The U.S. Senate, The Introduction of the Copyright Term Extension Act Of 1995 4-5 (March 1, 1995).

102. Guinan, *supra* note 15, at 32-33:

It can be argued that if commercial value is significant in regard to the length of term, it leads to a conclusion against, rather than for, a longer term. The argument might be stated as follows:

It is of little significance to the public at large what happens to works which have no commercial value at the end of the term. Few will wish to use them. Such works will not be exploited in a variety of editions, recordings, productions or the like. It is the works which still have commercial value which should fall into the public domain as soon as the constitutional purpose [of inducing creation by provision of an adequate incentive] has been achieved (rather than continuing protection for the benefit of remote heirs), for it is the works which still have commercial value from which the public will benefit in the form of more numerous and varied editions, recordings and productions.

See id. at 26, 32. In the case of the great work of lasting social value copyright's tendency, through higher prices, to impede dissemination is especially harmful to the cause of learning. *See generally* Braunstein, *supra* note 35, at IV-1-2 ("the sooner restrictions on use...are lifted, the more useful will that...item be to society"). After all, while copyright policy is designed to reward creative intellectual effort so as to induce talented people to pursue it, it also aims to make the results of their genius available to as many people as possible as quickly and as cheaply as possible. Its goal is not to supply income to descendants for the full economic life of the work. The constitutional concept of a limited term of copyright protection rests on the idea that we <u>desire</u> works to enter the public domain and become part of the common cultural heritage that provides a rich collective source on which to found new works. *See* Netanel, *supra* note 58, at 368-69.

In a similar vein Senator Hatch cited the historical significance of the 1927 movie "The Jazz Singer", the first sound film to be commercially released, in support of the term extension legislation. *See* 141 Cong. Rec. S3392 (1995). However, it is surely the historical importance of the movie that dictates allowing it to enter the public domain so that film historians and others can fully and effectively use it. As long as it remains protected, important uses will not occur due to the royalty and transaction costs involved in obtaining permission from the copyright owners. *See also* note 100, *supra.*

103. *See generally* Braunstein, *supra* note 35, at III-16 (assumption that appropriate length of protection does not exceed the expected economic life of the property); *id.* at I-11 n.1:

In general...the optimal period of protection will be less than the useful economic life of the item covered. This is necessary in order to make sure that the net gains from the project are shared by the investor and by the general public. Obviously, the latter's gains are limited until after the expiration of the copyright since before that time the copyright holder may be able to use the monopoly power it confers to extract the bulk of the gains flowing from the copyrighted product.

We do not mean to imply here that expiration of copyright on writings of no great popularity is socially insignificant. Books without commercial value, for instance, may nevertheless be of great scholarly interest or shed light on the social history of the day. The enactment of legislation to extend the copyright term, then, will insulate such works from exploitation--subject to the fair use privilege--for whatever scholarly value they may have for an additional twenty years and thus will deprive the public of any scholarly value such works might have during that additional period. Oscar Cargill & Patrick A. Moran, *Copyright Duration v. The Constitution*, 17 Wayne L. Rev. 917, 925 (1971). *See also* John P. Barlow, *The Economy of Ideas: A Framework for Rethinking Patents and Copyrights in the Digital Age (Everything You Know about Intellectual Property is Wrong)*, Wired, March 1994, at 84, (generally information is perishable, but yesterday's papers are quite valuable to the historian). Under the pre-1976 law such works of little commercial value would fall into the public domain after twenty-eight years.

Indeed, during the copyright revision process Congress was faced with proposals for retaining the renewal term or limiting the term for unpublished works in response to the concern that since a large majority of copyrighted works were not renewed, a life plus fifty term would tie up a substantial body of material of no commercial interest which would be more readily available for scholarly use if free of copyright restrictions. A large number of unrenewed works had scholarly value to archivists, historians, and specialists in a variety of fields. Ultimately, Congress concluded that the benefits of a life plus fifty term outweighed these disadvantages.

See H.R. Rep. No. 1476, 94th Cong., 2d Sess. 136 (1976). That conclusion is questionable, but it is surely dubious that the case for life plus seventy outbalances these interests. Such an extension will significantly impede the efforts of archivists and educators to preserve and transmit portions of our cultural heritage. *See* text at notes 159-182 *infra* on some of the difficulties copyright poses for the historical enterprise.

104. *See* Benjamin Kaplan, *Impact of Proposed Copyright Legislation: The Businessman, The Government and the Public,* 8 Idea Conference No. 154, 155, 157 (1964); Thomas, *supra* note 32, at 19, 46. *Cf.* Plant, *supra* note 98, at 6-7, 15.

105. Landes and Posner, *supra* note 73, at 362.

106. *See* Copyright Term Extension Act, *supra* note 3, at sec. 102.

107. *See* Ralph Blumenthal, *A Rights Movement With Song at Its Heart,* N.Y. Times, Feb. 23, 1995, at C13 (Amsong, group of heirs of songwriters, seeks legislation extending copyrights on pre-1978 compositions to 90 years after composition); John J. Fialka, *Songwriters' Heirs Mourn Copyright Loss,* Wall St. J., Oct. 30, 1997, at B1; *The Copyright Term Extension Act of 1995: Hearing on S. 483 Before the Senate Judiciary Comm.,* 104th Cong., 1st Sess. 65 (1997) [hereinafter *Senate Hearing*] (statement of E. Randol Schoenberg, grandson of Arnold Schoenberg); William F. Patry, *Copyright and the Legislative Process: A Personal Perspective,* 14 Cardozo Arts & Ent. L.J. 139, 149 (1996) (term extension bill not motivated by "life + 70" term or concern for obtaining European royalties but rather by desire to secure additional income for "old act works", particularly music composed in 1920s and 1930s); Shauna C. Bryce, *Recent Developments: Life Plus Seventy: The Extension of Copyright Terms in the European Union and Proposed Legislation in the United States,* 37 Harv. Int'l L.J. 525, 538-39 (1996). *See generally* Peter A. Jaszi, *Goodbye to All That--A Reluctant (and Perhaps Premature) Adieu to a Constitutionally-*

Grounded Discourse of Public Interest in Copyright Law, 29 Vand. J. Transnat'l L. 595 (1996) (alternative, and unwelcome, vision of copyright underlies support for retroactivity).

108. This legislative change holds out the real counterproductive possibility of a net decrease in the creation of new works. Application of a term increase to existing copyrights will, of course, have no positive incentive effects as those works have already been created. But such application can not be justified on equitable grounds either. And legislation which accomplishes this end is arguably unconstitutional. *See* text at notes 259-65 *infra*.

109. Miller, *supra* note 5.

110. Strictly speaking, interest represents the price of earlier availability, rather than later availability, of rights to use goods. The real rate of interest reflects the rate at which present consumption goods can be traded off for future consumption goods. *E.g.*, Armen A. Alchian & William R. Allen, University Economics 179 (3d ed. 1972).

111. Not surprisingly, in order to remove the distortive effects of inflation, economists generally analyze investment in inflation-corrected terms. That is, they examine the demand for investment by considering the effects of real output and real interest rates on real investment outlays, meaning that the references to the values of these variables are in constant prices. And the real interest rate, the interest rate that borrowers pay in terms of real goods and services, is defined as equal to the nominal (or money) interest rate less the rate of inflation.

112. Michael Kinsley, *The Thinker*, The New Republic, August 14, 1995, at 36 (book review of *To Renew America* by Newt Gingrich).

113. *See* Keyes & Brunet, *supra* note 35, at 59-63; Economic Council of Canada,

---

supra note 10, at 140-48 (lengthening of term of copyright unjustified; existing term of life + 50 provides ample time for income flow to copyright holders and surviving dependents).

Indeed, if anything, that analysis suggests that, based solely on domestic considerations, a decrease in the term would be desirable. However, The Berne Convention, to which the United States acceded in 1988, requires a minimum term of life plus fifty *pma* for most covered works. See text at notes 23-24 *supra*.

114. Comments of the National Music Publishers' Association, Inc. (NMPA), In the Matter of Duration of Copyright Term of Protection, Docket No. RM 93-8, Copyright Office, September 22, 1993, at 2. If extension would, in fact, be costless, one must wonder--why have any time limit on the protection? The assertions of costlessness are directly at odds with the claims of supporters of legislative change that they will be deprived of sizeable European revenues if the United States does not extend its term to match that of Europe. *See, e.g., infra* note 183.

115. Joint Comments of the Coalition of Creators and Copyright Owners, In the Matter of Duration of Copyright Term of Protection, Docket No. RM 93-8, September 22, 1993, at 10.

These trade groups have some esteemed company in their erroneous assertion about the costlessness of an extension of protection. Speaking of intellectual property Jeremy Bentham favored "an exclusive privilege" because it is "of all rewards the best proportioned, the most natural, and the least burdensome." He went on to argue, mistakenly, that such a privilege "produces an infinite effect and...costs nothing." Jeremy Bentham, Rationale of Reward 318 (1825). Similarly, John Bates Clark argued with respect to patents that "the inventor's monopoly hurts nobody. It is as though in some magical way he had caused springs of water to flow in the desert or loam to cover barren mountains....His gains consist in something which no one loses...." John Bates Clark, Essentials of Economic Theory 361 (1927). *See generally* Waldron, *supra* note 29, at 862-68.

Bentham, in proclaiming a patent system costless, neglected, among other costs, not only the cost of operating the system but also the cost of inventing, *i.e.*, the use for research and development work of personnel withheld from other activities. Advocates of copyright and patent protection often overlook as a cost of protection the alternative output which the resources would yield in other employment. *See* Alfred C. Yen, *Restoring the Natural Law: Copyright as Labor and Possession*, 51 Ohio St. L.J. 517, 543 n.164 (1990). Thus, if a shift of resources were induced by a reduction in protection, such a shift would not necessarily be harmful, for the resources may move into fields of at least equivalent social value. In the context of book publishing, for example, Breyer has speculated that a modest decline in college textbook revenue should not cause serious social concern. If the royalty income of authors, who are primarily college teachers, is threatened, he speculates, these authors may turn to writing scholarly articles or to devoting more time to teaching. Since these activities provide considerable spillover benefits, he concludes that substituting more of them for somewhat fewer college textbooks should not prove socially harmful. *See* Breyer, *supra* note 33, at 309. In the record industry context, though, it is impossible to even plausibly speculate as to the directions in which most of the "freed" labor and capital resources will move if protection were reduced or eliminated and as to whether the marginal performer will produce a more or less valuable social product in some other field.

116. Miller, *supra* note 5. A similar claim appears in the House Report accompanying the 1976 Act, being offered there to support the increase of the term of protection then to life plus fifty. H.R. Rep. No. 1476, 94th Cong., 2d Sess. 134 (1976). Perhaps not surprisingly, this dismissive and inaccurate view of the value of the public domain is not a recent phenomenon. *See* Ervin Drake, *Perpetuating Aid To The Arts*, Billboard, April 4, 1982, at 20, col. 2.

As we make clear in the following pages, we very seriously doubt that the general result of entrance into the public domain is "down and dirty" reproductions of works. However, if that output were the common response, one would still have to ask whether that outcome occurs because it is what the consumer wants.

117. *See* Comments of the NMPA, *supra* note 114, at 6.

118. These sentiments are not novel, though their older expression is no more persuasive. *See* Charles Morgan, The House of Macmillan (1843-1943) 174 (1944).

119. This error also appears in Cohen, *supra* note 10, at 1187, where it is mistakenly asserted that there is no significant connection between the existence or non-existence of copyright protection and the price of the good involved.

120. Even if Professor Miller's erroneous contention were accepted, we note that it speaks to only a small portion of the full range of values represented by the public domain. Whether or not public domain status tends to encourage republication of works, it does aid a wide range of other new uses, including translation, adaptation to new media, and scholarly criticism. Professor Jaszi makes this point well in his testimony before the Senate Judiciary Committee. He also notes that public domain status provides some works a new lease on popularity and offers examples to support the proposition that publishers do, in fact, compete to offer new editions of popular public domain works. *See Senate Hearing, supra* note 107, at 73 (statement of Peter A. Jaszi).

121. *E.g.*, Campbell R. McConnell & Stanley L. Brue, Economics: Principles, Problems, and Policies 54-62 (12th ed. 1993).

122. Paul Goldstein, *The Competitive Mandate: From Sears to Lear*, 59 Calif. L. Rev. 873 (1971); Robert A. Gorman, *Comments on a Manifesto Concerning the Legal Protection of Computer Programs*, 5 Alb. L.J. Sci. & Tech. 277, 285-86 (1996); Ralph Brown, *Unification: a Cheerful Requiem for Common Law Copyright*, 24 UCLA L. Rev. 1070, 1093, 1105 (1977).

123. Patrick Parrinder, *The Dead Hand of European Copyright*, 15 Eur. Intell. Prop. Rev. 391 (1993) (as soon as copyrights of D.H. Lawrence, W.B. Yeats, James Joyce and Virginia Woolf expired, competing paperback editions of their works appeared; for first time readers given choice of text and publishers had incentive to produce better and cheaper editions). In addition, the impending termination of copyright protection stimulates improved versions of classic works. Extension of protection will postpone the appearance of these improved editions. *See* John Sutherland, *The Great Copyright Disaster*, London Rev. of Books, Jan. 12, 1995, at 3.

124. Recent examples of the public benefit flowing from imaginative freedom to author derivative works from the public domain are the high quality films based on the works of Jane Austen, "Emma", "Persuasion", and "Sense and Sensibility".

125. *See* Parrinder, *supra* note 123, at 392 (literary scholarship significantly facilitated by expiration of copyright: "As authors approach classic status there is a growing need for definitive editions, for critical commentaries including quotation, and for extracts to be reprinted in anthologies. Where the work is in copyright, permissions for these acts of exploitation is very frequently refused.") *See generally* L. Ray Patterson, *Copyright and "The Exclusive Right" of Authors*, 1 J. Intell. Prop. L. 1, 4, 17-18, 25 (1993). Professor Patterson argues that the limitations on congressional power expressed in the copyright clause are designed to protect against the misuse of copyright. Misuse would take place if a copyright proprietor used copyright as a means of information control to inhibit rather than promote learning. The expiration of the term of protection removes the risk that historians and biographers will be inhibited from offering independent assessments of earlier authors and their writings by descendants who, for whatever personal reasons, employ copyright to prevent the publication of parts of protected writings. *See also* David Vaver, *Some Agnostic Observations on Intellectual Property*, 6 Intell. Prop. J. 125, 136-39 (1991) (examples of use of copyright for purposes of censorship by public and private agencies).

Attempts by copyright owners to use their proprietary rights to suppress personal, social, or political criticism are at odds with copyright's democracy-enhancing goals. Netanel, *supra* note 58, at 294-95. Contemporary examples of such use include infringement suits filed by Howard Hughes and J.D. Salinger to enjoin the publication of biographical material. *See* Rosemont Enterprises. v. Random House, Inc., 366 F.2d 303 (2d Cir. 1966); Salinger v. Random House, Inc., 811 F.2d 90 (2d Cir. 1987). The more expansive the definition of copyright the more likely and the easier its invocation to impede criticism. *See* text at notes 159-182 *infra*. *See generally* David Lange, *At Play in the Fields of the Word: Copyright and the Construction of Authorship in the Post-Literate Millennium*, L. & Contemp. Probs., Spring 1992, at 139, 142 ("What comes naturally to copyright...is the deliberate, if selective, suppression and advancement of speech").

126. Richard Morrison, *New Rights for all the Wrong Reasons*, The Times, Feb. 18, 1995, at 5. *See* Patrick Parrinder, *Who Killed Clause 29?*, Times Literary Supplement, Feb. 9, 1996, at 16 (cheaper, more definitive editions with copyright expiration); Guinan, *supra* note 15, at 26 ("greater probability of more varied editions of works of lasting value, and a wider opportunity to distribute existing works competitively, and use them as the basis for new creation, if they are freely available").

127. *See, e.g.*, Mike Trickey, *Russia: 'Pirates' Profit Selling Cut-rate Movies, CDs*, The Ottawa Citizen, July 24, 1995, at A6 (widespread duplication of computer software, videocassettes, and compact discs; the CDs sound just like the originals); Callan, *supra* note 36, at 27, 32-37. China and other Far Eastern countries, as well as Russia, have come in for particularly vigorous criticism. A focus of that criticism has been on how perfectly and quickly "pirates" can reproduce works. *See, e.g.*, Bryce, *supra* note 107, at 542-46; Linda W. Tai, *Music Piracy in the Pacific Rim: Applying a Regional Approach Towards the Enforcement Problem of International Conventions*, 16 Loy. L.A. Ent. L.J. 159 (1995).

The thrust of the digital revolution suggests that high quality or "non-inferior" reproductions are now easier to produce. One result, for example, is that the quality difference advantage vis-a-vis a duplicator that an original record producer enjoyed from being closer to the master tape disappears, as digital copies are as good as the initial copy from the master recording.

128. The erroneous contention that the absence of copyright protection will not yield a price decrease and therefore will be of no benefit to the consumer echoes some similar claims which recur in the history of congressional consideration of copyright policy. Thus, for example, in the House hearings on the bill which first extended federal copyright protection to sound recordings (the McClellan anti-piracy bill), it was suggested that if copying by duplicators (record pirates) were permitted, the response of the record companies would be to raise their prices in order to cover the loss of revenue to pirates. *See Prohibiting Piracy of Sound Recordings: Hearings on S.646 & H.R. 6927 Before Subcomm. No. 3 of the House Comm. on the Judiciary,* 92d Cong., 1st Sess. 21-22 (1971). This conclusion and the assumptions on which it is based are erroneous. *See* Jussawalla, *supra* note 33, at 25, 91. From the perspective of the initial producer, "piracy" is an activity which does not increase his cost but which does decrease demand for his product. If we assume the original producer was maximizing his return prior to the spread of copying, he would not rationally respond to a decrease in demand by raising his price. Indeed such a response might exacerbate the reduction in demand. The more likely response by the initial producer would be to decrease his price. An increase in price would be feasible only if we assumed--and we have no reason to so assume--that the original producer had some degree of monopoly power which he had not been previously exercising.

A similar error apparently appears in Barry W. Tyerman, *The Economic Rationale for Copyright Protection for Published Books: A Reply to Professor Breyer,* 18 UCLA L. Rev. 1100, 1120 (1971), where the author argues that in the absence of copyright protection reduced distribution (*i.e.* fewer copies) of each title at higher prices would result. It is hard to imagine a set of economic circumstances where this could be the result. Stephen Breyer, *Copyright: A Rejoinder*, 20 UCLA L. Rev. 75, 79-80 (1972).

129. *Hearing Held On Possible Extension Of Copyright Term*, 46 Pat. Trademark & Copyright J. (BNA), at 467 (Sept. 30, 1993) (remarks of Susan Mann, NMPA, and Bernard Sorkin, MPAA):

> Mann stressed that a work that enters the public domain does not necessarily benefit the public because the public may never see it. Without the market exclusivity that copyright protection brings, there is no incentive to distribute the work, she reasoned. Bernard Sorkin, appearing on behalf of the Motion Picture Association of America, agreed, calling public domain works 'essentially worthless.'

130. *See* Guinan, *supra* note 15, at 26 ("It is basic to our economic system that profits in this area should be gained by more efficient manufacture, better distribution and the like, rather than by perpetual protection, once the purpose of the protection for a limited times has been achieved.")

131. *See* text at notes 116-17 and notes 116-17 *supra*.

132. Magnetic recording tapes with metal particles or with "high bias", for example, generally produce superior sound recordings to other kinds of magnetic tape. For a technical explication of the different qualities of categories of magnetic audio tape, the process of production of compact discs as compared with pre-recorded tapes, and the differences between digital and analog sound recordings, see John M. Woram, Sound Recording Handbook 331-78 (1989); Delton T. Horn, DAT, The Complete Guide to Digital Audio Tape 75-97, 107-34 (1991); John Watkinson, The Art of

Digital Audio 1-30 (2d ed. 194).

133. In the terminology of the music industry this person is known as a "counterfeiter". Analogous behavior in the patent context would occur if a company produced a camera similar to a Polaroid and labeled and sold it as a Polaroid. In that instance of a "counterfeit" product, Polaroid's trademark as well as its patents would be infringed. Music industry terminology deems a "pirate" one who without authorization duplicates the sounds of an original recording; it labels a "bootlegger" one who without authorization records a live concert or a live performance broadcast on television or radio; and it dubs a "counterfeiter" one who without authority duplicates the original artwork, label, trademark and packaging of prerecorded music as well as the prerecorded sounds. *See* Recording Industry Association of America, Rewind, Fast Forward, 1995 Annual Report 35.

134. Rochelle Cooper Dreyfuss, *The Creative Employee and the Copyright Act of 1976*, 54 U. Chi. L. Rev. 590, 606 (1987). To the extent that the concern is about harm to an author's reputation while he is alive due to false attribution of words or other means of expression, tort law provides an adequate remedy in the form of a defamation claim for the injured author. *See* W. Page Keeton, et al., Prosser and Keeton on the Law of Torts 790-91 (5th ed. 1984) (professional injury due to false representations).

135. Condemnation of the practice of "palming off" or "passing off" one's goods as those of another lies at the heart of the law of unfair competition. See, *e.g.*, Restatement (Third) of Unfair Competition sec. 4 cmt. b (1985) (misrepresentations relating to source: passing off); Shaw v. Time-Life Records, 38 N.Y.2d 201, 341 N.E.2d 817 (1975). Such misrepresentation also provides the basis for an action of deceit as well as for a defense to contractual enforcement. *See, e.g.,* Restatement (Second) of Torts sec. 531 (1977) (liability of maker of fraudulent misrepresentation); Restatement (Second) of Contracts sec. 164 (1981) (contract

voidable due to fraudulent or material misrepresentation).

136. Legislative proscriptions, federal and state, aimed at this type of deceptive behavior provide for civil relief as well as criminal sanction and contemplate private and public invocation. *See, e.g.*, 15 U.S.C. sec. 1125(a) (1994) (Lanham Act sec. 43(a)); Conn. Gen. Stat. sec. 42-110a-q (1997) (Unfair Trade Practices Act); Tenn. Code Ann. sec. 47-18-104 (1997) (Consumer Protection Act; misdemeanor).

137. The Federal Trade commission, for instance, has broad authority over "unfair methods of competition...and unfair or deceptive acts or practices in or affecting commerce." 15 U.S.C. sec. 45(a)(1)(1994)(FTC Act sec. 5). Pursuant to that authority it has promulgated trade practice rules which define and proscribe the use of "palming off" and related deceptive promotional techniques in a variety of marketing settings. *See, e.g.*, 16 C.F.R. sec. 243.7 (1997) (wall paneling); 16 C.F.R. sec. 250.10 (1997) (household furniture); 16 C.F.R. sec. 301.10 (1997) (domestic furs).

138. Social support for the objective of an accurately and adequately-informed consumer is not limited to the enactment and enforcement of prohibitions against deceptive practices. If, for example, we think that the private provision of information will be inadequate and an accurate assessment by the individual buyer impossible, perhaps due to the complex characteristics of the good, we might intervene in other ways to facilitate the transmission of relevant data. For example, we might publicly define a set of grades and prescribe that these be used in identifying the product, as the United States Department of Agriculture does with grades of meat. *See* 7 C.F.R. sec. 53.201 *et seq.* (1997); 7 C.F.R. sec. 54.102 *et seq.* (1997).

139. The two different senses of inferiority are, quite clearly, not mutually exclusive. Both might apply to any particular reproduction.

140. *See* text at note 116 *supra.*

141. While we refer to the author's important personal interests, as distinguished from his commercial interests, in his work, we recognize that it is difficult to distinguish between the commercial and non-commercial aspects of an author's reputation.

For a succinct and insightful delineation of creators' non-pecuniary interests in their works and the parallel social concerns with respect to these creative works, see Dreyfuss, *supra* note 134, at 605-06.

142. *See generally* Hughes, *supra* note 83, at 330-365. The right of integrity is one of a set of personal interests, all of which are to some extent rooted in a concern for the author's professional reputation, which are generally referred to collectively in civil law countries as "moral rights." From a practical standpoint the right of integrity is the most important of the moral rights. In addition to the integrity right, they include the right of disclosure or divulgation--the right to decide whether and when the work is to be disseminated or displayed--and the right of paternity or attribution--the right to be acknowledged as the creator of a work and the right to prevent others from attributing to one a work one has not created. While these rights are generally grouped and protected under the term "moral right", the content of the creator's "moral right" varies in particulars among the civil law countries. Thus, though often referred to as a "doctrine", "moral right" is more appropriately viewed as a label for a number of rights and privileges to which many Latin American and European countries afford differing degrees of recognition, subject to a uniformity of minimal protection which these countries have undertaken to grant as members of the Berne Union. The common thread is a concern for the artist's reputation and a focus on the work as an extension of his personality. A prime presupposition is that an author stands in a peculiarly intimate relationship with his intellectual creative output. The two components of the moral right in the Berne Convention, the paternity right and the integrity right, are delineated in Article 6*bis* of the Convention.

While the United States acceded to the Convention in 1988, our lawmakers have not shown the same enthusiasm for recognition and expansion of the moral right. *See, e.g.*, Patty Gerstenblith, *Architect as Artist: Artists' Rights and Historic Preservation*, 12 Cardozo Arts & Ent. L.J. 431, 433-54 (1994); *see generally*, S. Rep. No. 352, 100th Cong., 2d Sess. 9-11 (1988) (Berne Convention Implementation Act of 1988); Weinreb, *supra* note 32, at 1219-21, 1245-46 (self-revelatory connection between author and work greatly weakened, if not broken, once work is published).

Some European countries recognize a further right to disavow or withdraw a work from circulation, for example when an author has changed his opinion on the subject. This right is largely theoretical. In France, for example, the right of withdrawal is neither well-established nor very useful. *See* Monroe Price, Resuscitating a Collaboration with Melville Nimmer: Moral Rights and Beyond 9-10 (1998); Raymond Sarraute, *Current Theory on the Moral Right of Authors and Artists Under French Law*, 16 Am. J. Comp. L. 465, 476-78 (1968). The considerable variation in the scope of authors' and artists' moral rights from one European country to another has led to difficulties in harmonizing law in this area among the European Union's Member States. *See generally* David Saunders, Authorship and Copyright 75-105 (1992) ("France: from royal privilege to the droit moral"; distinctive history of legal-cultural arrangements in France).

143. Without questioning the legitimacy of these personal interests, we can not help but suspect that performers and record companies dislike duplication primarily because they are worried about loss to their pocket rather than injury to their reputation. The history of experience under the compulsory licensing provision, section 1(e) of the 1909 Copyright Act (section 115 of the present law), seems to offer support for this proposition. Under that provision once the proprietor of a musical copyright has recorded or permitted his composition to be recorded, anyone else may record it subject to an obligation to pay the proprietor the statutorily-fixed fee. In the operation of this provision complaints from composers that their work

was being mangled by recording artists have been rare. The infrequency of such complaints may well be in large part due to the fact that the composer is compensated on the basis of records sold, and he is therefore willing to give the arranger and performer wide latitude in adaptation in order to maximize sales.

As noted previously, *supra* note 127, the revolution in digital technology means that high quality reproductions of certain kinds of artistic works are easier to achieve.

144. Sympathy for protection of the personal interests recognized by moral right doctrine does not justify copyright, *i.e.*, a general prohibition of duplication, much less a lengthening of the copyright term. *See* Breyer, *supra* note 33, at 289-91.

145. Berne Convention, art. 6*bis* (1) ; 17 U.S.C. sec. 106A(a) (1994).

146. Restatement (Second) of Torts sec. 560 (1976); *see, e.g.*, Saari v. Gillett Communications of Atlanta, Inc., 195 Ga. App. 451, 393 S.E.2d 736 (1990); Insull v. New York World Telegram Corp., 172 F. Supp. 615, 635-36 (N.D. Ill. 1959). *See generally* Jeremy Phillips, *Life After Death*, 20 Eur. Intell. Prop. Rev. 201 (1998) (no special legal protection should be given to post-mortem reputation of deceased celebrities). *But see generally* Swidler & Berlin v. United States, 118 S. Ct. 2081 (1998) (attorney-client privilege survives death of client). Of course, living relatives of the deceased author may bring a defamation action if the contested publication reflects poorly upon them. But the action would arise from the libelous reference to the living and would not be based on any principle that a cause of action exists for a third party when a deceased person is defamed. Keeton, *supra* note 134, at 778-79.

It is noteworthy that the Visual Artists Rights Act of 1990 (VARA), the first explicit federal recognition of moral rights, provides that for works of visual art created after its effective date the right of integrity "shall endure for a term consisting of the life of the author." 17 U.S.C. sec. 106A(d)(1) (1994). *See also* Note, *Copyright Protection, Privacy Rights, and the Fair Use Doctrine: The Post-Salinger*

114

Decade Reconsidered, 72 N.Y.U. L. Rev. 1376, 1379-80, 1405 (1997) (proposed privacy-based exception to fair use limited to life of author).

The integrity interest can be seen to safeguard the monetary interests of people other than the author, particularly in the case of works of fine art. Each work of an artist serves, in effect, as an advertisement for all of his other works. Protection of the artist's reputation, then, may serve to support the value of works that are held by other owners of the artist's work, and their financial interest may well last past the artist's death. Difficulties arise, though, in deciding who should have standing to assert this interest *pma* and for how long it should endure. *See* Henry Hansmann & Marina Santilli, *Authors' and Artists' Moral Rights: A Comparative Legal and Economic Analysis*, 26 J. Legal Stud. 95, 104-05 121-23 (1997).

147. It is sometimes said that a reason for tying the term of protection to the life of the author is that his family will be in a position to exercise responsibly and in the way the author would have wished his moral rights after his death. Stephen M. Stewart, International Copyright and Neighbouring Rights 89 (2d ed. 1989). And that thought may be credible as applied to heirs close in time (and in person) to the author. But how likely is it that the person holding the copyright fifty years after the author's death, much less seventy years *pma*, even if a distant relative, will have any knowledge of the author's attitudes and intentions towards his work?

In fact, of course, there is no reason at all to assume that an heir will control the copyright at the time of death, much less fifty or seventy years thereafter. The copyright interest, after all, is fully alienable, transferable in whole or in part.

148. The premise and purposes underlying recognition of a right of integrity may be conceptually related to those "personality" theories of property which proceed from an assumption of a human tendency to identify the self with its possessions and therefore to experience an intimate, painful loss from a loss of possession. Property, under these theories, functions to protect and nourish personality. *See* Olin L. Browder, Jr. et al., Basic Property Law 1196-99 (1966); Michelman, *supra* note 52,

at 1205; Lawrence C. Becker, Property Rights: Philosophic Foundations 65 (1977); Lawrence C. Becker, *Deserving to Own Intellectual Property*, 68 Chi.-Kent L. Rev. 609, 619-620, 626-27 (1993). *See also* Hughes, *supra* note 83, at 358-365 (expressive integrity and first amendment; free speech meaningless without assurances that the expression will remain unadulterated); Elie Kedourie, Hegel and Marx 104-14 (1995) ("Property and Personality"; significance of property for human self-realization in Hegel's thought--notion that property rights should be allotted in a way that best permits people to develop and exercise their talents). *But see generally* Sterk, *supra* note 70, at 1242-44 (Hegel furnishes, at most, limited support for the notion that personal dignity requires recognition of a right of integrity giving an author permanent control over the destiny of his work). For an insightful critique of the extended notion of the person which, in part, underlies moral rights doctrine, see Weinreb, *supra* note 32, at 1219-1222, 1245-46 (fact that person is creative source of work not make it part of himself; at most, may associate person with it as cause to effect). *See also* Tom G. Palmer, *Artists Don't Deserve Special Rights*, Wall St. J., March 8, 1988, at 34 (theory of moral rights ultimately incoherent).

In an essay entitled "Of the Injustice of Counterfeiting Books", Kant argued that a duplicator might alter or misrepresent a work; the author might then be put to the trouble of explaining to his readers what he in fact meant. Viewing authorship as an *act* and an author's work as an extension of his personality, Kant regarded the duplicator's activity as an unjustifiable infringement of the author's liberty and his attempt to express himself and communicate with his readers. *See* Immanuel Kant, *Of the Injustice of Counterfeiting Books*, in 1 Essays and Treatises on Moral, Political, and Various Philosophical Subjects 225 (1798). *But see generally* Fisher, *supra* note 32, at 1773 n.494. Similarly, the right of first publication in American law--the author's right to control the circumstances of the first public revelation of his work--and its equivalent in moral right doctrine, the right of disclosure, are also rooted, in part, in respect for autonomy, personality, and privacy. These rights guarantee to the author the decision of when a work is finished. He decides whether, when, and how his work will be made available to the public; and he can decline to expose his work to the public before he believes it is satisfactory. This right to control disclosure constitutes recognition of the fact that one's public persona is determined in part by the ideas one expresses and the way one expresses them. To compel public disclosure of one's ideas would distort personality and alter the nature of one's thinking. *See* Lynn Sharp Paine, *Trade Secrets and the Justification of Intellectual Property: A Comment on Hettinger*, 20 Phil. & Pub. Aff. 247, 251-52 (1991).

149. The core concern is that destruction of a work of fine art damages the richness and diversity of our cultural heritage by permanently removing a work from the collection. A possible related fear is that such a practice of destruction might discourage fame-conscious artists from creating new works.

150. *See, e.g.*, Cal. Civil Code sec. 987 (1982 & 1996 Supp.) (California Art Preservation Act); N.Y. Arts & Cult. Aff. L. sec. 14.03 (1991 & 1996 Supp.) (Artists' Authorship Rights Act); 17 U.S.C. sec. 106A (1994) (Visual Artists Rights Act).

151. In the recent campaign to block the colorization of black and white films, one major reason why it was difficult to work up much sympathy for the opponents of colorization is that generally the existence of a colorized version did not hinder entree to the original. Thus the result was a wider range of choice for the public as viewers could select between the black-and-white original and the colorized version. *See generally* Ralph S. Brown & Robert C. Denicola, Cases On Copyright, Unfair Competition, and Other Topics Bearing on the Protection of Literary, Musical, and Artistic Works 736-37 (7th ed. 1998)("Moral Rights and the Colorization of Films").

152. With respect to the focus of responsibility for enforcement, it is doubtful that strict reliance on the artist or the artist's heirs is sufficiently protective of the public interest in prevention of violations to the integrity of the cultural patrimony. It would

be fortuitous, to say the least, if the overriding motivation of the person holding the copyright fifty years after the author's death was a commitment to the preservation of cultural heritage. *See* Thomas F. Cotter, *Pragmatism, Economics and the Droit Moral*, 76 N.C. L. Rev. 1, 37-38, 84-85 (1997) (moral rights flawed as means of advancing cultural preservation); Price, *supra* note 142, at 13-17 (guidance from landmark preservation laws).

153. To be truthful, when referring to an author deceased for fifty years, it seems almost comical to speak of his personal interests at all; but it appears farcical to suppose that concern for these interests justifies copyright and the extension of the copyright term.

154. We are not suggesting that there will necessarily be no "inferior" reproductions, only that it is likely that there will be some quality ones and that the "remedy" for the others is not a general prohibition on duplication. *See* Pierre N. Leval, *Toward A Fair Use Standard*, 103 Harv. L. Rev. 1105, 1128-29 (1990).

155. *See, e.g.*, Copyright Statute of Uruguay, art. 37, 2 UNESCO, Copyright Laws & Treaties of the World (1992):

> The performer of a literary or musical work may oppose the dissemination of his performance if the reproduction thereof has been made in such a form as to produce serious or unjust prejudice to his artistic interest.

156. *See generally* Gilliam v. American Broadcasting Companies, 538 F.2d 14 (2d Cir. 1976) (presentation of edited version of Monty Python program which was altered without permission of comedy group violates section 43(a) of Lanham Act as misrepresentation of source of the product); Brown & Denicola, *supra* note 151, at 732-35 (Notes and Questions on "Integrity").

A system of direct protection would, of course, pose its own difficult issues

8

8

and impose its own costs. Thus, for example, the question of inalienability, whether the author could transfer his interest and if so under what formal conditions, would have to be faced, as well as the issues of duration of protection, who can assert a claim, and what remedies would be made available. And the entrepreneur putting together a project would likely incur larger transaction costs because he will have to deal with an increased number of people and/or secure additional permissions. Indeed these factors underlie the vocal opposition to moral rights by American movie companies; and presumably these costs represent some of the reasons behind the reluctance of American courts and legislatures to explicitly adopt moral rights. (As Judge Posner suggests, the saliency of freedom of expression in our legal traditions may also inform that reluctance, for what is a criticism to a user may be a "mutilation" to the author being criticized. Richard A. Posner, *When Is Parody Fair Use?*, 21 J. Legal Stud. 67, 75 n.15 (1992).) However, our point here is not that the United States should more enthusiastically embrace protection of the integrity interest, but only that if, after weighing the costs and benefits, it chose to, it could responsively react without putting in place a copyright scheme or an extension of the life plus fifty term under our copyright system.

157. *See generally* Edmund Cahn, The Moral Decision 199 (1955). These difficulties are likely to be particularly knotty in the case of works such as musical compositions or dramas which are written to be performed and where the introduction of some interpretive element by the performer (and director) is generally expected. A well-publicized example of such a conflict between dramatist and director was the clash between Samuel Beckett and the Harvard-based American Repertory Theater over its planned staging of his play *Endgame*. That production involved changes in stage setting and casting as well as the introduction of music. Beckett was incensed by the changes, claiming that they represented a travesty of his conception, and he threatened legal action. In the end that action was averted by a compromise under which an insert containing the first page of the text, which

includes Beckett's specific stage directions, disclaimers by Beckett and his American publisher, and a rejoinder defending the production by Robert Brustein, the director, were added to each program. *E.g.*, Sylviane Gold, *Theater: The Beckett Brouhaha,* Wall St. J., Dec. 28, 1984, at A10.

158. Copyright can, in part, be a vehicle for protection of integrity and related interests. Thus, the copyright proprietor's exclusive right to prepare derivative works, 17 U.S.C. sec. 106(2) (1994), approaches a right against distortion; and the author's successors as owners of the copyright can prevent what they view as distortions of the work by refusing to license them or by conditioning production licenses on their artistic approval. However, control of works by an author's descendants may cause harm in a number of ways, one of them being suppression. In addition, restrictive conditions, for example an insistence that performance of a dramatic work be done only in a particular manner, may lead to artistic frustration and sterility. This production of cultural atrophy by which famous works can not be reinterpreted by later creators will, of course, be facilitated by the increase in the length of the copyright term. *See* Benjamin Kaplan, An Unhurried View of Copyright 74-75 (1967) (headstart conferred should be moderate because of serious danger of "clogging the utilization of the [fresh] signals by other authors in the creation of further or improved signals for additional audiences").

Copyright does not provide direct protection of an author's personal interests. Instead, by forbidding unauthorized duplication, it provides a framework within which author and publisher can define safeguards for the author in their contract. *See generally id.* at 78 (copyright seems an awkward defender of artistic integrity); Dreyfuss, *supra note* 134, at 631 (copyright often gives sparse attention to author-based considerations). *But see generally* Hansmann & Santilli, *supra* note 146, at 112-16, 142-43 (copyright gives authors sufficient flexibility to protect against many of the harms to which moral rights are addressed, particularly if creation of reproductions is involved.)

159. *See, e.g.*, Sutherland, *supra* note 123, at 3 (permission denied to prospective books disliked by estate of authors, such as Eliot and Joyce); Caroline Fraser, *Mrs. Eddy Builds Her Empire*, N.Y. Rev. Books, July 11, 1996, at 53, 57 (Christian Science Church permits access to archives to only those with a sympathetic approach to Mary Baker Eddy and Christian Science, thereby exercising censorial control over critical uses of existing works); Religious Tech. Ctr. v. Netcom On-Line Communication Servs., 923 F. Supp 1231 (N.D. Cal. 1995) (Church of Scientology invokes copyright to impede critics from bringing to public view allegedly fraudulent Church practices). *See generally* David Garrow, *Stifling the Work of Dr. Martin Luther King*, N.Y. Post, Jan. 29, 1997, at 23; Vaver, *supra* note 125, at 136-39; Leval, *supra* note 154, at 1118 (strict limitation on fair use of unpublished documents creates new despotic potentate in politics of intellectual life, the "widow censor"; permission may be denied by heirs if the writing is not admiring of deceased figure). *But see generally* Lloyd L. Weinreb, *Fair's Fair: A Comment on the Fair Use Doctrine*, 103 Harv. L. Rev. 1137, 1145 n.38 (1990) (problem of "widow censor" overstated). Concern about the possibility of suppression of works deemed undesirable by the authors' successors in title was expressed in the mid-19th century British copyright debates. Lord Macaulay, speaking in opposition to a bill which would extend the term of copyright in a book to sixty years from the death of the author, gave a number of examples of what might have occurred if the descendants of certain famous British authors had been authorized to control the dissemination of their ancestors' works. For example, had the control of Samuel Richardson's novels passed to his grandson, "a most upright and excellent [clergy]man...[who] had conceived a strong prejudice against works of fiction", a reprint of *Clarissa* "would have been as rare as an Aldus or a Caxton." Similarly, the eldest son of Boswell, who disapproved of the entire relationship of his father with Samuel Johnson, might well have suppressed Boswell's *Life of Johnson* had the copyright passed to him with the result that "[a]n unadulterated copy of the finest biographical work in the world would have been as scarce as the first edition of Camden's *Britannia*." Thomas B.

Macaulay, 1 Miscellanies 246-49 (1901) (Feb. 5, 1841 speech). *But see generally* Morgan, *supra* note 118, at 174 ("it does not pass the wit of man to devise means of over-ruling an heir to copyright who should prove a curmudgeon and abuse his powers").

Macaulay's reminder is salutary, for "it must be recognized that even at its best copyright necessarily involves the right to restrict as well as to monopolize the diffusion of knowledge." Edward G. Hudon, *The Copyright Period: Weighing Personal Against Public Interest*, 49 A.B.A.J. 759 (1963). While it is impossible to know how many works are not created because of the new authors' inability to negotiate a license with present copyright holders, there is evidence that the instances are not insignificant. In his classic reflections on copyright law a half century ago, Professor Chafee offered examples in which descendants' veto power deprived the community of valuable works. *See* Zechariah Chafee, *Reflections on the Law of Copyright: II*, 45 Colum. L. Rev. 719, 725-30 (1945). Use of the veto power of copyright by authors' descendants is not just a historical curiosity. Troubling contemporary manifestations of such use persist. *See* Anthony Haden-Guest, *Picasso Pic Has Heirs Seeing Red!*, The New Yorker, Aug. 21 & 28, 1995, at 53 (assertion of rights by Picasso's estate to prevent the use of any of the artist's pictures in a film biography of Picasso the content of which is disagreeable to the estate); James E Person Jr., *Plath's "Bell Jar" Firmly Sealed*, The Virginian-Pilot & The Ledger-Star, May 22, 1994, at C3 (censorship by Ted Hughes, husband of Sylvia Plath, and his sister Olwyn, Plath's literary executor, of the work of serious biographers who wish to quote Plath's poetry; work quoting from written material by Plath must be cleared by the Hughes family; and the Hugheses have gone to extraordinary lengths to restrict and manipulate what is written about Plath); *Disputed Harding Love Letters Will Be Locked Up Until 2014*, N.Y. Times, Dec. 30, 1971, at 1. *See generally* Peter Jaszi, *When Works Collide: Derivative Motion Pictures, Underlying Rights, and the Public Interest*, 28 UCLA L. Rev. 715, 738-42 (1981).

160. *See, e.g.*, Simon Hattenstone, *Keep Open the Routes to the Past*, The Times, Nov. 5, 1991, at 14 (D'Oyly Carte Opera Company control of Gilbert and Sullivan comic operas after Gilbert's death; required production be staged in accord with original performances in every detail; not a note of music could be sung differently; result was a mummification of the works).

Judge Kozinski has noted our strong tradition of having things seep into the public domain and as a result make our world a richer place. The fact that we don't have to ask for permission from the descendants of Shakespeare and Beethoven, he observes, "enriches not only the public domain, but the creators themselves, or at least their legacies, because there are people out there who give their works new meaning, by giving them new twists, new interpretations, and new dimensions." Alex Kozinski, *Mickey & Me*, 11 U. Miami Ent. & Sports L. Rev. 465, 467 (1994). *See also* Phillips, *supra* note 146 (desirable to limit "disneyfication" of celebrity). If a purpose of copyright is to support learning and discourse, then at some point the public must be free to modify and reformulate the works that have become part of its cultural matrix. *See* Zeitlin, *supra* note 82.

161. Paul L. Latham, *Copyright Duration*, 50 A.B.A.J. 958 (1964):

> There is another aspect which deserves consideration. That is the stifling effect copyrights may have on other authors and would-be authors who may be restrained from giving full range to their fancy by the fear or threat of an infringement suit, not because they would reproduce a book on which copyright is claimed but because the work they would produce might have enough resemblance to a work on which copyright is claimed to incur an infringement suit or the threat of one.

162. The doctrine of fair use was developed by the courts and was codified for the first time in Section 107 of the 1976 Copyright Act.

Sec. 107. Limitations on Exclusive Rights: Fair Use

Notwithstanding the provisions of sections 106 and 106A, the fair use of a copyrighted work, including such use by reproduction in copies or phonorecords or by any other means specified by that section, for purposes such as criticism, comment, news reporting, teaching (including multiple copies for classroom use), scholarship, or research, is not an infringement of copyright. In determining whether the use made of a work in any particular case is a fair use the factors to be considered shall include--

(1) the purpose and character of the use, including whether such use is of a commercial nature or is for nonprofit educational purposes;

(2) the nature of the copyrighted work;

(3) the amount and substantiality of the portion used in relation to the copyrighted work as a whole; and

(4) the effect of the use upon the potential market for or value of the copyrighted work. The fact that a work is unpublished shall not itself bar a finding of fair use if such finding is made upon consideration of all the above factors.

As fair use involves a multi-factor test, as these factors have a good deal of play in the joints, and as the statutory criteria may, in the court's discretion, be supplemented by consideration of additional relevant factors, the outcome of application of the doctrine in any particular case is often uncertain. *See* H.R. No. 94-1476, 94th Cong., 2d Sess. 65 (1976). Determining what uses are fair has been described as "the most troublesome [issue] in the whole law of copyright." Dellar v. Samuel Goldwyn, Inc., 104 F.2d 661, 662 (2d Cir. 1939). The uncertainty and confusion generated by the fair use doctrine diminish the ability of authors and users of intellectual works to determine their rights and to adjust their conduct accordingly. Accordingly, the prospective author of a derivative work must necessarily adopt a cautious approach if a license is unavailable.

163. Unlike the situation with patent claims, a copyright registration certificate generally does not indicate which elements of a writing are protected and which are not. As a result, a prospective user who believes that he has copied only a work's unprotectible ideas takes the risk of later being found to have copied protectible matter as well.

164. *See* Daniel E. Wanat, *Fair Use and the 1992 Amendment to Section 107 of the 1976 Copyright Act: Its History and an Analysis of Its Effect*, 1 Vill. Sports & Ent. L.F. 47, 56 n.47 (1994) (making distinction between fact, unprotected by copyright, and expression, which copyright protects, may be extremely difficult). Facts are not within copyright protection, notwithstanding the effort expended by the original author in uncovering them.

165. The fountainhead case is the Supreme Court decision in Harper & Row, Publishers, Inc. v. Nation Enterprises, 471 U.S. 539 (1985) where the Court held that The Nation magazine's publication of a story about the pardon of President Nixon which quoted excerpts from President Ford's then unpublished memoirs was not fair use. In *Harper* apparently the copy of the manuscript made available to the magazine was stolen, publication of the memoirs was imminent, and a deal with Time magazine under which it would pay a sizable sum of money for the right to print segments of the work prior to its general release was canceled as a result of The Nation's use. In its opinion the Court majority built on the value, rooted in both economic and privacy considerations and historically recognized by our law via the doctrine of common law copyright, that an author should control release of his work, *i.e.* he generally should decide whether, when, and how his work is sent out in permanent form. Recognizing an author's interest in shaping the manner in which his creation is apprehended, the Court stressed the unpublished status of Ford's work, and the opinion's language indicated that any claim of a right to copy unpublished works on grounds of fair use would be evaluated quite skeptically.

Harper & Row was invoked in a set of subsequent suits brought against biographers who quoted from the letters, diaries, and other writings of famous authors. The Second Circuit's first opinion after *Harper* involved a suit brought by J.D. Salinger against Random House to stop publication of a biography that reproduced passages from unpublished letters Salinger had sent to friends and to his editor. Salinger v. Random House, Inc., 811 F.2d 90 (2d Cir.), *reh'g denied* 818 F.2d 252, *cert. denied* 484 U.S. 890 (1987). The letters had been donated to university libraries by their recipients, and the biographer obtained access to them through these libraries. (The sender of a letter continues to own the copyright.) The biography quoted approximately 200 words, but the court also found numerous passages that "closely paraphrase" portions of the letters. The issue was whether the biographer made fair use of his subject's letters. Reversing the district court and remanding for a preliminary injunction, the Second Circuit rejected the claim of fair use, placing "special emphasis on the unpublished nature of Salinger's letters." The appeals court also rejected the lower court's concern that a biographer desiring to use copyrighted unpublished material was confronted with the dilemma of either risking infringement by copying verbatim or distorting his subject's meaning by putting a passage in the biographer's own words. The court concluded that unpublished works "normally enjoy complete protection against copying any protected expression."

In the next round in the Second Circuit a corporation holding copyrights from the Church of Scientology founded by Ron Hubbard sued to enjoin publication of a biography highly critical of Hubbard. New Era Publications International, ApS v. Henry Holt and Co., 873 F.2d 576 (2d Cir. 1989), *cert. denied*, 493 U.S. 1094 (1990). The work, entitled *The Bare-Faced Messiah*, was a hostile expose of Hubbard's life, portraying him as a religious charlatan. To support this portrayal the defendant copied many excerpts from Hubbard's unpublished diaries and letters. The district court again refused an injunction, and Judge Leval found that quotation helped the biographer to make his point that Hubbard's very own words supported the biographer's critical judgments about Hubbard's life and character. The Second Circuit affirmed but only on the grounds that laches barred an injunction. The majority opinion explicitly rejected Judge Leval's fair use analysis, putting heavy weight on the unpublished status of the copied works and reaffirming the strong protection that *Salinger* and *Harper* gave to unpublished material.

(Another Hubbard biographer was shortly before the Second Circuit in New Era Publications International, ApS v. Carol Publishing Group, 904 F.2d 152 (2d Cir.), *cert. denied*, 498 U.S. 921 (1990), which upheld the defendant's fair use defense in connection with quotes from Hubbard's *published* works. The quotations were used to communicate Hubbard's "hypocrisy and pomposity, qualities that may best (or only) be revealed though direct quotation." *See also* Wright v. Warner Books, Inc. 953 F.2d 731 (2d Cir. 1991) ("sparing use" of unpublished writings in a biography of author Richard Wright held fair use.)

The *Henry Holt* court's remarks about the narrow scope of fair use for unpublished works and the availability of injunctive relief echoed the *Salinger* opinion and increased authors' fears that significant risks are involved in any history or biography using appreciable amounts of copyrighted expression. Authors complained to Congress that in reaction to these cases their publishers were prohibiting them from quoting unpublished sources. Congress responded with an amendment to undo the over-deference to the unpublished status of a work. Pub.L. 102-492, 106 Stat. 3145 (1992). The amendment added a new sentence at the end of section 107: "The fact that a work is unpublished shall not itself bar a finding of fair use if such finding is made upon consideration of all the above factors.", thus emphasizing the applicability of the traditional fair use factors to unpublished works. The congressional purpose was to make clear that there is no per se rule barring claims of fair use of unpublished works. *See* H.Rep. No. 836, 102d Cong. 2d Sess. (1992).

Of course, fair use remains an elusive concept, and accordingly one can not be at all confident that passage of the amendment will yield decisions that the biographers of authors such as Salinger, Hubbard, and Wright should be able to quote from unpublished works to the extent necessary to offer an accurate picture of persons who have influenced the public, as appropriate as such a judicial conclusion would be. *See generally* Wendy J. Gordon, *A Property Right in Self-Expression: Equality and Individualism in the Natural Law of Intellectual Property*, 102 Yale L. J. 1533, 1592-95 (1993). Moreover, a question which has to this point received little attention is what do the terms "published" and "unpublished" mean in this context. For purposes of the scope of fair use does "unpublished" mean the same thing as unpublished, and therefore protected by common law copyright, meant under the 1909 Copyright Act? That meaning of unpublished, which is carried forward in the definition of publication in sec. 101 of the present law, includes many works that are publicly known and available.

166. *E.g.*, Arthur Schlesinger Jr., *The Judges of History Rule*, Wall St. J., Oct. 26, 1989, at A16.

Sympathy with the historian's dilemma does not bespeak an ignorance or minimization of the strong creative value of generally securing authorial control over the decision to release his work. The possibility, or at least the frequent possibility, of premature release may inhibit an author's urge to experiment, move him to untimely destruction of early drafts, or lead him to take expensive precautions to keep his writing hidden. *See* Dreyfuss, *supra* note 134, at 632-33.

167. *Fair Use and Unpublished Works: Joint Hearing on S. 2370 and H.R. 4263 Before the Subcomm. on Patents, Copyrights and Trademarks of the Senate Comm. on the Judiciary and the Subcomm. on Courts, Intellectual Property, and the Administration of Justice of the House Comm. on the Judiciary*, 101st Cong., 2d Sess. 160 (1990). *See generally* Michael Les Benedict, *Historians and the Continuing Controversy over Fair Use of Unpublished Manuscript Materials*, 91 Am. Hist. Rev. 859 (1986). The Second Circuit's opinions showed little recognition of the need for quotation as an instrument of accurate historical method and of the value of accurate quotation as a necessary tool of historians and journalists.

---

168. For a piece which describes the Second Circuit's treatment of the vexing question of use of unpublished writings, criticizes the hysterical reaction to that treatment, and is skeptical of the claim that the ability to produce biographies has been seriously impaired, see Jon O. Newman, *Not The End of History: The Second Circuit Struggles With Fair Use*, 37 J. Copyright Soc'y 1, 12 (1989). However, Judge Newman himself expresses concern about the dangers of unwarranted self-censorship. He recognizes that publishers may go to great lengths to avoid the risks of litigation, imposing limits on their authors' use of unpublished materials which go beyond current legal requirements. Moreover, biographical subjects (or their descendants) may threaten litigation over unpublished writings as a bargaining chip to obtain elimination of unflattering passages.

The problems posed by unpublished materials are not new ones. *See* Luther H. Evans, *Copyright and the Public Interest*, 53 Bull. N.Y. Pub. Libr. 3, 8-9 (1949):

> The use by scholars of manuscript material of great historical and social significance years after the death of its author other than at peril of settlement with unknown and unascertainable claimants of remote consanguinity or tenuous proprietorship would seem a matter to which the ingenuity of counsel should be capable of better answer than has yet been given.

169. The difficulties presented by letters are perhaps not surprising. (Under the Copyright Act they are deemed "literary works" akin to unpublished manuscripts.) They fit awkwardly within the copyright model as typically their composition is not stimulated by prospect of financial remuneration, and they are written with neither the intention nor expectation of public dissemination and reproduction. Accordingly, the standard rationale for protection applies only in strained fashion. Thus, copyright legislation has proclaimed that it is in the public interest to guarantee authors property in their works in order to encourage them to produce and distribute books and to reap profits from sales. This justification, of course, can not be simply applied to writers of private letters. *See generally* Jon O. Newman, *Copyright Law and the Protection of Privacy*, 12 Colum.-VLA J.L. & Arts, 459 (1988) (author's interest in privacy should be explicitly recognized and weighed).

Our present conception(s) and legal treatment of letters are hardly universal or inevitable. For an examination of a decidedly different (18th century) set of social, political, and moral assumptions and a corresponding legal characterization rooted in the notion that letters are to be understood as the communal property of both the writer and recipient, see Dena Goodman, *Epistolary Property: Michel de Servan and the Plight of Letters on the Eve of the French Revolution, in* Early Modern Conceptions of Property, *supra* note 9, at 339.

170. The recent evolution of the judicial and legislative treatment of unpublished materials may well illustrate how the order in which cases arise affects significantly the direction in which the law moves. Thus, *Harper*, the first major case, featured an unattractive defendant who had procured a copy of the Ford manuscript in a questionable, surreptitious manner, clear economic injury to the plaintiff, and a manuscript which the copyright owner was not seeking to suppress but rather was about to be published. The Court's distaste for the plaintiff is manifest in the opinion which is marked by sweeping language about protection of unpublished works, language which in large part dictated the results and reasoning in *Salinger* and *New Era* and in turn stimulated the push for the 1992 amendment to section 107. How different might this scenario have been had the first case been a variant of *Salinger* involving the use of letters in a serious study of a dead, reclusive, prominent author whose estate or heirs seek to enjoin publication? Even if the result were similar, isn't it likely that the tone and language of the opinion would have been significantly different?

171. David A. Kaplan, *The End of History?*, Newsweek, Dec. 25, 1989, at 80

(hesitancy of publishers to publish books quoting from unpublished sources); Amy Gumerman, *Unfair Use: Copyright Decision Cramps Writers' Style*, Wall St. J., April 10, 1990, at A22. *See* Karen Burke LeFevre, *The Tell-Tale "Heart": Determining "Fair" Use of Unpublished Texts*, L. & Contemp. Probs., Spring 1992, at 153, 168-69, 173; Leval, *supra* note 154, at 1107, 1118 n.64 (publishers reluctant to undertake commitments for biographical or historical works that call for use of unpublished sources).

172. Professor Waldron denominates this individualist perspective which adopts the perspective of those who feel the impact of the putative owner's rights as "oppositional." In his article, *supra* note 29, he offers a suggestive oppositional analysis of the justifications for intellectual property, one which includes a plausible libertarian objection to intellectual property rights. *See generally* Nance, *supra* note 65, at 771 (using law to compel citizens to support creative efforts more strongly than would be the case under voluntary arrangements entails unacceptable constraints on the liberty that individuals would otherwise have). *See also* Patterson, *supra* note 125, at 21-22 (natural law rights of members of public as users).

173. *See generally* Gordon, *supra* note 40, at 157 (overbroad grant of rights to prior creators may retard development of new intellectual products and interfere with autonomous efforts by individuals to achieve cultural self-determination). *But see generally id.* at 216-18 (comparison of parties' autonomy stakes; unlike copyist, creator has foregone alternative investments of effort and reduced her available avenues of action, and therefore particular avenue remaining has great importance for her).

174. The historians' dilemma suggests the broader point of intellectual property's potential disruptive effects on the patterns of communication which groups create for themselves, including the processes of communication within scientific and artistic communities. *See* Drahos, *supra* note 70.

175. *See* Netanel, *supra* note 58, at 295-97.

176. The Copyright Office itself has shown some recognition that extension will exacerbate the difficulties involved in the use of unpublished materials. At the September 20, 1995 Senate Judiciary Committee hearings on the term extension bill, Register of Copyrights Marybeth Peters expressed opposition to the proposed amendments to section 303. Section 303 of the 1976 Act, which covers works created but not published before January 1, 1978, provided that all works in this category are guaranteed at least twenty-five years of federal copyright protection. It specified that in no case would copyright in such a work expire before December 31, 2002. In addition, if the work were published before that date, the term would extend another twenty-five years through the end of 2027. Works in this category may be quite old; the unpublished letters and diaries of the Republic's founding fathers, for example, would be included here. Under the Copyright Term Extension Act, the minimum term of protection guaranteed an unpublished work is extended ten years to December 31, 2012, and if the work is published by that date, the term of protection is extended another thirty-five years to December 31, 2047. Peters opposed these amendments because of the likely harmful effect on archivists, libraries and educational institutions. She offered concrete examples of worthwhile projects that would be seriously impeded and observed that difficulties for scholars are particularly severe in situations, such as letters, where ownership of the copyright interest and ownership of the physical document have become separated. Peters further noted that the fair use doctrine, as a limited exception, would not adequately give these kinds of institutions access to the works. *See Senate Hearing, supra* note 107, at 7, 14, 28, 32, 112 (statements of Marybeth Peters, Register of Copyrights); *see generally* Kanwal Puri, *The Term of Copyright Protection--Is It Too Long in the Wake of New Technologies?*, 12 Eur. Intel. Prop. Rev. 12, 16-17 (1990); Report of the Register, *supra* note 29, at 42-43 (manuscripts placed in archives). Most of the works addressed by section 303, of course, have only scholarly value because if they

132

were readily available and had financial value, they would already have been published. Presumably in response to the Copyright Office's misgivings, the Term Extension Act differs from the bills introduced in earlier congressional sessions with respect to changes in section 303. The expiration of the minimum term guaranteed an unpublished work remains at December 31, 2002. However, if the work is published by that date, protection will still be extended twenty years to December 31, 2047. *Compare* S. 483, 104th Cong., 1st Sess. sec. 2(c)(1)-(2) (1995) (Copyright Term Extension Act of 1995) *with* Copyright Term Extension Act, *supra* note 3, at sec. 102(c) *and* S. Rep. No. 315, 104th Cong., 2d Sess. 5-6, 14-15 (1996).

177. *See generally* Michael Holroyd and Sandra Jobson, *Copyrights and Wrongs: D.H. Lawrence*, Times Literary Supplement, Sept. 3, 1982, at 943 ("copyright period has gradually been lengthening until it is now in danger of benefiting the dead author at some expense to the living").

178. As noted, note 70 and text at notes 162-64 *supra*, these other vague limiting doctrines which define the scope of protection and permit a measure of copying include the idea-expression dichotomy, the fact-expression distinction, the merger doctrine, and the noncopyrightability of utilitarian articles.

179. Public domain status confers another benefit. It removes the possible "tie-in" cost in the situation where a user is faced with the choice of buying all or none when what he wants is a part, for example an article in a periodical or a chapter of a book.

180. Public domain status also translates into avoidance of the situation where the copyright owner chooses to withhold permission for use solely because the fees a particular user can afford to pay are too small to justify a licensing transaction. Thus, film scholars would be free of the clearance problems they encounter in attempting to license the use of stills and frame enlargements for critical books in the field of cinema studies. *See* Kristin Thompson, *Report of the Ad Hoc Committee of the*

Society for Cinema Studies, "Fair Usage Publication of Film Stills", Cinema Journal, Winter 1993, at 3; *House Hearings, supra* note 20, at 283-83, 287-89 (statement of Professor John Belton, Society for Cinema Studies).

181.   Brown, *supra* note 122, at 1093; Patterson, *supra* note 125; Robert W. Kastenmeier & Michael J. Remington, *The Semiconductor Chip Protection Act of 1984: A Swamp or Firm Ground?*, 70 Minn. L. Rev. 417, 459-61 (1985); Jaszi, *supra* note 159, at 804-05. On the tendency of our author-centered copyright discourse to undervalue the public domain, and the interests of both sources of and audiences for information, see Boyle, *supra* note 9; Keith Aoki, *(Intellectual) Property and Sovereignty: Notes Toward a Cultural Geography of Authorship*, 48 Stan. L. Rev. 1293, 1323-24 (1996) (U.S. law has erred consistently on side of overprotecting intellectual properties).   That author-centered vision also tends to downplay the importance of fair use, thereby encouraging an absolutist rather than a functional notion of intellectual property.

182.   *See* Hughes, *supra* note 83, at 323-25. If copyright's purpose is to support learning and discourse, then at some point the public must be free to copy, alter, and refashion the works that have become a part of its cultural matrix. The community of users of public domain materials, whose interests would be negatively affected by a copyright term extension, is numerous and diverse. It includes students, teachers, writers, filmmakers, reprint publishers, video distributors, film scholars, multimedia producers, teachers, and students. Testimony of Professor Jaszi, *supra* note 120. *See generally* Gordon & Postbrief, *supra* note 70, at 151, 154, 156.

183.   We can take a first step toward partial quantification of the cost that a twenty year extension will impose on American consumers and users of copyrighted works. And based on proponents' estimates of the likely European benefits a term change would yield for American producers, the cost would be considerable.   ASCAP projects that an additional twenty years will mean a present annual increase of $30

million from the foreign licensing of music public performance and mechanical reproduction rights. *See Senate Hearing, supra* note 107, at 138. The Motion Picture Association of America (MPAA) forecasts that an extension will produce additional foreign revenues of $1 million by 2000, rising to $160 million by 2020. *House Hearings, supra* note 20, at 211. Since it is reasonable to assume that Americans are greater consumers of domestic works than nationals of other countries, the American public will have to pay a multiple of dollars to American copyright proprietors for every dollar paid by Europeans. (If foreign uses equal 25% of the total use of American works, that multiple is 3:1). Thus, assuming a 3:1 multiple, by proponents' own estimates, American consumers and users of music and motion pictures will incur an immediate annual cost of approximately $93 million due to the term change.

184. As noted, text at notes 253-54 *infra*, retroactivity has no positive incentive effects as the works to which additional protection is being granted have already been created and published. The result will be a windfall to an assemblage of publishers, heirs, estates, and perhaps a few old authors at the expense of users (e.g. readers) and future authors. *See* Parrinder, *supra* note 126, at 16 (twenty year windfall, at public expense, to beneficiaries of H.G. Wells estate).

185. *See* 17 U.S.C. secs. 201(b), 302(c) (1994).

186. Directive art. 3(1)-(2).

187. *House Hearings, supra* note 20, at 210 (statement of Charlene Barshefsky, Deputy U.S. Trade Representative). In recognition of this state of affairs, the Recording Industry Association of America (RIAA), the trade group of record companies, opposed a move to life plus seventy. Adoption of the European Union standards, it says, will perpetuate the differential treatment of sound recordings internationally. Dorothy Schrader, Proposed U.S. Copyright Term Extension 19 (1995).

188. Similarly, American film producers, another major sector of the United States copyright industries, will not be aided directly by enactment of the extension bill, though they may secure added European benefits indirectly in some cases by contractual arrangements with the directors of their films. As with sound recordings, European protection of film producers is limited to fifty years from first publication or communication to the public. Directive art. 3(3). Thus, an increase in the American term for works for hire, will not confer directly any European benefit on film producers. However, in Europe directors are considered the authors of films and are given a term of protection of life plus seventy years. Directive art. 2. The contract between film producer and director can, and typically does, assign to the producer the authority to exercise all economic rights granted to the creator of the work throughout the world. The term of protection granted directors of American films in Europe is capped by the term granted the film in the United States. Accordingly, the life plus seventy European term was capped by the seventy-five year term granted in the United States. With the extension of the work for hire term to ninety-five years here, the term of life plus seventy granted directors of American films in Europe will be capped at ninety-five years rather than seventy-five years. Directors of these films will therefore receive, and the producers as assignees of their rights will therefore enjoy, up to twenty years additional protection in European countries, depending on the director's life span. Testimony of Charlene Barshefsky, *supra* note 187. But this interpretation of the effect of an assignment is not certain. And, at a minimum, the European Union may not make it easy for American film producers to benefit from the twenty year added term. *See* Schrader, *supra* note 187, at 11-13. Ironically, the European directive provides for the emergence of new copyright roles for film directors and others involved in film production, roles which the American film industry has vigorously opposed at home. *See generally* Gerald Dworkin, *Authorship of Films and the European Commission Proposals for Harmonising the Term of Copyright*, 5 Eur. Intell. Prop. Rev. 151 (1993).

Analysis of the likely European treatment of sound recordings and movies suggests that the most likely beneficiaries of a term extension will be the composers and publishers of musical works. The important general point is that it is misinformed to believe that the European Union will apply the life plus seventy term to all categories and types of copyrighted American works. To the contrary, the Directive sets different terms for particular categories (books and music v. sound recordings) and particular types of works (personal v. corporate), with shorter terms adopted for the less favored recordings and corporate works.

For another element of the term extension legislation which will produce burdens for domestic users and consumers while yielding no comparable gains abroad for American authors, see note 275 *infra*.

189. Professor Cargill and Attorney Moran have made a distinctive argument that the present term of protection is unconstitutional, though not because of excessive length. They contend that a term in the form of life + X years is unconstitutional because the constitutional reference to "limited times", when legislative history and state practice are taken into account, implies a "certain" length. Thus a term determined by a set numerical span of years, *e.g.*, fifty-six years from publication, is authorized; but a flexible term based on the life of the individual author violates the prescription. Cargill & Moran, *supra* note 103. Without passing judgment on the constitutional claim, their major points have merit as a matter of policy. Thus, they express concern about protection being transformed, via continual lengthening of the term, into a "near absolute property right", thereby depriving the "limited times" provision of any operative significance; and they observe critically that "Congress has twice increased duration seemingly without inquiring as to whether the longer term would encourage greater literary production." *Id.* at 922.

190. *See generally* Patterson, *supra* note 125, at 19, 37-38.

191. *See generally* Melville B. Nimmer, *Does Copyright Abridge the First Amendment Guarantees of Free Speech and Press?*, 17 UCLA L. Rev. 1180, 1193-

94 (1970); L. Ray Patterson & Stanley F. Birch, Jr., *Copyright and Free Speech Rights*, 4 J. Intell. Prop. 1 (1996).

192. *See* Joseph A. Lavigne, *For Limited Times? Making Rich Kids Richer Via the Copyright Term Extension Act of 1996*, 73 U. Detroit L. Rev. 311, 354-58 (1996). We believe that contraction rather than expansion of the copyright term is justified. However, as a practical matter such a reduction is precluded by the Berne Union, of which the United States is a member. Though the Convention permits countries some flexibility in determining what is protectable, *see* Jane Ginsburg, *Surveying the Borders of Copyright*, Address at the WIPO Worldwide Symposium on the Future of Copyright and Neighboring Rights 5-9 (June 1-3, 1994), it requires a minimum term of life plus 50 for most covered works.

The extent of the duplicator's cost advantage, the length and import of lead time, and the presence of offsetting advantages held by the original producer surely differ among different intellectual and artistic works, and accordingly the strength of the case for legal intervention will differ among these works. Under our analysis this fact suggests that the optimal period of protection will vary from case to case and that a different term of protection is desirable for different kinds of works. *See generally* Michael O'Hare, *Copyright and the Protection of Economic Rights*, 6 J. Cultural Econ. 33 (1982). Thus, production and dissemination of computer programs may be encouraged most effectively by a copyright lasting x years while a novel may call for protection lasting y years. *See* Dreyfuss, *supra* note 32, at 222-23 (choices in the definition of protection should be tailored to characteristics of the particular intellectual property industries); Jussawalla, *supra* note 33, at 103 (product cycle should be determinant for protection of intellectual property; as cycle shortens, there is less justification for protection in terms of social welfare). *See also* Gordon, *supra* note 75, at 2586. Indeed, the notion of different durational terms for different types of works fits with the efficiency-rooted view of the legislative (and judicial) task as the determination of the combination of grants and reservations that will yield economic gains that exceed by the maximum amount the accompanying efficiency losses. The problem with such discriminations is one of administrative complexity. The question is whether it would be possible to construct a feasible scheme of categories and to run the more complex system at a cost lower than the contemplated social benefits from increased access. *See generally* Evans, *supra* note 168, at 7-8. The presence of multi-media products which cut across traditional lines might appropriately make us cautious about differentiation. On the other hand, different terms for different kinds of works have not been uncommon in other countries; and in a situation where administrative simplicity calls for uniformity while other considerations point to variability, a small number of categories may add little to administrative costs and yet contribute greatly to efficiency. *See, e.g.*, Guinan, *supra* note 15, at 4-6, 31; 1 Stephen P. Ladas, The International Protection of Literary and Artistic Property 315, 317, 324, 330-38 (1938); Braunstein, *supra* note 35, at I-10-11. *Cf.* Fisher, *supra* note 32, at 1720 (categorizing copyrighted works for purposes of fair use determinations promotes allocative efficiency but creating too many subdivisions reduces efficiency). In fact, during the revision conferences which preceded the enactment of our 1909 Act, there was considerable sentiment for assigning different terms for different types of writings. *See* Barbara Ringer, Renewal of Copyright (Copyright Office, General Revision of the Copyright Law Study No. 31, 1960). *See generally* Lyman R. Patterson, *Copyright and the Public Interest, in* Copyright: Current Viewpoints on History, Laws, Legislation 47-48 (Allen Kent & Harold Lancour eds., 1972) ("uniform protection for all works is neither necessary nor appropriate"). *See also* Scherer, *supra* note 99, at 422, 426-27 (desirable patent policy would tailor life of each patent to economic characteristics of its underlying invention); Roger L. Beck, *Comment: Does Competitive Dissipation Require a Short Patent Life?*, *in* 8 Research in Law and Economics, *supra* note 32, at 121, 124-25 (optimal patent life longer for non run-of-the-mill inventions); William D. Nordhaus, Invention, Growth, and Welfare: A Theoretical Treatment of Technological Change 79 (1969) (patents for industries with more progressive (or easier) invention should have shorter lives); Ad Hoc Committee on the Role of Patents in Research, Nat'l Research Council, Pub. No. 980-A, The Role of Patents in Research: The Committee Report 39 (1962) (petit patent with term shorter than 17 years suggested when invention of little significance or when fair return on investment could be made in shorter period). A shorter term for photographs and sound recordings, in particular, is not unusual abroad. *See, e.g.*, Copyright Statute of Austria, sec. 60, 72, 1 UNESCO Copyright Laws & Treaties of the World (1988); Copyright Statute of Germany, art. 64, 85, 3 UNESCO Copyright Laws & Treaties of the World (1990); Denmark, Act No. 157 of 1961 on Rights in Photographic Pictures, sec. 15, 1 UNESCO Copyright Laws & Treaties of the World (1980); Silke von Lewinski, *EC Proposal for a Council Directive Harmonizing the Term of Protection of Copyright and Certain Related Rights*, 23 Int'l Rev. Indus. Prop. & Copyright L. 785, 794 (1992). The Berne Convention, art. 7(4), permits Member States to accord a shorter term of protection for photographs and works of applied art; the minimum term required is twenty-five years from the making of such a work. A similar provision in the Universal Copyright Convention requires a minimum term of ten years. *See* Universal Copyright Convention, arts. 2, 3 (Paris Revision 1971).

One might contend that an optimum copyright law should be highly flexible, tailoring the term (and other characteristics) of each grant to the incentive needs of each recipient. Arguably, it makes no economic sense to set the term absolutely in advance, and rather the term should be variable, depending on the size of and actual return on investment. However, such tailoring would involve formidable administrative difficulties, if not nightmares, and we must generally be content to select a uniform duration which will work well on the whole. *See* Maskus, *supra* note 43, at 14 (choice of apt protection level complicated by measurement problems; because of these problems intellectual property rights standardized by property type not tailored to specific products). The doctrine of fair use, though, may be seen as a device which, on an ad hoc basis, can modulate protection so as to bring it closer to the optimum prescription that creators not requiring remuneration for their efforts not be granted a monopoly on production of the physical embodiments of their work thus eliminating any deadweight loss for these products and that where remuneration is required for production the duration of monopoly be just enough to provide such remuneration. Fair use provides a vehicle for the courts, interested in employing the doctrine to increase efficiency in the use of scarce resources, to moderate the rules of copyright law in situations where the benefits of increased consumption appear to outweigh the harm from reduced production. *See* Liebowitz, *supra* note 64, at 188-191; Fisher, *supra* note 32, at 1698-1744. More generally, the fair use doctrine is designed to insure that future authors have a sufficient supply of raw materials available to them.

193. *See* Netanel, *supra* note 58.

194. *Id.* at 366-71.

Chapter V. Equitable Considerations

The Natural Right Argument

Most modern discourse about the justification(s) for copyright protection has viewed the copyright system as instrumental and has spoken in terms of economic incentive and efficiency.[195] Essentially utilitarian, the guiding principles seek to advance culture and learning by stimulating the generation and distribution of a wide array of intellectual and artistic works. A parallel thread of thinking which grounds justification for protection in a moral or natural right argument has always been present, though.[196] That presence is unsurprising, as in its various formulations--for example, a person's asserted entitlement to "the fruits of one's labor"[197]--this argument expresses a powerful intuition about the relationship between a person and his creations. Thus, proposals for recognition or extension of copyright protection have often been accompanied by reference to John Locke and his celebrated labor theory.[198]

Locke's position is deceptively straightforward.[199] Basically, he argues "that whenever one mingles his effort with the raw stuff of the world, any resulting product ought--simply ought--to be his."[200] Locke begins with the premise that people have a natural right of property in their bodies. Since people own their bodies, he reasoned that they also own the labor of their bodies and, by extension, the product of that labor.[201] Under this theory authors deserve legal protection as an inherent natural right attaching to the act of creation; protection is not provided as an inducement for effort. Rather property rights exist without regard to any need for the economic stimulation of creative activity.[202]

142

For our purposes, Locke's approach is problematic in a number of respects. One difficulty with the theory is its overbreadth and absolutist implications.[203] It suggests protection unlimited in time for it offers neither logical nor moral justification for temporally circumscribing that protection.[204] More generally, once it is accepted that reproduction and imitation are not inherently evil activities,[205] that all copying of intangibles is not illicit[206], Locke's undiscriminating ethical imperative offers us no guidance in deciding which intangibles to protect[207] and what scope of protection,[208] including duration, to provide.[209] It does not help us determine how large "the fruit" is.[210] The appeal of the natural right argument is also lessened by recognition of the contributions of others to the author's or artist's work.[211] While the perplexing question of the extent to which individual labor should be discounted by social factors in calculating desert is not unique to this context,[212] the author's debt to others is considerable. Unlike Locke's food gatherer, authors do not really work alone; authorship is not a solitary enterprise in which a single person creates an entire work from his imagination alone. Authors are members of an artistic community whose values and experiences shape their vision. Creative works represent not just the author's personality; rather they capture a mixture of his personality, the society in which he lives, and the works of other authors. All authors draw on the work of their predecessors and are usually stimulated as well by the ongoing efforts of their contemporaries.[213] Even acknowledging that the matter of individual versus social contribution is one of degree, the author's reliance on borrowed material provides the basis for recognition of a strong public domain. Moreover, the compensation a person receives for his services often depends on fortuities having no relation to the level or quality of his efforts. For example, before records a performer's (and composer's) compensation was limited by the number of people who could physically hear him. Now radio, television, movies and long-playing records multiply his audience a thousand fold.[214] These advances have dramatically increased the opportunity to exploit music and correspondingly the earnings potential of composers and performers, though these artists had nothing to do with the development of the technical changes.[215]

A more discriminating reading of Locke and the natural law tradition, one which removes the absolutist implications, is possible. But such a reading would likely be of scant aid to proponents of an increase in the copyright term. Thus, Professor Yen presents a well-argued case for copyright's historical and theoretical link to natural law and pleads for the utility of an explicit restoration of natural law thinking to our copyright jurisprudence.[216] However, partly in recognition of the author's substantial debt to those who preceded him, he infers significant limits on protection, resulting in an expansive public domain. While he does not address the issue of duration directly, the clear thrust of his argument goes against an increase of an already lengthy term.[217]

Copyright and Recognition of Great Works

One might try to justify a term extension as an equitable means of recognition of great works. The premise is that society should reward the author of a masterpiece of enduring social value for the contribution he has made to social progress,[218] a contribution that goes beyond the value he has provided purchasers of his work. And in the case of serious works of literature, art, and music, their excellence may take many years to be appreciated. However, such a rationale is at odds with the structure and assumptions of our copyright system, which imposes no aesthetic or imaginative qualification for protection, no test of literary or artistic quality as a condition of copyrightability.[219] Unlike inventors seeking patent protection who must demonstrate the novelty, utility, and non-obviousness of their invention or discovery, copyright attaches to authors' works which are "original" in the limited sense only that they originated with the author and were not copied from a prior work.[220] The extension of the copyright term will provide additional protection for the singular gem, but it will do so by lengthening protection for all works, distinguished and undistinguished,[221] with the significant costs attendant on such a change. Moreover, copyright's tendency to limit dissemination, via higher prices, is especially harmful when the work is a classic.

In any case, copyright as a general matter is a poor vehicle for assessing and insuring "due rewards". Economic success and cultural value do not perforce coincide. Under copyright there is no necessary correlation between the monopoly return to a copyright proprietor and the long-term social value of his work. Nor is there any necessary correlation between this return and the moral deserts of the creator.[222] The size of profits earned under the protection of copyright is not correlated with the efforts, funds, or sacrifices invested in the creative work.[223] Indeed, "sacrificial days" and "lasting benefit"[224] often are absent from precisely those works which copyright benefits most. In the case of book publishing, for example, the copyright system tends to favor the commercial popular work with large sales rather than important and serious works with limited marketability. Similarly, in the music industry, it is the high volume, ephemeral popular recording which gains most from copyright protection, for it is this work which has been duplicated and which would continue to be the prime object for duplicators in the absence of protection.[225]

Rather than paint with the crude, broad brush of copyright, a less restrictive device is available to express publicly admiration and support of works exemplary of human excellence. Prizes or grants from foundations, government, or universities are a practical alternative means by which to recognize works of genius. The cost burden of this means would be spread more widely, and it is not inequitable to finance through taxes the support of works that benefit not only those who purchase them but also many other members of the group as well. Such an arrangement will channel funds to the author without simultaneously limiting dissemination of the great work which enriches the cultural heritage. Reliance on the alternative means of prizes, then, singles out the meritorious work but avoids the costs incident to an extension of the copyright term.[226]

Longevity and Term Extension

Longevity, more precisely the increase in life expectancy among the population, is frequently cited by proponents as a ground for extending the term of protection.[227] It is difficult, at least at first glance, to see the bearing of this increase in the length of life on copyright policy. It is not immediately apparent why an author's longer life should affect the term of protection and particularly why it should affect the term after death. It appears irrelevant to the objective of providing adequate incentives to authors and publishers; and it will not alter the investment horizon they face. With respect to equitable considerations, the author's natural right entitlement, the claims of the public domain, and the implications of the mix of individual and social contributions to a work are also all unaffected by the fact of increased longevity.

References to increased life span may reflect a concern about authors possibly outliving their copyrights.[228] However, even if that scenario is somehow regarded as unseemly, the problem is removed by a term of protection defined by the life of the author. Under that approach, which is adopted by our present Copyright Act, an author can not outlive the copyright. Moreover, under a scheme which measures the term, in part, by the life of the author, any increase in longevity will automatically produce a longer term of protection. Thus, if authors are living twenty years more than they used to, that will necessarily yield twenty more years of protection than they had previously enjoyed.[229]

Of course, inherent in a life plus scheme is the possibility of (great) unevenness in the number of years of protection actually accorded to different works.[230] For example, under the present life + 50 formula, a work composed by a seventy year old author who dies at age seventy-five will receive protection for fifty-five years while a work authored by a twenty-five year old who lives to age seventy-five will be protected for 100 years. This possibility is disturbing to many observers.[231] However, this unevenness is built into the structure; and Congress chooses the number of years post mortem which it deems best over the full range of cases. In fact, large disparities and unhappiness with them do not provide grounds for extension of an already generous term to life + 70, but rather offer evidence of the relative desirability of a term measured by a fixed number of years from a set event such as publication[232].

What more, then, does the recurrent emphasis on the increase in longevity implicate? Perhaps it is a concern for the welfare of the author's grandchildren. There are frequent references by proponents of extension to the need to provide for subsequent generations.[233] But the reasons why a potential producer of intellectual products wants to earn more money--whether it is to support his grandchildren or increase his own standard of living--are irrelevant to the question of an appropriate length for copyright protection.[234] As we have indicated, the considerations pertinent to copyright length are the impact of a particular term on creation incentives balanced against the cost of a particular period of protection to consumers and the public domain.

Also, concern for poor progeny, just as concern for the poor aged author, would better be served by social welfare measures explicitly directed to this problem than by trying to refashion copyright as an income support vehicle.[235] In any case, the free alienability of copyright lends a distinct air of unreality to these contentions about assuring the welfare of later generations. Both during and after the author's life the copyright interest (or its component parts) is just as likely to be held by a stranger as a member of his family.[236] Indeed, often royalties go to a person who was unknown to the author.[237] There is nothing in copyright law generally which assures the financial benefits of copyright will inure to offspring or near relatives of the author.[238] And there is nothing in the specific proposal before Congress to extend the term that is designed to insure that the benefits of this extension are received by the author's heirs;[239] and the absence of any such provision renders suspect the life expectancy argument. Of course, one might contend that the identity of ultimate beneficiaries does not matter as long as the author receives the (present) value of the longer term. But that line of reasoning would shift us back to an incentive perspective,[240] and we have shown that the incentive-based argument for extension is a weak one. Finally, the longevity-concern-for-heirs line of argument (and most of the other equity-based contentions) have no relevance to works of corporate authorship, which comprise a substantial percentage of copyrighted writings.[241] Extension of the term for works made for hire can not be justified as benefiting natural authors and their dependents.[242]

In conclusion, even if one regards an increase in life expectancy as relevant to the determination of the copyright term of protection, there has hardly been a dramatic increase, much less a twenty year rise, in that statistic since 1976 when the generous term of life + 50 was put in place.[243]

Extent of Government's Duty to Guarantee Success

Finally, it is sometimes claimed that fairness requires that the legal structure be shaped to permit a person to support himself via exploitation of his particular talents.[244] Obviously, this claim would require drastic changes in our existing attitudes toward the kind of assistance individuals can expect from government with respect to their economic activity. Rather, under existing notions, so long as the rules are clear and adhered to consistently, the fact that, with respect to the market conditions applicable to a particular product, the protections provided by our legal system might be insufficient to permit financially rewarding commercialization of particular intellectual products is not deemed unfair in any sense to those unable to profitably use their talents in a particular way. Conceivably, a persuasive argument can be made supporting the creation of this kind of right; perhaps one rooted in the concept of the development of human personality.[245] But so far, our legal system has not recognized this kind of "right" and those seeking to justify additional copyright protection can not rely on it.

Notes

---

195. *See, e.g.*, H.R. Rep. No. 2222, 60th Cong., 2d Sess. 7 (1909) (House Report accompanying 1909 Copyright Act):

> The enactment of copyright legislation by Congress under the terms of the Constitution is not based upon any natural right that the author has in his writings...but upon the ground that the welfare of the public will be served and progress of science and useful arts will be promoted by securing to authors for limited periods the exclusive rights to their writings.

Wheaton v. Peters, 33 U.S. (8 Pet.) 591 (1834); Sony Corp. of Am. v. Universal City Studios, Inc., 464 U.S. 417, 429 (1984). In this instrumental focus the modern American copyright tradition differs philosophically from that of many other countries, including those in continental Europe, which ground intellectual property in the natural rights of individual creators. In the American system Congress need not accord intellectual property rights, but if it does, the purpose must be to promote the progress of science (in the broad eighteenth century sense of that term of "knowledge" or "learning") by providing the public with more, and more desirable, intellectual and artistic works. In the same vein, new rights are not established nor old ones strengthened just because it appears that a worthy person may gain. Such action is justified only when it appears that a public benefit, in terms of the increase and spread of knowledge, will result. *See* Evans, *supra* note 168, at 6-7; Leval, *supra* note 154, at 1107-09, 1124. *See generally* Richard Stallman, *Reevaluating Copyright: The Public Must Prevail*, 75 Or. L. Rev. 291, 292-93 (1996):

> [T]here are many alternative bargains that the public could offer to publishers. So which bargain is the best one for the public? Which freedoms are worthwhile for the public to trade, and for what length of time? The answers depend on two things: how much additional publication the public

will get for trading a given freedom, and how much the public benefits from keeping that freedom....Copyright is a bargain with the public; not a natural right. Copyright policy issues are about which bargains benefit the public, not about what rights publishers or readers are entitled to.

196. *See* Weinreb, *supra* note 32, at 1211-1216 (in United States sense that an author's property in his work is not only good but also right has been strong bulwark of instrumental arguments that might not have fared so well on their own might); Sterk, *supra* note 70, at 1203, 1227 (number of copyright doctrines more consistent with desert theory than incentive rationale). *See generally* Alain Strowel, *Droit d'auteur and Copyright: Between History and Nature, in* Of Authors and Origins 241-49 (Brad Sherman & Alain Strowel eds., 1994) (natural-positive law dichotomy). While there is some disagreement about the extent of influence this natural right strand, in fact, has exercised historically, it appears that any support for a broad proprietary entitlement rooted in natural right has operated, at best, as a secondary rationale for copyright protection in the twentieth century United States. *See* Netanel, *supra* note 58, at 307 n.97, 313 n.126. *But see* Weinreb, *supra* note 32, at 1216 n.291 (historical record contradicts Netanel's terse dismissal of influence of natural right thinking). For the well-considered argument that the landmark case of *Wheaton v. Peters*, 33 U.S. 391 (1834), rejects both common law copyright and the Lockean argument that underlies it, see Meredith L. McGill, *The Matter of the Text: Commerce, Print Culture, and the Authority of the State in American Copyright Law*, 9 Am. Literary Hist. 21 (1997). According to McGill, "Rather than confirming the author as the owner of a text that was clearly defined as a commodity, *Wheaton v. Peters* establishes going-into-print as the moment when individual rights give way to the demands of the social, and defines the private ownership of a printed text as the temporary alienation of public property. It is with the circumscription of individual rights and not with their extension that nineteenth-century American copyright law is primarily concerned."

197. Another common variation asserts that a person, and not someone else, should "reap where he has sown." *See generally*, Harper & Row Publishers v. Nation Enterprises, 471 U.S. 539, 546 (1985) ("The rights conferred by copyright are designed to assure contributors to the store of knowledge a fair return for their labors"). Elaborating on the basic contention, an author might assert that because he created the work himself and did not thereby reduce the opportunities available to other citizens, he should be entitled to fix the terms upon which others can gain access to his creation. That assertion is tellingly criticized in Weinreb, *supra* note 32, at 1217-19 & n.301, 1220-29, 1245-46.

198. *See Hearings on H.R. 4347, H.R. 5680, H.R. 6831, H.R. 6835 Before Subcomm. No. 3 of the House Comm. on the Judiciary*, 89th Cong., 1st Sess., pt. 3, at 1699 (1965). Not surprisingly, the argument that one has a "natural right" to "the exclusive control and benefit of what he has created" has been consistently and forcefully advocated by the organized representatives of authors. *See, e.g.*, Copyright Law Revision, Part 2, Discussion and Comments on Report of the Register of Copyrights on the General Revision of the U.S. Copyright Law, 88th Cong., 1st Sess. 247, 249 (Comm. Print 1963) (Authors League of America). Locke's core notion is that natural entitlements arise out of the activity of labor and that the positive law should enforce these entitlements. *E.g.*, A. John Simmons, *Original-Acquisition Justifications of Private Property, in* Property Rights 63, 76 (Ellen F. Paul et al. eds., 1994):

> Take...the central thesis...of Locke's OA justification: that your purposeful labor (using only what is yours) on what is either unowned or already owned by you, can yield property for you in the product of your labor (including as part of the product that which was labored upon, if it was unowned).

A. John Simmons, The Lockean Theory of Rights 223 (1992) (been no more widespread or enduring intuition about property rights than that labor in creating or improving a thing gives person special claim to it). *But see generally* John Rawls, A Theory of Justice 102 (1971) (rejection of Lockean notion that person entitled to fruits of his own labor; talented do not deserve to be rewarded for their talents).

For the "logic" by which perception of this natural property right leads to copyright protection as the appropriate way to socially recognize it, *see generally* Penrose, *supra* note 61, at 21. A possible source of discomfort with the natural right argument is that it is often put forth not on behalf of the author himself but rather on behalf of his publisher, record company, or film producer. When a commercial enterprise enters the scenario, much of the effect of the reap-where-you-have-not sown metaphor is dissipated. Weinreb, *supra* note 32, at 1245-46.

199. John Locke, The Second Treatise of Civil Government ch.5, sec. 27-30 (J.W. Gough ed., 1948) contains the classic statement of the labor-desert argument for tangible goods. For a thoughtful and detailed explication and critique of Locke's line of thought and the several strands to the Lockean argument, see Becker (1977), *supra* note 148, at 32-56 ("The Labor Theory of Property Acquisition"). On the idea of labor-mixing and its critics, see Hillel Steiner, An Essay on Rights 233 n.7 (1994).

200. Michelman, *supra* note 52, at 1204. *See generally* Simmons, *supra* note 198 (Locke's justification of private property rights as morally permissible rather than morally optimal).

201. In other words, since one's body is one's property, and its produce (labor) is also one's property, it follows as a matter of course that the product of the labor is also one's property. The chain of reasoning, however, is defective, as the conclusion does not necessarily follow from the premises. *See* Gopal Sreenivasan, The Limits of Lockean Rights in Property 59-62 (1995); Brian Barry, *You Have To Be Crazy To Believe It*, Times Literary Supplement, Oct. 25, 1996, at 28 (succinct criticism of notion of self-ownership; verbal trickery involved in move from grammatical truth

of man's property in his person to normative claim that laborer creates property in what labor is mixed with). *See also* John E. Roemer, Theories of Distributive Justice 208-10, 232-35 (1996) ("Neo-Lockeanism and Self-Ownership"); J.E. Penner, The Idea of Property in Law 200 (1997) (central flaw in Lockean analyses). Unlike one's labor which is inseparable from one's body, the product of one's labor is clearly separable from one's body, and therefore the transfer from ownership of labor to ownership of product is not warranted in the same way as the extension from ownership of the body to ownership of the labor. As Robert Nozick has questioned, why should anyone think that mixing of one's labor with a thing is a means of making the thing one's own rather than a way of losing one's labor. Robert Nozick, Anarchy, State, and Utopia 174-5 (1974); *see* Steiner, *supra* note 199, at 233-35. *But see generally* Stephen R. Munzer, A Theory of Property 67-75 (1990) (role of intention). (Admittedly, though, this objection that the Lockean theory lacks an explanation of why labor should give rise to ownership of the thing labored on is somewhat less forceful when applied to works of the intellect and imagination.) Moreover, there is a large gap between the claim that one has a natural right to possess and use personally the fruits of one's labor and the claim that one should receive for that product whatever the market will bear. Even if the labor theory demonstrates that a laborer has a natural right to the fruits of labor, that proposition does not establish a natural right to obtain the full market value of the resulting product. *See* Edwin C. Hettinger, *Justifying Intellectual Property* 18 Phil. & Pub. Aff. 31, 36-40 (1989); Sterk, *supra* note 70, at 1237-38 (market prices have little to do with merit; desert provides little basis for property right protection for authors or for other protection tied to market forces).

For criticism, on other grounds, of attempts to derive intellectual property rights by analogy to derivation of rights to tangible objects based on self-ownership, see Palmer, *supra* note 29, at 278-83. *See generally* Ferdinand Mount, *Soil Science*, Times Literary Supplement, March 7, 1997, at 13 (reviewing Colin Kolbert, ed., The Idea of Property in History and Modern Times).

202. We treat Locke's theory here as, in Professor Michelman's terms, a "desert" theory--one which justifies property by reference to an ethical postulate about individual merit, insisting that property is desirable because under its rule people can get and keep what is due them. A "desert" theory does not insist that property is desirable because it leads to consequences which are good for society "as a whole", such as maximizing social satisfactions. Michelman, *supra* note 52, at 1203-04. In this context, the notion is that authors deserve a reward for their labor and should receive it regardless of whether they would continue their effort in the absence of that compensation. Locke's theory, though, may also be viewed as a social utility theory. *See* Willmoore Kendall, John Locke and the Doctrine of Majority-Rule 69-74 (1941); James O. Grunebaum, Private Ownership 53-54 (1987).

The question of whether authors and artists deserve some reward other than the amount of compensation needed to keep them at their vocations has received little sustained attention in our copyright commentary.

203. *See generally* Penrose, *supra* note 61, at 20 n.1 (a chief defect of natural right argument for patents is that only the individual is considered and group interest is ignored). By the end of the nineteenth century, those seeking to offer justification for a patent system had largely abandoned natural law arguments. *Id.* at 24.

Those who argue for copyright (or patent) protection in terms of a natural property right must be somewhat uncomfortable with the seeming inconsistency with that notion reflected in the historically contingent nature of this protection, which amounts to a limited conditional monopoly grant. *Cf.* Machlup, *supra* note 36, at 53. *See also* Boyle, *supra* note 9, at 138-39. In fairness, one should recognize that talk of "property" or "natural rights" may as much reflect a judgment about legislative and semantic strategy in pursuit of legitimation as a belief in rationale. For a candid admission by some nineteenth century patent lawyers that they preferred to speak of "natural property rights" for propaganda purposes, particularly because the alternative concepts such as "monopoly right" or "privilege" were unpopular, see Machlup,

154

supra note 36, at 23 & n. 118; Fritz Machlup & Edith Penrose, *The Patent Controversy in the Nineteenth Century*, 10 J. Econ. Hist. 1, 16 (1950). *See generally* Augustine Birrell, Seven Lectures on the Law and History of Copyright in Books 10-14 (1899); Susan Stewart, Crimes of Writing: Problems in the Containment of Representation 12 (1991). For a similar observation about the strategic use of reference to the "natural rights" of "authors" by advocates in the history of copyright law and in particular with respect to the passage of the Statute of Anne, see Benjamin Kaplan, An Unhurried View of Copyright 8 (1967):

> Although references in the text of the statute to authors, together with dubious intimations in later cases that Swift, Addison, and Steele took some significant part in the drafting, have lent color to the notion that authors were themselves intended beneficiaries of parliamentary grace, I think it nearer the truth to say that publishers saw the tactical advantage of putting forward authors' interests together with their own, and this tactic produced some effect on the tone of the statute.

See also Strowel, *supra* note 196, at 40-41 (language chosen for debate tied to goal of expanding or limiting rights). A contemporary parallel is the manner in which the language of romantic authorship is utilized to justify intellectual property rights for large corporate entities. These entities who employ the creators and handlers of information support their own, derivative rights, in "works made for hire", through the rhetoric of original genius and individualism. *See* Boyle, *supra* note 9, at xiii ("Sony, Pfizer, and Microsoft tend to lack the appeal of Byron and Alexander Fleming"; ironic that large companies "can use the idea of the independent entrepreneurial creator to justify intellectual property rights *so* expansive that they make it much harder for future independent creators actually to create"). The irrelevance to works of corporate "authorship" of equity-based arguments for extended protection is noted at text at notes 241-42 *infra*. *See generally* Peter Jaszi,

Toward a Theory of Copyright: The Metamorphoses of "Authorship", 1991 Duke L.J. 455, 500-01:

> [I]n the domain of intellectual property, "authorship" has remained what it was in eighteenth-century England--a stalking horse for economic interests that were (as a tactical matter) better concealed than revealed, and a convenient generative metaphor for legal structures that facilitated the emergence of new modes of production for literary and artistic works.

204. With a less traditional reading, one might interpret the natural law approach in a way that avoids the criticism in the text. Professor Yen, for example, appeals to the natural law tradition; but, cognizant of the fear that the tradition will yield an unprincipled increase of authors' rights at the expense of the public interest in free access to works, he finds significant limits, recognizing a strong public domain, implicit in the approach. *See* Yen, *supra* note 115. Yen's argument, though, does not offer much solace for proponents of an extension of the copyright term. *See* text at notes 216-17 and notes 216-17 *infra*.

205. *See* Gordon, *supra* note 40, at 167-70. Indeed, to some thinkers the right to imitate has seemed more of a natural right than the property right:

> That ideas should freely spread from one to another over the globe, for the moral and mutual instruction of man, and improvement of his conditions, seems to have been peculiarly and benevolently designed by nature, when she made them, like fire, expansible over all space, without lessening their density in any point, and like the air in which we breathe, move, and have our physical being, incapable of confinement or exclusive appropriation. Inventions then cannot, in nature, be a subject of property.

The Invention of Elevators, Letter from Thomas Jefferson to Isaac McPherson (Aug.

13, 1813), *in* The Complete Jefferson 1015 (Saul K. Padover ed., 1943). *See also* Boyle, *supra* note 9, at 52-53; Drahos, *supra* note 89, at 24-28.

206. *See generally* Gordon, *supra* note 40, at 167-170.

207. In 1971, for example, Congress was faced with the question of whether to extend federal copyright protection to sound recordings. Locke's intuitive proposition about people's entitlement to the product of their own industry and initiative offers no clear answer to that question, for we are dealing here with matters of degree. The relevant inquiries, then, would include: Do sufficient incentives already exist? If not, what detailed set of institutional arrangements will most efficiently satisfy the want for recordings? *See generally* Economic Council of Canada, *supra* note 10, at 224-25.

208. The Lockean intuition does not help us determine, for example, whether to provide legal protection by means of a liability rule or a property rule. *See generally* Gordon, *supra* note 40, at 280 (reap/sow argument, even when constrained by restitutionary principles, "does not describe with specificity the particular acts that would constitute actionable copying of an eligible intangible, nor does it provide a list of those intangibles that would be eligible or ineligible for protection.") Put more generally, the approach is essentially indeterminate.

When we move from copyright protection as a means to encourage creative activity to protection as a means to provide rewards for deserving authors, we move from a rationale which provides a discernible though imprecise measuring rod to one which offers virtually no aid in drawing lines with respect to the appropriate scope of protection.

209. Alternatively, Locke might be viewed as espousing a labor theory of value. Thus, in the music industry context, record duplicators obtain the benefits of a huge input of skilled labor at a much lower price than they would have to pay if the

duplicator were forced to purchase the services of the record producers on the open market. When sales are made to duplicators for the purpose of reproducing the record and selling it at cut rate prices, the original producer remains uncompensated for the initial labor and is precluded from recouping his labor costs from other consumers. Thus, it is plausible to argue that unrestricted duplication leads to the uncompensated appropriation of the labor of the record producers. But whatever the merits of labor theories of value, very few societies, including our own, have adopted any. In capitalistic countries property rights ordinarily are not created or modified nor is compensation awarded solely on the basis of labor expended. And innumerable governmental and private actions continuously alter property values without reference to human labor, with the result that wealth and income normally are not directly proportional to the amount of work put forth. *See generally* Hettinger, *supra* note 201, at 39 ("To what extent individual laborers should be allowed to receive the market value of their products is a question of social policy; it is not solved by simply insisting on a moral right to the fruits of one's labor"). More broadly, our practices belie any assumption that a creator has a claim on the benefits of anything that would not have existed but for the initial creation; no entitlement of producers to a productive opportunity is recognized.

210. *See* O'Hare, *supra* note 192, at 38-39 ("The moral right of creators to the 'fruits' of their labor is correctly recognized...to be so difficult to determine (does the author of a book on investment advice have a moral right to collect the profits of readers who apply his methods successfully?) and probably impossible to apply in practice outside fairly narrow limits...."). *See generally* Weinreb, *supra* note 32, at 1226 (if author's claim based on labor, need first to establish he has labored in relevant sense; no solid basis by which to distinguish compensable labor from uncompensated play); John P. Dawson, *The Self-Serving Intermeddler*, 87 Harv. L. Rev. 1409, 1412 (1974) ("[A]n effort to retrieve all forms of unearned increment, for no better reason than that it is unearned, could not succeed. Uncompensated gains are pervasive and

universal; our well-being and survival depend on them....merely by living we reap what we did not sow.")

Similarly, in 1976 Congress explained the new and longer Revision Bill term as designed to insure an author "the fair economic benefits" from his works, H.R. Rep. No. 1476, 94th Cong., 2d Sess. 134 (1976), but it gave no standard to determine what are the fair benefits which should be allocated to an author and his dependents. As is often the case with references to "fairness", the difficulty here is in giving content to a normative standard from which we can then infer the apt entitlement owed to an author. As with the Lockean intuition, the ambiguity of the norm limits its operational utility as a guide to the resolution of contemporary problems of copyright policy. *See* Sheldon W. Halpern et al., Copyright 559-61 (1992). *See generally* Guido Calabresi & A. Douglas Melamed, *Property Rules, Liability Rules, and Inalienability: One View of the Cathedral*, 85 Harv. L. Rev. 1089, 1098 & n.21 (1972) (no adequate theory of desert currently available).

211. *See* Hettinger, *supra* note 201, at 36-39 ("If laboring gives the laborer the right to receive the market value of the resulting product, this market value should be shared by all those whose ideas contributed to the origin of the product"; laborer entitled only to value he added and not to total value of resulting product). Moreover, and in the same vein, the labor argument's intuitive appeal--"I made it; therefore it's mine"--is undercut when it is employed to try to justify owning something others are responsible for, *i.e.*, market value, which is a socially created phenomenon.

Our copyright terminology with its focus on the "original author", and its implicit suggestion that the author creates his work from nothing, mistakenly tends to lead to an undervaluation of the sources of the author's material and fails to recognize sufficiently the importance of the raw materials from which intellectual, informational, and artistic works are constructed. Culture grows by accretion, and the creation of knowledge is a cumulative undertaking. As previously noted, one key purpose of the fair use doctrine is to insure that future creators have a sufficient supply of raw materials available to them.

212. *See* Becker (1993), *supra* note 148, at 610-11:

> We know that intelligence, industriousness, health, motivation and opportunity are all crucial determinants of what we produce, and are arguably not the sorts of things that contribute to the claim that we are entitled to (or deserve) the things that we produce. Yet the thought that people do *sometimes* deserve reward (or blame) for their achievements is unshakable. How are we to solve this puzzle in the case of property rights?

213. *See, e.g.*, Posner, *supra* note 32, at 340-49 ("literary imagination is not a volcano of pure inspiration but a weaving of the author's experience of life into an existing literary tradition. The more extensive copyright protection is, the more inhibited is the literary imagination"); Patterson, *supra* note 125, at 21-24 (fallacious that author creates work out of private materials that he owns as carpenter owns wood out of which he fashions furniture).

214. *See generally* Arnold Plant, *supra* note 98, at 6-9, 23; Kozinski, *supra* note 160, at 466-67. In addition, the character of artists' recorded performances may owe as much to advances in recording technology as to their rhythmic inventiveness and lyrical skills.

215. *Cf.* Puri, *supra* note 176, at 18 (new technologies increasing channels for distributing works both raise returns of copyright owners and also permit them to receive those returns in a very short time span).

Our observations and critique in this section are not meant to deny that the romantic conception of authorship and its accompanying rhetoric of entitlement offer an attractive idea of creative labor--"transcending market norms, incorporating both work and play and entailing a world in which workers have a real connection to and control over the fruits of their labours." Boyle, *supra* note 9, at 176.

216. *See* Yen, *supra* note 115.

217. *See id.* at 553 ("If anything, the natural law of possession suggests a stronger public domain than the one courts might discover through our present economic model.") *See generally* Becker (1977), *supra* note 148, at 55 (defensible version of labor theory rooted in principle of desert calls for sharp limitation of patent and copyright arrangements). *See also* Gordon, *supra* note 40, at 249 (fairness rationale supports limited term and may excuse some quantitatively significant uses); Patterson, *supra* note 125, at 21-24, 26 (persons in free society have as much natural law right to learning as author has to exclusive publication). *But see generally* Adam D. Moore, *A Lockean Theory of Intellectual Property*, 21 Hamline L. Rev. 65, 101-05 (1997) (prospect of perpetual rights for intellectual works not alarming).

Another recent interpreter of Locke and his explicators, and the implications of their writings for copyright law, also does not provide great comfort for advocates of a lengthened term. R. Anthony Reese distinguishes two readings of Locke which have developed over time. The first, libertarian Lockeanism, associated primarily with Robert Nozick, emphasizes the natural, pre-political right flowing from the individual's labor, but offers no obvious answer to the intellectual property question of which sticks are in the bundle of sticks owned by the creator. While the libertarian view may offer support for a lengthy term, it also implies a very narrow scope of protection, one more restrictive than that provided by present copyright doctrine. Rent-theory Lockeanism, on the other hand, insists on an exacting separation of the individual and social components in the creation of a work and justifies intellectual property rights only to the extent they compensate an author for the sacrifice involved in the creation of the work. Thus, under this second theory, in the case of a book, for example, the author would be entitled to earn enough income to pay for the value of the time he invested in writing the book plus the cost of his materials as well as a fair return on his investment of those costs. Any value in a copyrighted work beyond that needed to compensate an author for his sacrifice belongs, according to rent-theory Lockeanism, to the community as a whole. This approach not only argues against lengthening the term of protection but suggests that a life plus fifty term is too long. R. Anthony Reese, *Reflections on the Intellectual Commons: Two Perspectives on Copyright Duration and Reversion*, 47 Stan. L. Rev. 707 (1995).

218. *See* Robert M. Sherwood, Intellectual Property and Economic Development 37 (1990) ("public honoring of the effort of the individual, an acknowledgement of achievement").

219. *Mazer v. Stein*, 347 U.S. 201 (1954), for example, makes it clear that copyright is not confined to works of high art, but includes some aspects of utilitarian design. In a decision which validated the age of commercial design copyright, the Court there held that copyright protection is available for works of art embodied in industrial objects. Accordingly, under the Copyright Act works of art include all original pictorial, graphic, and sculptural works that are intended to be or have been embodied in useful articles, regardless of factors such as mass production or commercial exploitation.

220. See text at note 88 and note 88 *supra*. Works need only exhibit the minimal creativity sufficient to meet a generous standard of originality. Copyright's low originality standard for protection reflects, in part, the practical difficulties of determining novelty in intellectual and artistic works. As Professor Goldstein notes, as compared with the technical arts in which the scope of an invention can be described discretely and with relative precision, the arts do not lend themselves to precise verbal or mathematical boundaries. The task of an inventor searching technical descriptions of the prior art in order to determine whether his work will duplicate earlier efforts is far easier than that of a novelist searching all existing literature to be sure that his work will not duplicate earlier writings. Indeed, often the

cost of such a search would be greater than the potential economic returns to be garnered from the work and thus would "discourage authors and publishers from producing and distributing any copyrighted works at all." Goldstein, *supra* note 56, at 15.

221. *See* Plant, *supra* note 98, at 12:

> If it could be shown that the writing of works of enduring and exceptional literary value had depended upon long periods of copyright, and extended terms had been confined to them (on the lines of the permissive extensions of patent rights now so rarely granted to exceptional inventions), a reasonable justification for the extensions might be advanced; but that does not seem to me to have been the case.

As Cargill & Moran, *supra* note 103, at 923-24, observe, increased protection especially favors authors of exceptional durability "not because of the immortality of their work but because of the superiority of their vascular equipment." *See also* W.R. Cornish, *Authors in Law*, 58 Mod. L. Rev. 1, 7 (1995).

222. Sam Ricketson, *The Copyright Term*, 23 Int'l Rev. Indus. Prop. & Copyright L. 753, 759 (1992) (arbitrary and ephemeral character of reward promised); *cf.* Plant, *supra* note 98, at 15 ("there is no logical case for making the period over which we might wish to assure a continuing income to successful authors coincide with that for which a monopoly might reasonably be accorded to the first publisher of a new work").

223. *See* Hettinger, *supra* note 201, at 41-43 (1989) (mistake to conflate the created object which makes a person deserving of reward with what that reward should be, particularly if value of property rights in object produced is disproportionate to effort expended by laborer and alternative forms of reward are possible); Frank Curtis,

Protecting Authors in Copyright Transfers: Revision Bill Sec. 203 and the Alternatives, 72 Colum. L. Rev. 799, 819 (1972); *cf.* Machlup, *supra* note 36, at 29-30, 54, 60-1; Penrose, *supra* note 61, at 26-7, 30-1; John Jewkes, David Sawers & Richard Stillerman, The Sources of Invention 252 (1959).

The utilitarians strongly believed that copyright and patent protection would benefit creators in proportion to their social contributions. Thus, John Stuart Mill, favored "an exclusive privilege, of temporary duration...because it leaves nothing to anyone's discretion; because the reward conferred by it depends upon the invention's being found useful, and the greater the usefulness the greater the reward." John Stuart Mill, Principles of Political Economy, Book V, Ch. X, at 933 (Sir William Ashley ed., 1909). Though his faith in such proportionality was misplaced, Mill's concern with the amount of discretion that may be safely entrusted to government is well-taken, as the principal alternatives to copyright have serious drawbacks. See note 58, *supra*.

224. Mazer v. Stein, 347 U.S. 201, 219 (1954):

The copyright law...is intended to afford...encouragement to the production of literary works of lasting benefit to the world....Sacrificial days devoted to such creative activities deserve rewards commensurate with the services rendered.

225. *See generally* Weinreb, *supra* note 32, at 1241 & n.370 (market favors commercial success over artistic achievement; copyright favors imitative or eccentric over truly novel or profound). It is sometimes stated that the reward due to an author is the social value of his work, a value which might be assessed in terms of what those who benefit from the work would be willing to pay for it rather than do without. However, it is not self-evident that a creator is entitled to participate in every profit which is derived from his creation. *Hearings on S.1006, Copyright Law Revision--CATV, Before the Subcomm. on Patents, Trademarks, and Copyrights of*

the Senate Comm. on the Judiciary, 89th Cong., 2d Sess. 213 (1966). Workers commonly receive compensation which is significantly less than the total value of what they produce.

One of the prime difficulties for analysis of copyright issues, and therefore for formation of copyright policy, lies in our inability to measure the value of the benefits conferred by intellectual and artistic works, for example records, and to compare these with the losses incurred through eliminating record duplication. Under a free market economy, there is no accepted method of assessing the contribution to a society's welfare of any particular record or of all records combined. The recording will vary in value to different listeners including purchasers and all others who might gain access to a particular recording. Recordings also benefit people who sell record and tape equipment or other record-tape supplies to listeners. And radio stations which program recorded music substantially benefit. In fact, no existing theory purports to tell us in absolute terms how much a particular good is worth to any individual or to the buying public in general. Classical economic theory only purports to explain the reaction of and impact upon buyers and sellers to changes in costs and tastes in terms of more or less. It does not attempt to quantify these phenomena. Thus, according to economic theory, for records, and for every other economic good, a given number of consumers will pay a given price rather than do without it; as the price increases, potential consumers decrease and vice-versa; and at any price there are some buyers who are getting the record at less than they would be willing to pay for it rather than do without the product.

The difference between the price which a consumer would be willing to pay rather than go without the product and the price he actually pays is termed by economists the "consumer's surplus". Samuelson & Nordhaus, *supra* note 32, at 91-92. (The existence of a consumer's surplus derives from the fact that market price is determined by the aggregation of demand by many consumers in relation to the cost of production under market conditions where everyone pays the same price. Since some users would pay much more than the going price rather than do without the good, the total value of the product, as measured by the sum of the price each user would pay, can be considerably greater than the total return to the factors of production, including labor.) A supplier who, through market position or legal action, is the only source of supply of a good can increase his profits over those available to sellers in a competitive situation by cutting into this consumer surplus through higher prices and restricted output. But since we have no way of measuring the absolute value of the pleasure conferred by the record to each potential consumer, there is no way of allocating the consumer surplus between the purchaser and the record producer. Nor is it clear that the musical artist's claim to such surplus is stronger than that of other participants in the record's production and sale. That is, it is not evident that the artist's moral claim to be paid more than his inducement price--the minimum price necessary to call forth the desired level of services--is any weightier than the claim of others also responsible for producing and selling his recording--the record company, the record presser, the distributor, or the retail record store. Thus, there is nothing intrinsically immoral in the fact that workers are paid less than the social value of what they produce, as much of the excess of that value over inducement cost is transferred to consumers in the form of lower prices. *See* Becker (1993), *supra* note 148, at 623-26; Breyer, *supra* note 33, at 285-86.

226. *See* Becker (1993), *supra* note 148, at 621-23; Breyer, *supra* note 33, at 286-87.

227. *See, e.g., Senate Hearing, supra* note 107, at 134-35 (statement of Coalition of Creators and Copyright Owners in Support of S. 483); *id.* at 59 (statement of Ellen Donaldson, Vice President, AmSong). Congress offered the growth in life expectancy as a reason for adoption of the life + 50 term in the 1976 Revision Bill. *See* H. R. Rep. No. 1476, 94th Cong., 2d Sess. 134 (1976): "Life expectancy has increased substantially, and more and more authors are seeing their works fall into the public domain during their lifetimes, forcing later works to compete with their own early works in which copyright has expired." Copyright law, however, is designed only to protect an author from competing sales of the same title; it is not

intended to interfere with competition between titles. As Breyer notes, if buyers are at least equally satisfied with X, a public domain work, calling forth the production of Y by restricting the reproduction of X wastes resources, at least where the restriction is greater than needed to induce X's initial production. Breyer, *supra* note 33, at 327 n.180. On the alleged "problem" of author's outliving their copyrights, see text at notes 228-29 251-52 *infra*.

228. *See* Blumenthal, *supra* note 107.

229. Accordingly, if authors today are living twenty years more than they did at some past reference point, the net effect of the enactment to raise the number of years of protection after death by twenty will be to extend copyright by forty years beyond what prevailed at the time of the historical reference point. N. Dawson, *Copyright in the European Union--Plundering the Public Domain*, 45 Northern Ireland L.Q. 193, 204 (1994). *See* Cornish, *supra* note 19, at 490; 1 Hugh Laddie et al., The Modern Law of Copyright and Designs 513 & n.4 (2d ed. 1995) (logically, increased life span dictates shortening of the protection period because author lives longer to enjoy the benefit of his copyright); William Patry, *The Failure of the American Copyright System: Protecting the Idle Rich*, 72 Notre Dame L. Rev. 907, 931-32 (1997) (lifespan argument is internally contradictory; increasing term by twenty years leads to protection for four and perhaps five generations, not two).

Recognition that increased longevity is automatically reflected in a life plus regime suggests that longer life expectancy supports keeping the present term or perhaps even reducing it.

230. Guinan, *supra* note 15, at 28.

231. *See* Comments of the National Music Publishers' Association, Inc., *supra* note 114, at 4-5. This reaction is not surprising. Making the duration of protection turn on the author's longevity will produce a result which appears "arbitrary", as we do not

know when the author will die and the time of his death is not connected to any principle.

232. *See* Royal Commission on Patents, Copyright, Trade Marks and Industrial Designs (Canada), Report on Copyright 20-21 (1957) (term which runs for definite number of years from publication is "fairer than one which is based upon the death of the author in that it makes for greater equality in the treatment of authors").

Early in the copyright revision process, the Register of Copyrights compared the advantages of a term measured from the death of the author and one measured from the time of dissemination and concluded that the latter was preferable. *See* Report of the Register, *supra* note 29, at 47-49. Of course, if the life plus scheme itself is of questionable desirability, one might be reluctant to extend it.

In the past, a number of European countries have extended their terms to compensate for the disruption caused by war to right-owners. Thus, after the two world wars, France, Italy, and Belgium provided extensions to their copyright terms to make up for the loss of exploitation opportunities that resulted from wartime conditions. *See* Belgian Sole Article of the Law of June 25, 1921, M.B., Aug. 20, 1921; French Law of Feb. 3, 1919, J.O., Feb. 5, 1919; French Law No. 51-1119 of Sept. 21, 1951, J.O., Sept. 25, 1951; Italian Decree-Law No. 440 of July 20, 1945, Gazz. Uff., Aug. 16, 1945, No. 98; Ricketson, *supra* note 26, at 334-36; Dietz, *supra* note 91, at 165-68. For an in-depth explanation of these enactments, see Claude Masouye, *Les Prolongations de Guerre*, 3 Revue Internationale Du Droit D'Auteur (RIDA) 49 (1953) (Part I), 4 RIDA 80 (1954) (Part II), 9 RIDA 82 (1956) (Part III), 14 RIDA 109 (1957) (Part IV), 20 RIDA 59 (1958) (Part V) (1953-58). As a matter of policy, these steps are of questionable utility. Unless the term extension is confined to those works which have suffered an objective loss due to war, the extended period will apply to a great many works that would not have been exploited during this time in any event. In addition, why single out war as a disruptive factor? Ricketson, *supra* note 222, at 770-71. In any case, this kind of compensatory impulse does not justify a general extension of the term of protection, and no comparable disruption has recently affected the United States. *See* Cornish, *supra* note 19, at 490 (difficult to see bearing of such temporary measures resulting from particular disasters on question which must be settled on long-term basis).

233. *See, e.g., Senate Hearing, supra* note 107, at 55, 65.

A rise in life expectancy, however, does not necessarily indicate that the second generation of descendants loses something in comparison with earlier times. The critical figure is the number of years grandchildren survive after the grandparent-author's death. While those grandchildren are living longer, so are the grandparents. Thus, we should expect the current group of authors' grandchildren to remain alive for approximately the same length of time after their grandparents' deaths as at other times in the twentieth century. *See* Parrinder, *supra* note 123, at 393.

234. Imagine a worker who declares, "Pay me five times more than the going rate since I want to provide for my family." A person's desire to take care of his family is irrelevant to the shaping of the economic structure. From an incentive perspective, what motivates a person to be productive is of no concern, and there is nothing "unfair" about the resulting wage the worker receives. Policy makers in this area need to be careful not to conflate the distinct questions of how much a person earns or should earn and what he does with the money once he has earned it.

235. *See* Breyer, *supra* note 33, at 328. As a matter of analysis, to the extent that the focus is on incentives and identifiable ends, one can talk about whether a present or proposed scheme is well designed or not to accomplish these ends. To the extent the focus is on the impact on production, one has accepted standards for criticism of proposed measures. However, once noneconomic and moral concerns are offered separately or mixed in, such as the claims based on references to longevity and the care of grandchildren, it is difficult to fashion reasoned responses to such claims.

236. Of course, these family considerations have no relevance to works of corporate authorship, which represent a substantial percentage of registered writings. *See* text at note 241 and note 241 *infra.*

237. Holroyd and Jobson, *supra* note 177. And these recipients are frequently eccentrically situated. Of course, as the term of protection is lengthened, there will often be more years of protection after the author's death than during his life.

238. Indeed, if support of two generations of descendants were really the objective, Congress should be thinking about prohibitions on copyright transfers or stronger termination rights rather than a longer period of protection.

239. *House Hearings, supra* note 20, at 312-14 (testimony of Professor William Patry); Patry, *supra* note 107, at 149-52. *But see* J.H. Reichman, *The Duration of Copyright and the Limits of Cultural Policy,* 14 Cardozo Arts & Ent. L. J. 625, 649-50 & n.144 (1996). The Term Extension Act provides for the retroactive application of the extension to existing copyrights. (For analysis of this retroactive feature, see Chapter VII. *infra.*) Imagine a person who purchased a copyright on the assumption that what he was buying would last for the life of the author plus fifty years (or for seventy-five years from publication). The retroactive application of the increase will provide him with twenty more years of protection, and of course these are twenty years that he never expected and did not pay for; thus it would not be inaccurate to classify the addition as a windfall to him. Yet nothing in the Act attempts to assure "recapture" of these twenty years for the benefit of the author or his heirs. *See* Jeffrey L. Graubart, *Music Industry's Rights Battles Not Over,* Billboard, Nov. 4, 1995, at 8 (without assertion of their own determination to have right to reclaim all or portion of the proposed additional 20 years via termination provision, songwriters and their heirs have had their rights compromised); David Grossberg, *Extending Copyright Term Isn't Enough,* Billboard, Oct. 12, 1996, at 10. In his congressional testimony

Professor Patry suggested that this windfall could and should be prevented by vesting the proposed additional twenty years automatically in the author or his heirs. The objective would be to insure that any prolongation of the term of protection would actually accrue to the descendants of authors rather than to the individuals or firms to whom their predecessors assigned their rights. *See* William F. Patry, *The Copyright Term Extension Act of 1995: Or How Publishers Managed To Steal the Bread from Authors*, 14 Cardozo Arts & Ent. L.J. 661-68, 691 (1996). *But see generally*, Schrader, *supra* note 188, at 9-10. The enacted legislation manifests some modest sympathy for authors and heirs in this context by subjecting some copyrighted works still in their renewal terms to a termination right with respect to the additional term of twenty years even though the existing termination right has not been exercised and has expired. *See* Copyright Term Extension Act, *supra* note 3, at sec. 102(d)(1)(D); S. Rep. No. 315, 104th Cong., 2d Sess. 5-6, 17-18 (1996).

This issue was consciously faced in the process of enactment of British legislation implementing the European Union directive. In deciding that the twenty year extension would inure not to the author's estate but to the benefit of the person holding the copyright interest at the end of the present term, the Government there emphasized the value of "simplicity" and "the greatest legal certainty" as more weighty than any equitable claim of authors and their heirs to share in any windfall. *See Debates in British House of Commons on Extension of Copyright Term*, 43 J. Copyright Soc'y of USA 198, 200, 206, 218 (1995).

240. That is, we would be returned to the economic question of what incentive structure is necessary to generate a socially desirable output (and mix) of intellectual and artistic works. Ricketson, *supra* note 222, at 784:

> The commercial and practical reality now is that most copyrights are transferred by authors to intermediaries--publishers, producers, promoters and the like--who then undertake the marketing and dissemination of the work.

In these circumstances, the interests of the author in relation to termbecome of secondary importance, and the real issue is what length of protection is necessary to ensure the continuance of investment by these intermediaries.

241. A Copyright Office survey of registrations during the first six months of 1955 revealed that approximately 40 percent of registrations were for works made for hire. Corporations or other group organizations were the "authors" of 92 percent of motion pictures and 94 percent of periodicals registered. In view of the relative commercial importance of periodicals and movies, it is likely that these works of corporate authorship represented more than 50 percent of the commercial value of all registered works during the covered period. *See* Borge Varmer, *Study No. 13: Works Made for Hire and on Commission*, April 1958, *in* 1 Studies on Copyright 717, 731, 733 (Copyright Society of the U.S.A. ed. 1963); Guinan, *supra* note 15, at Appendix A. The 1961 Report of the Register of Copyrights also stated that about 40 percent of all works registered in the Copyright Office are "corporate works"-- works prepared for corporations or other organized bodies by their employees. *See* Report of the Register of Copyrights, *supra* note 29, at 48. While, unfortunately, the Copyright Office does not keep more recent statistics on the number of work for hire registrations, there is no reason to doubt that, in terms of both numbers and commercial value, works of corporate authorship still constitute a substantial percentage of copyrighted writings. Mark A. Lemley, *Romantic Authorship and the Rhetoric of Property*, 75 Texas L. Rev. 873, 883 (1997) (book review) (with growth of software industry, percentage has likely increased since 1955). *See generally* Reichman, *supra* note 239, at 645-48, 653 (existing domestic term of protection for works for hire already appears overly long and empirically unjustified when viewed either as product of incentive rationale or, more generously, through the lens of cultural policy.)

242. *See generally* Hettinger, *supra* note 201, at 45-46 (most copyrights are owned by institutions; that fact undercuts argument for protection rooted in promotion of

individual security, independence and autonomy). Not only does the argument that extended protection is necessary to benefit the author's surviving family and heirs make no sense for corporate copyright ownership, the harmonization argument for uniformity fails here as well since the American term under the 1976 Act of seventy-five years from publication for works for hire already exceeded that of most European countries. To move to ninety-five years of protection for works for hire, as the Term Extension Act does, will just increase the divergence between American and European Union standards. *See House Hearings, supra* note 20, at 355-56, 372 (statement of Professor J.H. Reichman; Epping, *supra* note 99, at 195-97; text at notes 185-87 *supra* and note 276 *infra.*

In a May 1966 executive session of the Senate Judiciary Committee Senator Hank Brown offered an amendment to the Copyright Term Extension Act which would deny any extension of copyright term to corporate copyright owners. The amendment was defeated by a 12-4 vote. S. Rep. No. 315, 104th Cong., 2d Sess. 5, 19 (1996).

243. Between 1980 an
d 1994 life expectancy rose by two years. National Center for Health Statistics, Monthly Vital Statistics Report, Vol. 43, No. 13, October 23, 1995, at 17 (Table 7). The average American in 1996 could expect to live 76.1 years, up from 75.8 in 1995. Sheryl Gay Stolberg, *U.S. Life Expectancy Hits New High*, N.Y. Times, Sept. 12, 1997, at A14. Of course, the duration of protection enacted in 1976 significantly increased the term as compared with the prior law. *See* text at notes 17-18 and note 18 *supra.*

244. *Cf.* Chafee, *supra* note 61, at 509 ("only equitable that the publisher should obtain a return on his investment"). *See generally* Margaret J. Radin, Contested Commodities 79-101 (1996) ("Human Flourishing and Market Rhetoric"). This argument is to be distinguished from what we have called incentive arguments--that in order to induce the desired level of intellectual creation and dissemination,

conditions must be established which will permit producers of intellectual and artistic products to profit from their activities.

245. *See generally* text at note 148 & note 148 *supra.*

Chapter VI. Extension Limited To European
Union Works: Wealth Transfer

Extension of the United States copyright term has been justified as an opportunity for United States producers of intellectual and artistic products to achieve significant financial benefits at little or no cost to American consumers. This kind of justification differs sharply from those normally made for copyright extensions by American producers in that it is not primarily based on the need for additional incentives to potential producers or some sort of fairness argument. The factual basis of the argument is that the European Union, in response to internal political pressures, has decided to impose a uniform copyright term equal to the longest term then in force in any member of the Union--life plus seventy years. Moreover, the lengthened term will be available to foreign producers as well if the country of which these producers are nationals gives reciprocal treatment to EU produced products. More specifically, if the United States were willing to extend the copyright term for EU producers to life plus seventy years, American producers of intellectual property exported to EU countries would enjoy the same length of protection.[246] Since the United States exports far more intellectual property to Europe than Americans import European intellectual property, the result of such an arrangement would be large gains for American producers with minimum impact on American consumers. (The only "losers" would be American consumers or users of European produced products.)

A key point in determining the appropriate response to this situation is that in order for United States producers to be eligible for the European level of protection it needed only amend its copyright law to extend the period of protection to life plus seventy for works produced by Europeans--the copyright period for domestically produced intellectual products sold within the United States need not have been changed. Such an arrangement--under which non-European works, including those of American authors, would still enter the public domain fifty years after the death of the author--appears to be constitutional and would indeed have resulted in American producers gaining at minimum cost to American consumers or the public domain.

But this potential gain did not seem to satisfy American producers of intellectual property. Consistent with their practice of using their political power to aggrandize their financial interests, they sought to use the EU changes as cover to justify legislation which will yield them even greater benefits than would have resulted from extending the copyright period for European produced works. Thus they sought and obtained extension of the copyright period for all intellectual and artistic works. Rather than adding twenty years to the copyright period only for intellectual property created by EU producers they secured legislation which will "simply" extend the copyright period for all intellectual property producers, both European and American. Furthermore, they made the extension retroactive so that all existing copyrights will be extended by twenty years.[247] Presumptively, the proponents of these amendments would have us believe that this change also will benefit American producers with little harm to American consumers. In addition, they have offered some rather weak harmonization and balance of payments based arguments to support the change.

The claim that the legislation will not harm American consumers and users is patently false. American consumers and users will be substantially injured by a general lengthening of the copyright period for the same reason every such lengthening injures consumers; the period copyrighted works will remain subject to control of copyright holders rather than become part of the public domain will be extended for twenty years without any compensating benefits.[248] All the benefits of the extension will go to producers in the form of increased revenues. Of course, producers benefit and consumers suffer any time copyright control is extended, but, at least some effort is made to justify these costs by an alleged necessity of providing additional incentives to producers or correcting some unfairness in the existing schema. In this case no convincing arguments of that sort have been made and making the changes retroactive adds insult to injury.

If it were the case that producers only could benefit from the EU copyright law changes by lengthening the copyright period for American as well as European works, one would have to grapple with some very difficult fairness problems. It is not at all uncommon that government action benefits one group but the costs are shared among all citizens. Indeed, most government action would be precluded if all public actions had to benefit everyone equally. Therefore the fact that only producers will benefit from an extension does not necessarily render such action improper. But, in this case American producers can obtain all the benefits of the EU actions without imposing any substantial costs on American consumers by limiting the extension to EU produced works; and therefore the attempt to use the opportunity for relatively costless gain created by the EU action as an opportunity to enact legislation that lengthens the copyright period for all American produced intellectual property and, in addition, to make it retroactive is a particularly brazen attempt by producers to use their very considerable political clout to further their interests at the expense of the general public. This exhibition of naked greed should induce opposition from those who take seriously the policy and constitutional limits on copyright protection.[249]

The excessive political power of the music and film industry is a given. This power is similar to the advantages enjoyed by well-organized groups with sharply focussed political agenda, and there is no easy cure for it. Conceivably, there are ways of compensating consumers for some of their losses stemming from political weakness. Thus, the deleterious impact of excessive copyright length could be partially remedied by positive action by the Government to insure that important ideas are disseminated. Subsidies of important users, such as libraries, universities, and museums, are examples of such action. The desirability of these steps is underscored by the realization that the dissemination of some portion of the creative work being subsidized is critical to the optimum operation of our democracy.

Notes

---

246. There may be a technical objection, rooted in the wording of the EU Directive, art. 7(1), to such a limitation of extension to EU works, though it is highly doubtful that this reason played any role in congressional deliberations and decision-making. *See* Patry, *supra* note 229, at 925-26 & n.84.

247. As we demonstrate, neither incentive nor equity considerations warrant retroactive application of a term change. *See* text at notes 250-65 *infra*.

248. While public benefits are absent, the substantial costs, as we have seen, include both the wealth transfer payments to copyright holders during the extension period from those who otherwise would have unrestrained use of the works and the writings that are not created because of the reduced public domain. The public forgoes lower prices and a larger supply of new works.

249. Senator Christopher Dodd has proposed legislation--the "Arts Endowing the Arts Act of 1994"--which would establish a procedure whereby American producers could "purchase" a twenty year copyright extension for copyrighted works with the proceeds to be used for promoting the arts and humanities. This arrangement, however, would not permit American producers to take advantage of the EU extension because neither American nor EU producers would be granted a life plus seventy period of protection. Pursuant to the Dodd bill, at the time copyright protection would expire under existing law, the right to extend the copyright for an additional twenty years would be sold via public auction with the proceeds going to a federal trust fund to benefit the National Endowment for the Arts and the National Endowment for the Humanities. *See* S. 2423, 103d Cong., 2d Sess. (1994). (It is not clear whether European producers would be eligible for this scheme. But even if they were deemed eligible, it is very unlikely that the EU would consider this reciprocal treatment to warrant giving American producers the benefits of the EU extension.)

Given our strong opposition to any extension of the copyright term, our instinct would be to oppose this plan. However, under this arrangement the benefits would go to organizations which are likely to be supported by those likely to be injured by an extended copyright period. In fact, it is almost impossible to evaluate the merits of this proposal because its effect would depend upon who bids for these extensions, how high the price will be, and what will be done with the proceeds. *See generally* Justin Watts, *New Labour, Privatisation and Nurturing Talent*, 8 Ent. L. Rev. 279 (1997).

Chapter VII. Extension of Existing
Terms--Retroactivity

The drive for an increased term also received support from existing copyright proprietors whose protection would expire in the near future and who sought the application to their existing works of any enacted increase.[250] For example, the children of famed composers Irving Berlin and Richard Rodgers, who benefit from copyright, lobbied for the change so that they could continue to receive this benefit for a longer period. The arguments they offer for a continued wealth transfer from the American public to themselves, though, are ill-defined and insubstantial, with support neither in economics nor equity.

One notion to which this group appeals is a distaste for the phenomenon of an author outliving the copyright on his work. The disapproval seems to be as much of an aesthetic as an economic character; that is, it is somehow unseemly for the copyright to expire before the author.[251] But it is not clear why this scenario should offend us any more than an inventor outliving his seventeen or twenty year patent. (Also, the author, of course, will not necessarily be the owner of the copyright in the years approaching death.) However, even if the scenario is widely considered offensive, the phenomenon is ruled out by a copyright term which is defined by the life of the author plus some number of additional years. By definition, under a life + X years measure, the term will never expire before the death of the author. Thus, the concern to which the Berlin and Rodgers heirs (and others) advert is largely a red herring and can not arise with respect to any works created after January 1, 1978.[252]

More generally, there is no justification for applying any enacted increase in the term of protection to then-existing copyrights. One can hardly argue that an artist's creativity or a publisher's investment is encouraged by such an extension, since the work for which the term is extended has already been produced; obviously, additional incentive to produce and disseminate, in the way one usually conceives of incentives, is irrelevant. However, retroactivity might have some (very) small positive incentive effect upon the future production of intellectual and artistic works. Unless there is reason to believe that retroactivity was the result of special circumstances and any future extensions will not be retroactive, potential producers of intellectual and artistic products should assign some weight to the possibility that future extensions also will be retroactive. Obviously, the weight assigned will vary with each individual possible producer. More importantly, the incentive involved stems from the further possible extension of what would be an already very long protection period. Accordingly, the incentive impact will be minimal at best.[253]

However, even recognizing the possibility of some small additional incentive effect cannot justify making the extension retroactive. While the positive incentive effect is minuscule at best, the retroactive application imposes an immediate increase in the cost of expression.[254] By far the most significant and unambiguous impact of retroactivity will be to increase producers' revenues at the expense of consumers and the public domain. Indeed, since retroactivity will apply only to existing works and the incentive with respect to future works is so uncertain, the imbalance between possible desirable incentive effect and wealth transfer between producers and consumers is particularly unfavorable.

As for equity, where is there any inequity with respect to existing copyrights? The holders of these interests will receive exactly what they assumed they would when they purchased (or inherited) these copyrights. Indeed, lack of sympathy, on equitable grounds, for their lobbying efforts derives, in part, from the fact that they are looking to gain more than they had any reason to expect.[255] Retroactive application of a term increase, thenill simply give a varied set of descendants, estates, publishers, assignees, and perhaps a few aged authors a windfall gain at the expense of consumers.[256]

It is worthy of note that the potential windfall to current owners of copyrighted works has been argued to add weight to the case for retroactivity. The "reasoning" here is that any increase in the earnings of copyright holders contributes to the creation of valuable knowledge and artistic work because copyright holders are likely to use these additional monies to increase the production of desirable intellectual and artistic products.[257] This is a pathetic argument and provides further evidence of the extent of misunderstanding of the negative aspects of copyright. The biggest hole in the argument is ignoring the fact that the source of the additional revenues that retroactivity will produce for current holders of copyrights will be consumers and the public domain. In other words, the effect of retroactivity is to prolong the period in which copyright owners possess legal monopolies, with all that entails. Secondly, it cannot be presumed that the additional revenues generated by retroactivity will be spent to produce additional intellectual and artistic works valued by the public. Perhaps some would be spent that way, but it is also possible that most of it will be spent on wine, women, song, and increased salaries for top officials. The reaction of each recipient will differ in accordance with a myriad of factors pertinent to its situation, and no prediction regarding the impact of additional revenues to copyright holders can be made.[258]

Proponents of retroactive application may look for support by analogy to Section 304 of the 1976 Revision Act which added nineteen years to the term of subsisting copyrights[259] and to the prior series of congressional enactments which provided for interim extensions of the renewal terms of copyrights about to expire pending the passage by Congress of the general revision bill.[260] However, in view of the incentive and equity considerations previously canvassed, neither of these congressional actions is defensible. In fact, Professor Nimmer, the leading commentator on copyright, questioned the constitutionality of both these actions.[261] And Congressman Kastenmeier, the long-time, thoughtful chairman of the House subcommittee which dealt with copyright matters, captured well the lack of merit in the interim extension bills in his dissent from the passage of one: "[T]here is no discernible equity underlying their claim for an extension. The legislation makes what amounts to a retrospective reward for authorship at the expense of the public domain, in a situation in which the constitutional prescription '... to promote the progress of useful Arts...' cannot directly be served."[262] He noted further and tellingly that the extension would afford a windfall, at the expense of readers, to the assignees of authors who had bargained and paid for their interests on the assumption of the existing, shorter term.[263] All of Kastenmeier's (and Nimmer's) criticisms apply to the legislation to increase the term of existing copyrights. Accordingly, even if the term of protection is lengthened prospectively, a measure of which we disapprove, that change should most certainly not be given retroactive effect.[264]

Notes

250. As previously noted, *see* text at note 106 and note 106 *supra*, the Term Extension Act does provide for retroactive application of the twenty year increase in the term of protection. As we argue in the text of this chapter of the book, such application is mistaken.

251. *See* Blumenthal, *supra* note 107.

252. Even with respect to works created before 1978 the scenario will be rare since under the 1976 Act those works generally received 75 years of protection from the date of publication; accordingly, a combination of a (very) young author and a (very) long life would have been needed to produce the feared scenario.

253. The prospective producer's calculation would include not only the possibility of a future retroactive extension but also the likelihood that the copyright in his work would still be in existence at the time the extension was enacted. (Neither the Term Extension Act nor the 1976 Copyright Act operate to revive domestic copyrights which had expired at the time of the legislation's effective date.) In addition, any income to be earned more than seventy years after the author's death would have to be discounted to its present value. *See* text at note 99 and note 99 *supra*. Thus, the incentive effect of the possible provision of additional copyright protection for a period so far into the future will be minuscule.

254. Landes & Posner, *supra* note 73, at 362:

> If the increase [in term] applies retroactively, that is, to existing works as well as to works not yet produced, the increased incentive to create will be limited to a subset of the affected works (those not yet produced), while the increase in the cost of expression will apply to borrowing from all works, existing and

not yet produced. This is a strong argument against making increases in copyright term retroactive.

255. Works which were about to enter the public domain under the 1976 Act's scheme were created in 1923. (Works published before 1978 received seventy-five years protection rather than life + 50 for individual authors.) Society's "bargain" with the authors was a period of exclusive rights for a maximum of fifty-six years. Authors and publishers distributed their works then under the assumption that the works would enter the public domain fifty-six years later. Notwithstanding that bargain, the period was extended by nineteen years in 1976 to seventy-five years. Now, these same copyright owners have returned to Congress seeking, and obtaining, another extension in order to maintain royalty revenues from the relatively few works from the 1920s and 1930s that continue to have significant economic value today. Continued payment of these royalties constitutes a wealth transfer from the American public to current owners of these copyrights. No equitable consideration supports the continuation of this wealth transfer for another twenty years.

Moreover and unfortunately, to maintain royalty revenues on those few works from this period that have contemporary economic viability it was necessary to extend the copyrights on *all* works. Thus, letters, manuscripts, forgotten movies, out-of-print books, and other potential sources on which current scholars and authors can base new works will have been removed from the public domain for an extra twenty years in order to insure continued protection for Irving Berlin songs. Robert A. Gorman, *Intellectual Property: The Rights of Faculty as Creators and Users*, Academe, May-June 1998, at 14, 18. As a result, the historian, for example, who wishes to make use of any work from this period will have to conduct complex negotiations to do so. *See* text at notes 90-91 and notes 90-91 *supra*. Faced with the complications of tracking down and gaining consent from all those who may have a partial interest in the copyright, the historian may well elect to pick a topic that poses fewer hurdles and annoyances.

256. The conflict presented is between the heirs and assignees of copyrights in old works and the interests of today's public in lower prices and a larger supply of new works. As previously noted, the creation of new works depends on a vibrant, rich public domain. The term increase enactment will diminish rather than enrich the public domain. With no good reason to expect a material compensating public benefit, we should not tie the hands of current authors and risk making them less competitive in domestic and foreign markets simply to supply a windfall to owners of copyrights in works produced long ago.

257. *See, e.g.,* S. Rep. No. 315, 104th Cong, 1st Sess. 12 (1996) ("extended protection for existing works will provide added income with which to subsidize the creation of new works").

258. Professor Jaszi has argued insightfully that support for retroactive measures is grounded in an alternative vision of the goals of copyright which is gaining credence among congressional supporters of term extension. That vision sees copyright as designed to improve the competitive position of companies that have significant investments in inventories of copyrighted works. The focus is on promoting the well-being of the copyright industries rather than on providing incentives to specific acts of creativity or distribution. This vision, which assumes that whatever makes information and entertainment businesses more financially secure contributes to the progress of knowledge, is misguided and should be resisted. *See* Jaszi, *supra* note 107.

As noted in the text, to the extent that this alternative vision is rooted in an assumption that extended protection for existing works will provide added income with which to subsidize the creation of new works, its implicit economic predictions about how producers will use these "extra" revenues are off base. In the case of sound recordings, for example, record companies will not necessarily use supernormal profits to fund more recordings. They might distribute that money to shareholders or use it to increase the perquisites enjoyed by management. If they

188

decided to invest the funds, whether within or without their industry, they will look to maximize the return consistent with the level of risk they are willing to run. And that investment-risk analysis will not be influenced by the value of other financial assets held by the investor.

If it were deemed socially desirable to lend financial support to the entertainment and related industries, that subsidy could be accomplished more directly, openly, and efficiently through means other than retroactive extension of the copyright term.

259. 17 U.S.C. sec. 304(a),(b) (1994). The bill increased the then-present 56 year term to 75 years in the case of copyrights subsisting in both their first and their renewal terms.

260. Pub. L. No. 87-668, 89-142, 90-416, 91-147, 91-555, 92-170, 92-566, 93-573. In anticipation of passage of the comprehensive revision bill, Congress, in these resolutions, acted to keep alive copyrights which were about to expire in order for these interests to gain the benefits of the revision bill when it was, in fact, enacted. Brown & Denicola, *supra* note 151, at 481-82. As we have indicated, this congressional action was unwarranted.

261. Nimmer suggests that the extension of existing copyrights is not only beyond Congress's copyright power but also is in conflict with the First Amendment. Nimmer, *supra* note 191, at 1194-96. The criticism is repeated in Melville B. Nimmer & David Nimmer, Nimmer on Copyright sec. 1.10[C][1] (1995). *See also* Lavigne, *supra* note 192, at 352-54.

262. H.R. Rep. No. 605, 92d Cong., 1st Sess. 4 (1971).

263. *Id.*:

Although I have supported interim extension legislation on a number of occasions I have reached the conclusion that this may have been a mistake.

In any event, I now believe that Senate Joint Resolution 132 affords a windfall to the holders of copyrights in their renewal term, where such term would otherwise expire this year. I find it impossible to identify any public interest that would be served by the enactment of this measure.

264. An exceptional instance of copyright extension was enacted in 1971 when a new copyright extending protection for an additional period of seventy-five years was granted in all editions of Mary Baker Eddy's *Science and Health with Key to the Scriptures*, the central theological text of the Christian Science faith. Priv. L. No. 92-60, 85 Stat. 857 (1971). Senator Hart questioned the bill on First Amendment grounds of free speech ("limits what may be freely said and heard in public") and objected to the term extension as an infringement on "the rights of scholars, lay people, and members of the Christian Science and other religions to engage in textual and historical criticisms of the work in question." 117 Cong. Rec. 26,822 (1971) The Act was challenged as violative of both the copyright clause and the religion clauses of the First Amendment, and it was held unconstitutional as an establishment of religion in United Christian Scientists v. Christian Science Board of Directors, First Church of Christ, Scientist, 829 F.2d 1152 (D.C. Cir. 1987). Interestingly, the Christian Science Church generally gives access to its archives, which contain most of Eddy's unpublished correspondence and other writings, only to those who can assure it that they have a sympathetic approach to Eddy and Christian Science. Fraser, *supra* note 159.

Chapter VIII. "Harmonization"--The Case for Uniformity *Per Se*

It is also argued that extending the length of copyright protection will benefit the United States by equalizing its protection period with Europe's.[265] That is, independent of what the particular length of term is, harmonization will be beneficial. But since lengthening the copyright period will impose substantial costs on domestic (and foreign) consumers, harmonization must be proved to bestow substantial benefits to justify that cost. It turns out, however, that these benefits are quite small and that this small added convenience for those engaged in international copyright transactions does not alter our conclusion that an increase in the term is undesirable. The benefits are small because international harmonization of the length of copyright protection does not provide the gains to non-EU countries that internal harmonization affords to the European community. This differentiation in gains is the case because the EU has critical objectives which are irrelevant to United States international trade policy. The slightness of benefits also reflects the distinctive economic characteristics of copyrighted intellectual and artistic works as compared with patents and more conventional economic goods. And, finally, the limited nature of the benefits of harmonization stems from the fact that individual countries cannot gain advantages for domestic producers of copyrightable products via manipulation of their copyright protection period in the same way that countries might favor domestic producers via tariffs or export subsidies.[266]

The harmonization directive of the European Union is a poor model for United States action. The EU required a single copyright length in order to respect the core treaty commitment to the creation of a single, internal economic market.[267] This commitment to a single trading unit reflects the existence of a strong political connection among the member countries. Though the European arrangement does not fit within an established organizational category, the relationship among EU countries is better described as a commonwealth[268] than a customs union.[269] But the relationship between the United States and Europe is one between distinct political entities.[270] Though the two obviously interact with each other, and we favor a strong cooperative relationship with Europe, American political ties with the countries of Europe do not exhibit the characteristics of a commonwealth. Moreover, in contrast to those states, in our dealings with the EU we are not critically motivated by a desire to achieve economic interdependence in order to avoid armed conflict.

Moreover, considerations of political and economic cohesion among the states of the United States (and within the membership of the European Union) are not relevant to the United States-Europe relationship. We have in mind here, for example, the concerns and values expressed in dormant commerce clause jurisprudence in American constitutional law. That body of law reflects concern with the kind of parochialism that permits one state to take advantage of another by such devices as exclusionary discriminatory taxation of or "tariffs" on non-local businesses. Such measures affect economic efficiency by inducing production at other than the cheapest site.[271] These protectionist measures also cause political friction and undermine national solidarity. Faced with these kind of practices, the citizens of different states perceive each other as predators employing "unfair" tactics.[272]

Copyright policy decisions, however, can not be used destructively, and therefore differing copyright terms should not, and probably do not, generate the controversy and the harmful economic and political effects which accompany differential subsidy, tariff, and tax schemes. Unlike export subsidies which, if unmatched by other countries, can result in export gains at the expense of other countries' exports or domestic producers, manipulation of the copyright term can not be used to gain "unfair" advantage. So long as domestic and foreign producers receive the same level of protection, establishing a copyright term which differs from those of other countries can not be an instrument for achieving advantages for domestic producers over foreign ones; only the balance of benefits and detriments between producers and consumers is relevant.[273] Moreover, if countries adopt different protection terms, it is highly unlikely that this difference would result in any substantial shift of capital investment and labor opportunities. In other words, continuation of the twenty-year difference in the level of American and EU copyright protection would not distort the trade or investment decisions of American or European music producers. Finally, the term chosen would not discriminate against foreign authors in that both American and foreign authors would be protected in the United States for the same period of time.[274]

While the word "harmony" always carries a positive charge, considered evaluation of any significant economic decision, particularly decisions certain to raise the price of a product, require us to avoid being seduced by terms instinctively conveying positive values.[275] In this case the only clear positive impact of a uniform copyright period is trivial: since all lengths will be identical, no one need determine the length with respect to a particular country.[276]

Although the benefits of harmonization have been assumed, there has, in fact, been no clear statement of the advantages of uniformity *per se*. The upshot is that uniformity, *i.e.*, the fact of difference, is insignificant.[277] It is insignificant with respect to international political cooperation, with respect to economic efficiency, with respect to the intentional infliction of harm on one country by another, and with respect to costs imposed on copyright transactions. Accordingly, it should carry no weight in the argument about an increase in protection,[278] and the question remains as to whether a term extension is justified on its own merits.

Notes

---

265. *See, e.g., Senate Hearing, supra* note 107, at 27-28, 132-34.

266. Because of these distinctive characteristics copyright term measures do not implicate our traditional concern about economic localism measures which increase the price of imported goods compared to domestic goods and thereby produce an inefficient distortion of comparative geographical advantage.

267. *See, e.g.,* Treaty Establishing the European Economic Community, March 25, 1957, arts. 3a, 8a, 12-13, 48, as amended by Single European Act, reprinted in Office for Official Publications of the European Communities, I Treaties Establishing the European Communities 207, 223, 227, 234-35, 265 (1987); D. Lasok & K.P.E. Lasok, Law and Institutions of the European Union 379-410 (6th ed. 1994). As noted previously, note 19 *supra*, the term directive is one of a larger set of enactments designed to harmonize copyright law within the European Union.

268. The extent of economic and political interdependence existing and aspired to and the recognition of the authority of supranational institutions such as the Court of European Justice by members of the European Union bespeaks an arrangement that has moved well beyond the simple abolition of customs duties between Member States. *See, e.g.,* Treaty on European Union (The Treaty of Maastricht), 1993 O.J. (C224) 1, Feb. 7, 1992, art. 8 (common citizenship); art. F (respect for fundamental rights as recognized in European Convention for the Protection of Human Rights and Fundamental Freedoms); Protocol on Social Policy (annexed to treaty of Maastricht; this protocol incorporates the 1989 Social Charter which mandates a minimum wage and allows Union intervention in domestic social policy; although the protocol is not binding most Member States have chosen to adhere to it, though Great Britain has conspicuously opted out); Treaty Establishing European Economic Community, *supra* note 267, arts. 164, 177-82, as amended by Treaty of Maastricht (role and

jurisdiction of Court of Justice); Nathaniel C. Nash, *Europeans Agree on New Currency*, N.Y. Times, Dec. 16, 1995, at 1 (European Monetary System, Central Bank, and attempt to move to single currency); Edmund L. Andrews, *Mark-Devoted Germans Gradually Come to Terms with the Euro*, Int'l Herald Tribune, June 22, 1998, at 13 (Euro, single European currency, to be introduced Jan. 1, 1999; three year transition period).

269. The European objective of a single internal market represents a stronger commitment to economic integration than a free-trade area and a customs union because, in addition to the unimpeded movement of goods and common customs tariffs for goods imported into the union, it implies the free movement of all the elements required for economic production, people, services, and capital. Pursuant to the Single European Act, Feb. 17, 1986, art. 13, 1987 O.J. (L. 169), reprinted in Office for Official Publications of the European Communities, I Treaties Establishing the European Communities 1005, 1026 (1987) (adding Art. 8a to the EEC Treaty), virtually all trade tariffs and border controls were eliminated as of January 1, 1993. A prime result is that Europeans may now live and work where they please, regardless of nationality.

270. Consistent with this proposition, it is noteworthy that the rule-making bodies of the European Union and its Member States are not limited in power by the copyright clause of the United States Constitution nor is free speech as high in the hierarchy of values in these polities as in the United States.

271. *See, e.g.*, Fort Gratiot Sanitary Landfill, Inc. v. Michigan Department of Natural Resources, 504 U.S. 353 (1992) (protectionist Michigan Waste Import Restrictions invalidated; commerce clause condemns economic protectionism which illegitimately isolates state from the national economy; clause prohibits states from advancing own parochial commercial interests by curtailing movement of articles of commerce into or out of state); American Trucking Assns., Inc. v. Scheiner, 483 U.S. 266, 280-82

(1987) (commerce clause by own force creates area of trade free from state interference; clause prohibits state from imposing heavier tax on out-of-state businesses than it imposes on own residents); H.P. Hood & Sons v. Du Mond, 336 U.S. 525, 539 (1949).

272. Such a perception is inconsistent with viewing problems as joint ones. *See, e.g.*, Baldwin v. G.A.F. Selig, Inc., 294 U.S. 511, 523 (1935) (Constitution framed "upon the theory that the peoples of the several states must sink or swim together and that in the long run prosperity and salvation are in union and not division.") *See generally* Laurence H. Tribe, American Constitutional Law 416-17 (2d ed. 1988) ("[T]he negative implications of the commerce clause derive principally from a *political* theory of union, not from an *economic* theory of free trade. The function of the clause is to ensure national solidarity, not economic efficiency.")

273. A significant political constraint on damage to foreigners results from the fact that decisionmakers must take account of the interests of both domestic producers and consumers. Therefore, a measure harmful to another country can not be enacted without hurting some domestic group as well.

274. *See* 17 U.S.C. sec. 104(a)-(b) (1994). Curiously, one effect of passage of the Term Extension Act is to grant a term of life plus seventy years to works of foreign authors without requiring the foreign country to grant American authors the same term. Thus, Japanese authors, for example, will enjoy the life plus seventy term in the United States, (as the United States does not apply the rule of the shorter term), while American authors will only receive life plus fifty years in Japan. *See* David Nimmer, *Nation, Duration, Violation, Harmonization: An International Copyright Proposal for the United States*, L. & Contemp. Probs., Spring 1992, at 211, 233-34; Brownlee, *supra* note 27, at 590, 603-04. If a motivating force behind the change is a desire for uniformity in light of the reciprocal provisions of the European Union term directive, it is surprising that the extension legislation is not also reciprocal.

Such reciprocity beyond life plus fifty is consistent with our obligations under Berne. *See* Berne Convention, art. 7(8). *See generally* Reichman, *supra* note 239, at 633-38, 653.

Of course, one straightforward way to achieve uniformity in the treatment of American and European authors with respect to duration of protection would be for the Europeans to provide national treatment (and thereby eliminate invocation of the rule of the shorter term and the differential treatment of domestic and foreign works.)

275. *See* Comment of Copyright Law Professors, *supra* note 98, at 12:

We need not...seek uniformity for its own sake, if it means compromising other important principles. If the United States determines that works should belong to the public domain after life + 50 years, no transaction cost problem is posed to United States authors by the longer period in Europe. The ultimate owners of their copyrights will, of course, be able to exploit them for a shorter period, but that is the result of the policy choice to make the works freely available and not because of the absence of harmonization.

Ironically, in one important area, that of works for hire, the Term Extension Act will yield increased divergence rather than convergence between Europe and the United States. The American term under the 1976 Act of seventy-five years from publication or 100 years from creation, whichever expires first, already exceeded the considerably shorter terms for corporate works in European law. With the United States' move to ninety-five years of protection by adding an additional twenty years, the prior divergence will grow larger and "disharmony" will increase. Moreover, the upshot will be the imposition of domestic burdens without achievement of any foreign gains. As Professor Reichman has observed, the change will compound pre-existing differences and destabilize any de facto harmonization that may already have occurred in the context of United States-EU relations. In addition, he points out that whatever its effects on American-European legal relations, the change will do nothing to promote harmonization between American law and the laws of developing countries, which have little reason to increase copyright terms under their domestic laws. *See House Hearings, supra* note 20, at 356, 372 (statement of J.H. Reichman); *id.* at 281-82, 286 (statement of Professor John Belton on behalf of Society for Cinema Studies); text at notes 185-88 *supra*. With all the talk of "harmony" and "uniformity", these important points about works for hire have received inadequate attention.

Indeed, the more sweeping observation is that the apparent uniformity pursued by the extension legislation is offset by the divergent terms of protection that the United States and the European Union will continue to grant holders of rights in sound recordings, performances, cinematographic and audiovisual works, and computer programs, as well as in the bulk of works made for hire. And, except for music, the pre-existing American copyright terms for works produced by the commercially significant copyright industries already exceeded protection in the European Union and other countries. *See* Epping, *supra* note 99, at 189-201; text at notes 186-89 and notes 186-89 *supra*; Netanel, *supra* note 58, at 367 & n.380. In other words, not only is harmonization overvalued, but it will not be achieved under the Term Extension Act. *See id.*, at 367 & n.379. *See generally* Reichman, *supra* note 239, at 639-42 ("the unattainable goal of uniform law").

276. Epping, *supra* note 99, at 218-19 & n.215. In short, the practical benefits of uniformity, a reduction in the information costs of determining the amount of protection of intellectual property, are meager. With harmony, there is less here than meets the eye; and the extent of uncertainty incident to different terms is greatly overstated. With the United States' move to life + 70, the copyright entrepreneur and lawyer will know that both domestic and foreign works are treated the same in the United States. But they already knew that, with the life + 50 term. What they previously needed to know and would need to know in the future if the United States

had not harmonized its term is that in Europe American works are protected for life + 50 and European writings for life + 70. The work would be in monitoring, but once a chart was created reflecting this information about the rules in each country, that would be the end of "uncertainty". Businesses would not face any significant increase in overhead costs or enlargement of risks. In short, these differences in legal rules do not create substantial transaction costs that hinder otherwise beneficial exchanges.

For approximately thirty years prior to the EU directive the (West) German term of protection was life + 70 while the term in most other Member States was life + 50. The fact that the European countries were able to live so long with separate schemes without evidence of any great advantage to shorter or longer term countries suggests that no significant disruptions or distortions were occurring and therefore argues against the "need" for harmonization.

277. In practice, it is difficult to speak of harmonization without consideration of the specific term being proposed. Thus, for the European Council harmonization for the purpose of creating the internal market could not be divorced from the choice of the direction in which to harmonize. At the time of the Directive's promulgation, the general term of protection was 70 years *pma* in Germany and, for musical compositions only, in France; 60 years *pma* in Spain, and 50 years *pma* in all other Member States. The Council had a choice of harmonizing upwards to life + 70 (by increasing the protection to the highest level of any national regime) or downwards (by decreasing the protection to the lowest level of any national regime) or in between; the longer term of life + 70 was not dictated by the quest for uniformity, though it did constitute the politically most convenient choice. *See* Dietz, *supra* note 91, at 171; Patry, *supra* note 239, at 688-89; Dworkin, *supra* note 188, at 152 (increased life expectancy unconvincing reason for increasing term; only explicable reason is convenience, easier to harmonise up). Of course, had the Directive opted for the shorter term, transitional provisions would have been required to protect those

who had relied on the then-existing longer term (in Germany, Spain, or France) in making financial decisions and negotiating deals. It turns out that even with the decision to adopt life + 70, some such transitional provisions are necessary because the adopted term is to be given retroactive effect with the result that the copyright on public domain works may be revived. *See* Jean-Francois Verstrynge, *The Spring 1993 Horace S. Manges Lecture--The European Commission's Direction on Copyright and Neighboring Rights: Toward the Regime of the Twenty-First Century,* 17 Colum.-VLA J.L. & Arts 187, 194-97 (1993); *Clarification Sought on EU Directive on Copyright Term,* J. Proprietary Rts., Dec. 1995, at 33; Peter Schonning, *The New Copyright Act in Denmark,* 27 Int'l Rev. Indus. Prop. & Copyright L. 470, 473 (1996).

Similarly, even if harmonization is desirable, the question for Congress is who should harmonize with whom. At the time the Copyright Act of 1976 was enacted, life + 50 constituted an international standard and was required in order to join the Berne Convention. Life + 70, however, is not an international standard today nor is it likely to become one without United States support. It was not even the standard in Europe before the Directive that the Member States adopt a uniform term equal to the longest of any of its members. If the cost/benefit analysis required by our copyright tradition does not justify changing the social policy balances we have drawn--and it surely does not--, the United States might better use its influence to urge the rest of the world to remain with the life + 50 standard, rather than adopt a "monkey-see, monkey-do" approach and mimic a European decision that was made apparently without consideration of the factors we have always deemed crucial to copyright policy analysis. Comment of Copyright Law Professors, *supra* note 98, at 12-13.

278. More broadly, there is no guarantee that global harmonization of intellectual property rights would be optimal. Harmonization differs significantly from liberalizing traditional trade barriers such as tariffs and quotas. Economists generally

agree that these trade barriers damage both the country imposing them and its trade partners. Removing them raises global income by improving economic efficiency, and all countries will likely share in the resultant gains from greater trade. However, while reducing global tariff levels would provide welfare gains for all concerned countries, strengthening and harmonizing intellectual property rights would generate costs and benefits that are likely to vary across countries. Maskus, *supra* note 43, at 20-21. *See generally* Judith C. Chin & Gene M. Grossman, Intellectual Property Rights and North-South Trade (1988); *House Hearings, supra* note 20, at 384-87 (statement of Professor J.H. Reichman). Recognition of the existence of these differential effects suggests the need for caution against undiscriminating international harmonization of intellectual property laws.

Chapter IX. The Balance of Payments

Proponents of the extension argue that expected benefits to the balance of payments support their case.[279] Since the United States sells more intellectual property to the EU countries than it imports from them, extending the copyright period should produce a net increase in American exports.[280] This increase will contribute to a positive trade balance, and "improve" the balance of payments.[281] This argument is beset with difficulties, and the combined impact of these difficulties strongly implies that the possible benefits from export expansion do not overcome the clear drawbacks to an extension.

The starting point for analyzing this proposal is that extending the copyright period raises the price of intellectual and artistic products produced by Americans to both domestic and EU buyers and raises the price to American consumers of intellectual products imported into the United States from EU (and other foreign) producers. Without regard to the trade impact, we have concluded that any increased price to American consumers or contraction of the public domain as a result of extending the copyright period is unwarranted. Supporters of the extension point to the positive trade impact of copyright extension, resulting from the fact that after a short period the United States probably will export more intellectual property to EU countries than it will import from them. To determine whether these alleged benefits provide significant support to the pro-extension argument it is necessary to quantify the extra benefits conferred by increased exports on the American economy.[282] Since it is unlikely that increased American exports of intellectual products will enhance employment opportunities, this kind of argument differs from arguments for export promotion in order to produce more employment for American workers by expanding the markets for their products.[283]

To be relevant to the extension issue, exports must have a special value to the American economy. That is, goods sold to foreigners must be deemed to be worth more than goods sold to domestic consumers. Extending copyright protection, in effect, operates as a tax on American consumers, which is paid to producers of intellectual and artistic products rather than the government.[284] Therefore, proponents of the extension on export promotion grounds must argue that American consumers benefit more from the tax via enhanced exports than it costs them. In fact, no one has made a coherent case for the value *per se* of increased exports unrelated to increased domestic employment. Thus, those arguing for the importance of enhanced foreign exchange earnings must demonstrate the benefits of exports *per se*, unrelated to job creation, and that these benefits are sufficiently large to overcome the loss to consumers and the public domain of extending copyright.

Secondly, one must resolve the disagreement among economists regarding the impact of the balance of payments on a country's economic well being.[285] The concern with the balance of payments is a phenomenon of the past fifteen years. Prior to 1982 deficits in the United States current account were small and temporary. Since then the country has run large and chronic current account deficits. Yet during this period of time economists have differed over whether these developments represented a national problem or not, particularly in light of the economic growth experienced during the same period. It is clear that a deficit *per se* is neither desirable nor undesirable. (Put differently, there is no agreement that exports are inherently better than imports.) At a minimum, the deficit's economic impact, and our assessment of that impact, depend on how it is financed, more particularly on what the associated net capital inflow is used for. Thus, a large and persistent current account deficit is not problematic if the capital inflow is used to finance productive investment since such investment will boost living standards (and offset the interest payments on the inflows). On the other hand, future living standards may be eroded if the capital inflow is used to finance current consumption.[286]

The broader point is that the shape of the current account, and of the larger balance of payments, is rooted in macroeconomic factors, both domestic and foreign, and therefore any effective response lies in macroeconomic policy, not in a change in the copyright term. Thus, if one thinks that the deficit poses a serious short term risk (via pressure on interest and exchange rates) and a long term problem (via reduction in living standards) for the United States, a fit reaction would not lie in an increase in the level of copyright protection but rather would involve changes in federal fiscal and budgetary policy to encourage domestic savings and to reduce the budget deficit.[287]

Yet another problem is that even if improving the balance of payments is deemed beneficial, this kind of benefit cannot be quantified. First, one can't confidently predict the impact on the balance of payments.[288] Moreover, no algorithm exists for translating a specific balance of payment benefit to enhanced national income, consumer benefit, wages, profit or employment opportunities. Therefore, even if one concludes that increased exports will be beneficial via their positive balance of payments effect, one is unable to say how large the benefit will be and therefore one can't easily compare this kind of benefit to the expected losses from copyright extension.

In addition to all these problems, we lack a clear methodology for combining the direct effects of a change in legal rules with respect to copyright protection--*e.g.*, the costs to consumers--with possible benefits of such action in another, unrelated realm. More seriously, there is good reason to believe that there are much more effective methods for improving the balance of payments than increasing the level of copyright protection.

With respect to the problem of combining impacts in unrelated areas, it seems plausible that the enhanced export impact of copyright extension only adds to the case for copyright extension if it can be demonstrated that the benefits in the unrelated realm--the balance of payments--are positive and sufficiently large to overcome the negative impact of copyright extension on consumer welfare and the maximum availability of useful ideas. Since, in our judgment, the case for extension is quite weak, it would require that copyright extension provide very large balance of payments related benefits to make a positive case for the extension. Furthermore, it is necessary to resolve the question of the efficiency of promoting exports by copyright extension compared to other available methods for increasing exports. That is, before deciding whether or not the trade impact of copyright extension adds to the case for such extension sufficiently to overcome its drawbacks, one must conclude that the cost of increasing exports via copyright extension is cheaper than the next cheapest way of accomplishing this end.

In fact, export expansion via copyright extension seems to be a relatively undesirable modality for this purpose. Export expansion can be better and more equitably achieved by reducing trade barriers and/or by public subsidy. Calculating the cost and benefits of reducing trade barriers, like any change in trade rules, is tricky. Though no public expenditures are required, removing foreign export barriers usually requires the country seeking to expand exports to make difficult-to-quantify trade concessions or other allowances in other areas.[289] Exports also can be expanded by various kinds of subsidies. Programs which directly subsidize exports must justify the cost of such programs to taxpayers compared to their benefits. But assuming a reasonably equitable tax system, the cost would be equitably distributed among the beneficiaries. Moreover the decision to enhance exports would be made by those responsible for the nation's trade policies and fiscal soundness. However, expanding exports by increasing copyright protection imposes the cost entirely upon consumers of intellectual property and shrinks the public domain.[290] Thus, enhancing exports by increasing copyright protection may be viewed as imposing a covert tax on both domestic and foreign consumers of intellectual property. Moreover, unlike direct subsidies, the amount of the subsidy is concealed, and this concealment prevents citizens from comparing the benefits and costs of the subsidy.[291]

In sum, passage of the extension legislation and the resultant increased protection of American works in Europe will probably have a beneficial impact on the United States balance of payments, though the magnitude of that impact is difficult to gauge. That goal, however, will be achieved by the imposition of additional, considerable costs on American consumers and users of copyrighted works. And it is not at all clear that an improvement in the payments balance will translate into a gain in domestic economic welfare. While the balance of payments argument may have more substance than some of the others offered in support of change, it too does not justify an increase in the term of protection.

Notes

---

279. *See, e.g., Senate Hearing, supra* note 107, at 2, 25 (statements of Senator Orrin G. Hatch and Commissioner Bruce A. Lehman); Joint Comments of the Coalition of Creators and Copyright Owners, *supra* note 115, at 6-8, 10.

280. Actually, it is not clear that failure to match the European term would have a negative impact on our trade balance in the short run. After all, increasing the term does not mean that European users alone will pay longer; rather, American users will also pay longer, and not just to domestic copyright owners but to proprietors worldwide. Accordingly, the trade impact will depend on the patterns of usage on the two continents. While Europeans presently take more of our works than we consume of theirs, that was not the case at the turn of the century. Works which were about to enter the public domain here were created in 1923. Therefore an additional twenty years of protection, if retroactive, would include European works dating back to 1904. American use of European works of classical music and plays from the turn of the century through the 1920s and 1930s may be larger than the use Europeans make of United States works from that same era; and if so, our use of such works that will continue under protection under the enacted extension will cost more than we will receive in return. Comment of Copyright Law Professors, *supra* note 98, at 13. In the long term, though, if present behavior persists, the United States is likely to experience a net gain in revenues and a positive impact on the balance of payments, as the United States today is the world's largest exporter of copyrighted works. American musical and audiovisual works, for example, are widely disseminated and performed in Europe.

Of course, even thinking in the long term, the practical economic bite of an extension (and avoidance of the rule of the shorter term in Europe) will not take hold until about 2030 at the earliest. If the United States had maintained the life plus fifty term, the earliest date for application of the European rule of the shorter term would have been fifty years after 1978, assuming an author died immediately after life plus fifty became effective in the United States under the 1976 Copyright Act. Thus, the benefit of avoiding the rule of the shorter term will not be felt until 2028 and much later. Schrader, *supra* note 187, at 19.

Moreover, the generous treatment of American works by Germany and Great Britain, two of the largest consumers of United States works in Europe, further undermines the case for term extension in order to receive benefits in Europe. As previously noted, see note 27 and text at notes 22-27 *supra*, the EU Directive contains an exception to the mandatory rule of the shorter term for Member States who are bound by pre-existing treaty obligations recognizing a longer term. Germany is bound by such a bilateral agreement with the United States. Accordingly, American works, at least works published after U.S. accession to Berne, are protected in Germany for the full life plus seventy term even if term extension legislation were not adopted in the United States. *Agreement Between the German Reich and the United States of America*, 27 Stat. 1021, Jan. 15, 1892, art. 1 (unrestricted national treatment); *see* Wilhelm Nordemann, *The Term of Protection for Works by U.S.-American Authors in Germany*, 44 J. Copyright Soc'y of USA 1 (1996). In Great Britain, which did not apply the rule of the shorter term until it was mandated by the EU Directive, the regulations adopted to comply with the Directive grandfather existing works to the life plus fifty term that they enjoyed prior to the amendments. *See* Duration of Copyright and Rights in Performance Regulations 1995 sec. 15(1) (S.I. 1995 No. 3297). As a result, American copyright owners will receive protection there even after the term expires in the United States. For example, if an American author published a book in 1935 and died in 1975, the copyright will terminate in the United States in 2011 under current law, but it will remain in effect in Britain until 2026. Accordingly, the rule of the shorter term will not apply in these two countries to the old American works that were the stimulus for term extension legislation.

For the expression of serious skepticism, however, about the beneficial trade balance effects of increasing protection of corporate works to ninety-five years, *see House Hearings, supra* note 20, at 414 (1996) (testimony of Professor J.H. Reichman); Reichman, *supra* note 239, at 646-47. Moreover, as we have argued, a shorter term of protection in the United States, with its attendant expansion of the public domain, would encourage rather than deter the creation and publication of new works for worldwide markets, thereby generating export gains.

281. The "balance of trade" refers to the value of a country's exports minus the value of its imports. When imports exceed exports, it is said that the balance of trade is negative, unfavorable, or in deficit. When exports exceed imports, the trade balance is positive, favorable, or in surplus. In speaking of the trade balance our focus is on the "current account" portion of the nation's international transaction statistics. The balance of payments is the summary statement of a country's financial transactions with the rest of the world, often divided into the current account, the capital account, and the reserve account. As a matter of bookkeeping, all of a country's international transactions, those involving goods and services as well as those involving capital inflows and outflows must sum to zero. This accounting convention reflects the economic fact that the flow of goods and services measured by the current account is inextricably connected to the flow of funds for capital accumulation measured by the capital account; *i.e.*, the international flow of funds to finance capital accumulation and the international flow of goods and services are two sides of the same coin. N. Gregory Mankiw, Macroeconomics 178-89 (1992). The current account section of the balance of payments is usually subdivided into a merchandise measure and a services measure. In 1996 the United States current account was in deficit in the amount of $-114,300,000,000; the goods (merchandise) component totaled $-187,800,000,000 and the services figure was $73,500,000,000. Council of Economic Advisers, Economic Indicators, May 1997, at 35 (Table: U.S. International Trade in Goods and Services). As an absolute matter, a term extension's impact on

the balance of payments will likely be insignificant in two senses. First, the increase in annual foreign sales and royalty revenues will be small, reflecting the fact that few works are valuable generators of income seventy years after the author's death or seventy-five years after publication. Second, although it is growing, the intellectual property component remains only a small part of the overall merchandise and services accounts; and the amounts involved for works that will profit from term extension are tiny as compared to the overall United States trade in intellectual property. *See, e.g.,* International Monetary Fund, Balance of Payments Statistics Yearbook, pt. 1, at 824 (1966) ("royalties and licence fees"); *id.,* pt. 3, at 163. Of course, the United States' favorable trade balance in intellectual property depends on current works such as blockbuster movies, *e.g.,* "Forrest Gump" and "Independence Day", not on the few works from the 1920s and 1930s whose owners will benefit from term extension.

282. Presumptively, a substantial proportion of the benefits to the economy will benefit consumers thereby counter-balancing the negative effects upon consumers.

283. We have argued that extension of the copyright term will have little, if any, incentive effect on the creation and distribution of artistic and intellectual works. Moreover, whatever incentive effects it may have, they are not of the sort that leads to the kind of investment that produces substantial job expansion.

284. *See generally* Thomas Macaulay, 1 Speeches, Parliamentary and Miscellaneous 292 (1853) ("copyright is a tax on readers for the purpose of giving a bounty to writers"); Aoki, *supra* note 181, at 1335 (copyright as delegation of public power to tax to private copyright owners so that they receive income stream from users of copyrighted work).

285. Whether an improvement in the balance of payments is necessarily a "good"

objective is a highly contentious question among economists. There appears to be no consensus about the desirability or undesirability of a trade deficit and the pursuit of a payments surplus. *See, e.g.*, Samuelson & Nordhaus, *supra* note 32, at 683 (trade deficit not necessarily harmful; "unfavorable" balance of trade may be a fine thing for a country); Mankiw, *supra* note 282, at 190 (can't judge economic performance from current account alone, deficit not necessarily a reflection of economic malady, deficit may be sign of economic development). What seems clear is that an increase in export revenues does not automatically mean an increase in domestic well-being. *See* Laura D. Tyson, *Trade Deficits Won't Ruin Us*, N.Y. Times, Nov. 24, 1997, at A23 (trade deficit greatly flawed as gauge of economic health; no simple link between nation's net trade position and its overall economic health). That translation from more foreign earnings to improved domestic well-being is a complicated one and can not simply be assumed. *See generally* Peter Passell, *Economic Scene: America's Trade Gap Is (1) a Disaster (2) a Sign of Success*, N.Y. Times, April 17, 1997, at D2.

286. Craig S. Hakkio, *The U.S. Current Account: The Other Deficit*, Federal Reserve Bank of Kansas City Economic Review, Third Quarter 1995, at 11.

287. *See id. See generally* David Tufte, *Communications: Why Is the U.S. Current Account Deficit So Large?*, 63 S. Econ.J. 515 (1996).

288. It is difficult to quantify any predicted gain in the balance of payments. While one can be confident about the direction of the impact, similar confidence is not warranted with respect to an estimate of the absolute amount of the gain. The empirical magnitude is not likely to be large, though.

289. A good example of the necessity for making concessions to obtain concessions is provided by current negotiations with China regarding record piracy which feature trade-offs between more vigorous enforcement of Chinese copyright laws and

continuation of favorable American treatment of imports from China.

290. Any positive impact on the balance of payments, of course, will not be costless. After all, in the absence of change, the twenty years during which Europeans do not pay copyright royalties on American works are also twenty years during which Americans do not pay royalties on foreign (and American) works. Accordingly, every time we extend copyright protection in order to achieve more coverage for our exports overseas by imposing a higher cost on foreigners, we also levy an additional cost on American consumers and users. Though this cost can not be precisely quantified, it is real. (Indeed, the substantiality of this cost is demonstrated by the very claims of the legislation's supporters that they would be deprived of a sizeable European windfall if the United States did not extend its term to match that of Europe.) And these costs, large and certain, to the American public will greatly exceed even the gains to the relatively few copyright proprietors who will benefit from the term extension. Throughout the effort to secure enactment of the term change, a profound misconception was recurrently expressed--*i.e.*, more foreign protection is obviously good for Americans. In fact, it is probably beneficial to many American producers, but it is harmful to American consumers.

Perhaps, if Congress could extract additional revenues from European consumers without taxing Americans, a change would be attractive. But that costless scenario is not possible. In this context Congress can not just tax foreigners. If Europeans are required to pay for the right to use American works in Europe, Americans will be paying to use both domestic and European works here. Indeed, since it is reasonable to assume that Americans are greater consumers of domestic works than nationals of other countries, the American public will have to pay a multiple of dollars to American copyright owners for every dollar paid by Europeans. (For example, if foreign uses amount to 25% of the total use of American works, the multiple is 3:1.) However, if the United States produced certain intellectual or artistic works which were principally consumed in Europe and not here, at least some part of the impact of a term extension would be largely felt abroad and not at home and therefore the change would appear more attractive. Yet such a general lack of overlap does not exist under present behavior. The works which produce large sales in the United States, *e.g.*, movies, musical works, recordings and computer software, are typically the same works which sell well abroad.

291. Another international consideration that is put forth occasionally by supporters of a term extension is that enactment of an extension will enhance the United States's bargaining position in future international negotiations both in the copyright domain and in the field of trade more generally. We can generate political capital to be drawn on later. Undoubtedly, when it comes to bargaining, anything can be traded for anything else. And given the growing importance of information-based goods and services in international trade, countries may well increasingly view copyright policy and other trade issues as closely related and not consider international copyright protection in isolation from other international arrangements. (The inclusion of intellectual property in the Uruguay Round negotiations of the GATT multilateral trade agreement is a recent example of this phenomenon.) However, if the thinking is about bargaining chips, it is one thing to argue in the context of a specific negotiation that if the Europeans seek a concession such as a term extension we should give it to them in exchange for value, and quite another to argue that we should make a change now for free just in order to accumulate debating points for the future. In addition, this situation does not fit well the model case for earning political capital. In the model situation another country desires some action very much and we "concede" the strongly-sought change in order to earn its help in the future. In the present circumstances, though, the European Union was not lobbying for change here nor was it arguing forcefully on the merits for the life plus seventy term. Its move to that term was heavily driven by the objective of uniformity (and minimizing transitional adjustments), and even with that drive several member countries dissented from the change.

Chapter X. An Extended Term and the Making
of Copyright Policy

Determination of an appropriate period of protection involves resolution of the conflict between the establishment of incentives for creative activity and the desire for a free flow of the results of that activity. The tradeoff is between increasing the incentive to authorship and increasing the use of that which has already been authored. Optimally, calculation of the term consists of a balancing of these two considerations to figure that duration of copyright, neither too long nor too short,[292] which maximizes its net contribution to social welfare.[293] As we previously recounted,[294] the history of copyright in the United States has been marked by a continual lengthening of the term of protection, part of what one analyst has called "the seemingly inexorable expansion of copyright from the enactment of the first statute in 1790 to the present."[295] The duration of protection has increased with each comprehensive revision of the law. One probable reason for this direction of change is that the cost of copying has declined over time. As Landes and Posner point out, the lower the cost of copying the greater the optimal scope of protection.[296] But that change in copying cost hardly explains fully the magnitude of the historical record of term extension.[297] Rather the prime explanation likely lies in the characteristics of the political process generally and of policy-making in the copyright area in particular. Our reference here is to the differential attention given to and action taken on behalf of organized interests with concentrated benefits riding on the passage of legislation and diffuse interests which are shared by a large number of people with each person's projected benefit from legislative action small. This difference is manifest in the discourse attending the legislative process as well as in the lobbying efforts and the congressional results which emerge from the process.

Discussion of the extension legislation is full of references to the expected gain for American interests and to how the European benefits sought can be achieved at no cost to ourselves. The commentary speaks as if "American interest" is equivalent to the interest of American producers.[298] Of course, that equation expresses a profound misconception. Longer protection is better for certain Americans, perhaps, but it is costly to others. In speaking of an undifferentiated "us" or United States, no account is taken of the interests of consumers and users, of the broader public interest in ease of widespread dissemination of writings, of facilitation of the work of authors such as biographers and historians. Such talk avoids the complexity of a situation in which obtaining the benefit of an important foreign market requires a domestic change which hurts consumers and restricts the public domain. Thorough analysis requires explicit consideration of the extent and incidence of the benefits and costs of that change to various domestic groups. After all, producers prefer a system that generates the largest incomes for them, and therefore they will (almost) always favor an increase in the length of protection. The challenge is to assess proposed legislation in terms of its impact on the well-being of all Americans and to determine whether the social benefits of a change exceed its social costs.[299]

That assessment is hampered by a legislative process which is skewed to take account of organized interests and to discount or disregard diffuse, unorganized interests.[300] The result of this structural bias is that more broad-based values such as the competitive mandate[301] in favor of the production of desired goods at the lowest possible price receive scant attention, and the real and substantial costs to the public that would result from adoption of the term extension legislation are largely ignored. Similarly, the time limit on protection is one key way in which copyright law accommodates to the first amendment interest in people's ability to express themselves freely; but that interest has little institutional voice. As a result, the process of copyright legislation has been marked by meetings among those with vested interests, who negotiate compromises which are then ratified by Congress.[302]

Rarely do representatives of the broader public interest participate in these meetings and negotiations; that interest therefore receives only passing attention; and Congress has not proved an effective protector of the public interest, which winds up shortchanged.[303]

The structure of this process and the outcomes it produces are not surprising. A substantial body of economic and political science literature, in particular that of interest group theory, predicts such results.[304] According to this learning, in situations where individuals have high per capita interests in legislation--e.g., the small group of movie and music producers--those people are likely to incur the monitoring, research, and communication costs of effective political organization.[305] On the other hand, individuals with a low per capita interest--e.g., the large group of consumers and users of copyrighted works--will not find it worth their while to undertake these costs to oppose a legislative change (or judicial litigation)[306] which contracts the public domain.[307] One frequent result of these facts of political life is the passage of legislation which provides concentrated advantages to a small group even though the total costs to others are larger than these benefits and the action therefore represents a net social loss.[308]

Consider this example. Suppose a proposed piece of legislation will transfer $250 million to a particular interest group. Suppose further that the legislation imposes direct costs (such as taxes) and indirect costs (such as reductions in the efficiency of the economy) totalling $20 on every man, woman, and child in America. Clearly, passage of the legislation results in a net reduction of social welfare. Nevertheless, the economic theory of regulation suggests that the legislation will pass. While the interest group will expend resources up to the full amount of the prospective gain to ensure passage of the legislation, no individual will be willing to spend more than $20 to ensure its defeat. However, by the time any individual spends the resources to (1) learn about the existence of the proposal, (2) understand its merits and implications, (3) search for and discover others willing to oppose the legislation, (4) mobilize like-minded individuals to voice their opposition, and (5)

signal legislators that defeating the legislation is the price of their support, the costs
to the individual probably far outweigh the expected savings ($20) of defeating the
legislation. Consequently, the rational course of action of an individual citizen under
such circumstances is not only to refrain from organizing to oppose the legislation
but also to remain ignorant of its effects and possibly even ignorant of its existence.
Hence, an interest group seeking to obtain legislation with highly concentrated
benefits and diffuse costs can generally count on little popular opposition.[309]

We do not mean to suggest that the diffuse social interest always goes
unvoiced or is ignored.[310] In the early 1990s, for example, writers, particularly
biographers and historians, and their publishers were sufficiently concerned about
judicial decisions limiting the use of unpublished materials to petition Congress in
organized fashion for clarification of the reach of the fair use doctrine. The result
was the 1992 amendment to section 107.[311] Also, on occasion the interests of a
small, organized group may coincide with the broader public interest and this group
therefore serve as a surrogate voice of that broader interest. For example, for many
years the Electronic Industries Association (EIA), the trade association for
manufacturers of home audio and video recording equipment, championed the
interest of home recorders as it resisted royalty schemes which would place a levy on
the sale of recording equipment.[312] Similarly, the professional interests of educators,
archivists, and librarians have at times served as a reasonable proxy for the public
interest. But the coincidence of interests may prove temporary[313] and betray a less
than sincere appreciation for the value of an expansive public domain. Thus, in 1992
the EIA negotiated a compromise deal with representatives of the music and record
industries which resulted in passage of the Audio Home Recording Act,[314] legislation
which put in place a system of levies on the sale of recording equipment and blank
tape with the proceeds to be distributed among makers of musical works and sound
recordings. Moreover, unauthorized duplicators, "pirates" of intellectual and artistic
works, are unlikely to surface and present themselves as lobbyists to Congress,[315]
although their commercial interests are often congruent with the broader social

interest in widespread dissemination of works.[316] We need a more inclusive and deliberative legislative process to decide copyright policy issues, one in which the voices of those who desire to protect the public domain can be heard and as a result the existing dramatic undervaluation of the interests of audiences for intellectual, informational, and artistic works can be avoided.[317]

At a minimum we should be able to assure that relevant data and analyses produced by one agency of the federal government are made available to other bodies obviously interested in the topic--in the copyright context, the staff of the Copyright Office and the staffs of the Senate and House Judiciary subcommittees. In 1986 Timothy Brennan, an economist with the Antitrust Division of the Department of Justice, prepared a discussion paper for the Economic Analysis Group of the Division.[318] Entitled "Taxing Home Audio Taping", it closely examined the harms caused by home taping and evaluated at length the efficiency and equity of various royalty schemes which would place a levy on the sale of recording equipment and/or blank tape. Brennan was skeptical about the desirability of such legislation, and he concluded that in light of the certain administrative costs and the inability to guard against inefficient restriction of non-infringing uses, a taping fee was "ill-advised". With one abbreviated exception[319], a look through the legislative history of the Audio Home Recording Act, however, reveals neither awareness of nor reference to the Brennan study!

Congressional determination of a desirable term of protection--one which constitutes an appropriate mean between encouragement of authorship and publication and facilitation of widespread availability--is a formidable task. In light of the number and indefiniteness of the variables which need to be identified and assessed, one can not sensibly speak in terms of a single correct or optimal term that is the only acceptable period. However, one can speak of more or less.[320] In that respect, the "more" direction of the extension legislation is aided by the 1976 Copyright Act's adoption of the Berne minimum term of life of the author plus 50 years. In enacting that generous period Congress was motivated, in part, by the desire to bring the United States in line with what appeared to be the prevalent international standard and to make possible American membership in Berne.[321] The Berne term now seems to be treated as an accepted, normative reference or starting point. But any such deference is mistaken.[322] The analytic foundation for the Berne provision is not as solid as has been assumed. The term is quite arbitrary and the product more of historical accident and ideology than of sustained analysis of justification for protection. Just as the American political process is biased against the thorough consideration of all affected interests, so the Berne term has not resulted from a critical inquiry which analyzes its economic or other benefits and disadvantages.[323] As the leading scholarly commentator on the Berne Union has put it:

> While [the Convention's] prescriptions as to duration are quite precise, there has never been any real effort made to justify why, or to explain   how, these terms have come to be adopted, particularly in an era where the author is generally no longer directly involved in the exploitation of his works....[D]oubt must remain over two of the linchpins of the Berne Convention provisions on duration: the tendency towards a uniform term for all works, and the length of that term....[T]here has never been any attempt during the life of the Convention to examine these questions. The reason for this has been suggested above: the strong emphasis that has always been placed on the natural property rights of the author in his work. In this respect, ideology has replaced critical inquiry, and has led to a long period of protection--the life of the author plus 50 years--becoming enshrined as an absolute value that has seldom been challenged, except where there have been moves for its further extension.[324]

Notes

292. A very short period will fail in its purpose by being inadequate to stimulate any significant amount of investment in the authorial and publishing processes. On the other hand, a very long copyright period can extract an excessive price from society by granting monopoly power to investors for an excessive period. Thus, the goal is to find an optimal compromise between the two extremes of too short or too long a lag period during which protection via copyright is granted to the producer; the content and scope of protection should be such as to obtain the necessary return at the minimum social dislocation. Braunstein, *supra* note 35, at I-10.

293. *See generally* Cooter & Ulen, *supra* note 41, at 136-37 (graphical representation, in the context of patents, of costs and benefits of lengthening term and specification of optimal life at intersection of curves of net marginal social costs and net marginal social benefits).

294. See text at notes 8-18 *supra*.

295. Weinreb, *supra* note 32, at 1154, 1211 (inexorable expansion from narrow range and limited protection of first Copyright Act to current open-ended form). Another scholar notes critically that this historical trend, including the EU Directive, reflects "a policy of indiscriminate kindness to copyright interests." Cornish, *supra* note 221, at 7.

296. *See* Landes & Posner, *supra* note 73, at 344, 363. Of course, the same technical developments that make copying easier also furnish other ways for producers to recover their investments (or to encourage further innovation). This complexity is characteristic of the digital environment; yet it has received little recognition in early efforts to prescribe a legal framework for the internet. *See* Boyle, *supra* note 9.

222

297. Comparing the historical record of copyright and patent treatment to the beginning of the twentieth century, John Kasdan speculates: "It might be that the willingness to extend the term of copyright was based on a feeling that copyrighted works were not as essential to the economy as were patented ones, but it is also possible that the extension reflected a realization that the mis-allocative effects of copyright were not as great as those of patent law." Kasdan, *supra* note 73, at 8. Again, even accepting that the longer term of protection for copyright, with its more limited scope of protection, sensibly reflects the lesser social costs it imposes as compared with patent, this observation can hardly account for the absolute length of its protective term. With enactment of the Term Extension Act, copyright will last for life + 70 or, in the alternative, ninety-five years while the patent grant lasts only twenty years from the day of filing of the patent application.

298. Extension proponents also look to capture the high ground of discourse by consistently portraying the legislation as beneficial to creators and authors. In fact, the twenty year extension benefits copyright owners rather than creative authors, who will already have been deceased for fifty years.

299. *See* Keyes & Brunet, *supra* note 35, at 37-38. *See generally* U.S. Congress, Office of Technology Assessment, Copyright and Home Copying: Technology Challenges the Law 191-207 (1989). After all, the American public, as opposed to individual copyright owners, is not damaged by the absence of protection in Europe fifty years after the death of the American author. If the Europeans choose to burden their consumers, it does not automatically follow that we should do the same. From an economic perspective, copyright is intended to provide economic returns to producers but only when that is also in the long run interest of society as a whole. Copyright owners themselves, of course, will always prefer to maximize their own control over the works they produce. The net social welfare effect of lengthened protection, though, is a function of the effects on both producers and consumers.

300. *See* Patry, *supra* note 107; Sterk, *supra* note 70, at 1244-46 ("Copyright and Interest-Group Politics"). *See generally* James Boyle, *A Sense of Belonging*, Times Literary Supplement, July 4, 1997, at 3, 4:

> [I]n the United States, copyright has been described as the most technically perfect example of "industry capture" of the legislative process. The use of the legal system for industry rent-seeking is often so obvious that it is embarrassing.

301. See text at note 122 *supra*.

302. Patterson, *supra* note 125, at 26-27 ("industry plays a dominant role in shaping copyright legislation with small-minded concerns, weighted as they are by the desire for control and profit"). The Audio Home Recording Act of 1992, for example, represents codification of agreements between the record industry and the manufacturers of audio equipment. *See* Joel L. McKuin, *Home Audio Taping of Copyrighted Works and The Audio Home Recording Act of 1992: A Critical Analysis*, 16 Hastings Comm. & Ent. L.J. 311 (1994). Professor Litman has written broadly and insightfully about the political dynamics underlying copyright legislation and has shown that Congress has largely abrogated its role as representative of the general public in such legislation by allowing the various interest groups involved to fight it out, reach a compromise, and then have Congress adopt the negotiated result. *See* Litman, *supra* note 72; Jessica Litman, *Copyright and Information Policy*, L. & Contemp. Probs., Spring 1992, at 185; Jessica Litman, *Copyright Legislation and Technological Change*, 68 Or. L. Rev. 275, 357 (1989) ("The inquiry relevant to copyright legislation long ago ceased to be 'is this a good bill?' Rather the inquiry has been and continues to be 'is this a bill that current stakeholders agree on?'"); Jessica Litman, *Copyright, Compromise, and Legislative History*, 72 Cornell L. Rev. 857 (1987). In not subjecting industry (rent-seeking) claims to critical scrutiny, Congress fails to exercise its unique capacity to unearth salient facts via empirical inquiry. *See*

Marci A. Hamilton, *Copyright Duration Extension and the Dark Heart of Copyright*, 14 Cardozo Arts & Ent. L.J. 655-58 (1996) ("Congress and Factfinding").

303. *See* Litman (1989), *supra* note 302. We do not mean to suggest that interested industry groups can or should be excluded from a central role in the legislative process. Rather, the problem is one of incomplete, narrow vision. The process is skewed to disproportionately and consistently privilege powerful, well-organized owner interests at the expense of the interests of the public in use and reuse of copyrighted informational and imaginative works. *See* Economic Council of Canada, Report on Intellectual and Industrial Property 143 (1971) (inadequate attention to general public interest in information system); Antoon Quaedvlieg, *Copyright's Orbit Round Private, Commercial and Economic Law--The Copyright System and the Place of the User*, 29 Int'l Rev. Indus. Prop. & Copyright L. 420, 432, 435-38 (1998) (no institutional voice for freedom of information issues in European copyright systems; users' interests receive no serious attention). One result is the passage of laws which are unworkable from the point of view of people who were not among the negotiating parties. And the need is for a renewed attempt to bring the public interest to bear on administrative and legislative decision-making. Professor Litman has suggested that the Copyright Office has the interest, expertise, and institutional memory to function as the public's copyright lawyer and that the Office should redefine its role accordingly. *See* Litman (1994), *supra* note 72, at 52-54; Mackaay, *supra* note 40, at 22-23 (public discourse does not necessarily reflect the interests of people in the field; should be wary of idea that legislature balances all relevant interests fairly).

Greater public interest involvement in the development and implementation of intellectual property law may have the additional benefit of increasing the incidence of voluntary compliance with the legal rules. *See* Tom R. Tyler, *Compliance With Intellectual Property Laws: A Psychological Perspective*, 29 Int'l L. & Pol. 219, 229-33 (1996-97).

304. The seminal, classic presentation is Mancur Olson, The Logic of Collective Action (1971) (new theory of groups and organizations centered on the problem of the free rider). *But see generally* Donald P. Green & Ian Shapiro, Pathologies of Rational Choice Theory 72-97 (1994).

305. *See* Einer R. Elhauge, *Does Interest Group Theory Justify More Intrusive Judicial Review?*, 101 Yale L.J. 31, 37, 49 (1991). Monitoring costs refer to the expense of tracking the legislature and agencies to determine new proposed laws and to ascertain how individual congressmen are voting. Research costs include the expense of researching proposals to determine to what extent these items harm or benefit the group. Communication costs refer to the expense of communicating this information to the group's voters and convincing them to mobilize to voice their opposition or support. *See generally* William A. Niskanen, *Why Our Democracy Doesn't Work*, The Public Interest, Summer 1994, at 88, 90:

> The dilemma posed by the evidence from both political behavior and polls of opinion is that while most people oppose a higher level of total government spending, they are even more vocal in support of spending for programs from which they especially benefit! The calculus of concentrated benefits and diffused costs creates a strong incentive to organize political activity in support of specific programs, even if the sum of the diffused costs is much greater than the benefits. As a consequence, almost all the witnesses at legislative hearings favor higher spending for the specific program being reviewed.

This structural bias of the process also facilitates "expert" presentation of "mythical" numbers pointing to the existence of a problem and the easy acceptance of these figures in the absence of an informed opponent to challenge them. *See* Max Singer, *The Vitality of Mythical Numbers*, The Public Interest, Spring 1971, at 3.

306. The same barrier to expression of the diffuse social interest operates in the judicial arena:

> [L]itigation contains a structural bias against the articulation of a community interest in free access, for the community as such cannot be a litigant. Against an articulate plaintiff who is enunciating what sounds like a moral interest in reaping what she has sown often stands a commercially motivated defendant who may be an unsympathetic figure poorly situated to communicate what the community has at stake. Spokespersons for the community interest in nonownership exist, but, given the likely structure of the relevant litigation, their voices may go unheard.

Gordon, *supra* note 40, at 279.

307. The terms "small" and "large" refer only to the number of independent members which compose a group, not to the number of individuals a group represents or to the size of the group's funds. Thus, a "small" group has few independent members, while a "large" group has many independent members. A few corporations which comprise an interest group would be deemed a small group.

Although this analysis contrasts large groups with diffuse interests with small groups with concentrated interests, there can exist some large groups with high per capita interests. This type of group would be capable of greater collective action than large, uniformly dispersed groups and perhaps even greater collective action than smaller groups with less concentrated per capita interests. Russell Hardin, Collective Action 40-42 (1982). The reason for this capability is because "a group's willingness to devote resources to collective action will ...turn not only on group size and on average intensity but on the distribution of intensity throughout the group." Elhauge, *supra* note 305, at 38 n.22.

Both large and small groups confront the problem of free-riding, a problem which produces a group tendency to not spend the level of resources needed to effect the highest return from lobbying. But the small group still has advantages in dealing with free-riding. In contrast with large groups, one or most of the members of a small group have such a large stake in the legislation that they have an independent motive to spend the requisite funds; small group members perceive a direct correlation between their support and the desired outcome. *See* Mancur Olson, The Rise and Decline of Nations 29-34 (1982). Moreover, free-riding is easier to detect in a small group; the absence of funds from a member would be immediately noticed. Free-riding can also be curbed in a small group if the members who notice such a failure threaten to withdraw their own funds. Thus, small groups are better able to detect and remedy free-riding than large groups with dispersed interests. *See* Elhuage, *supra* note 305, at 38.

308. *See, e.g.*, James Q. Wilson, *The Politics of Regulation, in* The Politics of Regulation 369 (James Q. Wilson ed., 1980). These structural conditions are not unique to the American political process. A British observer of copyright revision there, for example, observes:

> The basic problem is clear enough. Authors' rights and interests are ferociously guarded (and aggressively enlarged) by agents acting on behalf of writers' estates and by the Society of Authors. Publishers' interests are protected by the cartelised might of the Publishers' Association. No one, least of all the politicians (who are more worried about threats to the British banger than to English literature), safeguards readers' rights as they are enshrined in the concept of the public domain. Any erosion of the public domain is a serious matter. What is needed, in the short term, is a commando as fierce in the protection of public domain as the Ramblers' Association is of public right of way. In the long term there should be a body as well organized as the Performing Rights Society, devoted to lobbying for the

extension and pro-bono exploitation of public domain.

Sutherland, *supra* note 123. Sutherland, though, does not indicate how this new public interest lobbying organization will be financed.

309. Henry N. Butler & Jonathan R. Macey, *Health Care Reform: Perspectives From The Economic Theory of Regulation and the Economic Theory of Statutory Interpretation*, 79 Cornell L. Rev. 1434, 1437-38 (1994).

310. Nor do we mean to suggest that interest-group (economic) theory provides a complete account of political behavior and citizens' motivation. *See generally* Albert O. Hirschman, Shifting Involvements: Private Interest and Public Action (1982); Richard Swedberg, Economics and Sociology: Redefining Their Boundaries: Conversations with Economists and Sociologists 159-160 (1990) (interview with Albert O. Hirschman). But the descriptive and explanatory power of the approach is evident, particularly in its application to the copyright policy-making process.

311. *See* text at notes 165-71 and notes 165-71 *supra*.

312. *See, e.g., Home Recording of Copyrighted Works: Hearings on H.R. 4783, H.R. 4794, H.R. 4808, H.R. 5250, H.R. 5488, and H.R. 5705 Before the Subcomm. on Courts, Civil Liberties, and the Administration of Justice of the House Comm. on the Judiciary*, 97th Cong., 2d Sess., pt. 1, at 202; *id.*, pt. 2, at 763 (1982) (statements of Jack Wayman, senior vice president, Consumer Electronics Group, EIA).

313. One difficulty is that a group typically looks at proposed legislation through a narrow lens and views proposals which do not immediately and obviously affect it as not worthy of its resistance. Much of the material that librarians, for example, work with is of recent origin and therefore is under copyright anyway, even without a term extension. Accordingly, they believe that their fight is to halt the expansion of the scope of copyright rights rather than the length of time they are in effect.

Similarly, the American Association of Law Libraries and the American Library Association initially opposed proposals for the partial repeal of the "first sale" doctrine as it applied to computer programs and sound recordings. (These proposals, which were ultimately enacted as amendments to section 109 of the Copyright Act, provided that commercial rental of programs and recordings requires the permission of the copyright owner.) However, both groups changed their positions when the proponents of the changes agreed to exempt non-profit libraries from the reach of the legislation. Their opposition to copyright amendments of general application was dropped in exchange for narrow provisions addressed to their specific concerns. Litman (1994), *supra* note 72, at 33 & n.23. Thus, the negotiation process incident to the passage of copyright legislation tends to divide users of works into discrete interests. And as businesses and institutions who are at the negotiating table ask for and obtain specific privileges, the result is that nobody winds up being a surrogate for the general public.

314. Pub. L. No. 102-563. 106 Stat. 4237 (1992).

315. *See generally* Thomas P. Olson, *The Iron Law of Consensus: Congressional Responses to Proposed Copyright Reforms Since the 1909 Act*, 36 J. Copyright Soc'y U.S.A. 109, 111, 118 (1989) ("pirates'" lack of political resources). An exception to this proposition, though, occurred in the early 1970s when several record "pirates", unauthorized duplicators of sound recordings, appeared at congressional hearings to argue against the extension of federal copyright protection to sound recordings. *See Prohibiting Piracy Of Sound Recordings: Hearings on S. 646 & H.R. 6927 Before Subcomm. No. 3 of the House Comm. on the Judiciary*, 92d Cong., 1st Sess. 67-116 (1971). Congress was unsympathetic to their efforts and enacted the Sound Recording Amendment of 1971, which for the first time brought protection for sound recordings within the federal Copyright Act.

Of course, advocates of protection have usually won their battle as soon as they gain acceptance of the designation "pirates" for their opponents.

316. Consideration of the term extension bill featured a depressing absence of representation of this social interest by public officials. Bruce Lehman, Assistant Secretary of Commerce and Commissioner of Patents and Trademarks, for example, offered precisely the same erroneous contentions about the economic effects of term expiration as did the representatives of movie and music producers. *Compare Senate Hearing, supra* note 107, at 25-26 *with* Comments of the NMPA, *supra* note 114, at 6. It is one thing for industry representatives to make transparently dubious arguments in service of their narrow interests; it is quite another for a public official to replicate and endorse such arguments. The basis for concern here is not simply that advocates of changes that will benefit them make poor arguments, but that these arguments seem to be so uncritically accepted by their audiences. Professor Sterk suggests that this paucity of criticism of copyright expansion reflects a stake of the nation's elite, including Congress, in believing and acting on the copyright rhetoric of desert. *See* Sterk, *supra* note 70, at 1198, 1247-49.

317. *See generally* Jeremy Phillips, *The Diminishing Domain*, 8 Eur. Intell. Prop. Rev. 429 (1996).

Failure of passage of a term extension bill until October 1998 did not reflect congressional recognition that the proposal was ill-advised. Rather, the lack of success was a result of political maneuverings with respect to other, unrelated copyright initiatives involving the reach of the public performance right in music. Those interested in restricting the reach of the music performance right tied the political fate of the term extension proposal to their initiatives to reform music licensing of bars and restaurants. That reform, which addresses music licensing complaints by small businesses, was strongly opposed by the music performing rights societies, ASCAP and BMI, which represent composers and music publishers and which fear significant revenue loss from the proposed changes. At the same time, these societies are among the principal proponents of term extension. The result was a lengthy political stalemate. *See, e.g.*, S. 28, 105th Cong., 1st Sess. (1997) (Fairness in Musical Licensing Act of 1997); Bill Holland, *Music Biz Bills Await Action--WIPO Treaties' Ratification at Stake*, Billboard, Sept. 19, 1998, at 8. The breaking of this logjam with the inclusion in the term extension bill of an expanded music licensing exemption for food service and drinking establishments led to the passage of the Act in the waning hours of the 105th Congress.

318. Timothy J. Brennan, Taxing Home Audio Taping (1986). The study, in somewhat different form, was published in Timothy J. Brennan, *An Economic Look at Taxing Home Audio Taping*, 32 J. Broadcasting & Electronic Media 89 (1988).

319. In his prepared statement for the October 1991 hearings on the Audio Home Recording Act of 1991, the Register of Copyrights made brief reference to the 1988 Brennan Journal of Broadcasting and Electronic Media article. *See The Audio Home Recording Act of 1991, Hearing on S. 1623 Before the Subcomm. on Patents, Copyrights, and Trademarks of the Senate Judiciary Comm., 102nd Cong., 1st Sess. 32-34* (1991). The reference, though, was quite truncated and misleading in that it omitted any mention of Brennan's negative views--his very serious reservations about this type of legislation and his conclusion that, on balance, it would be wise not to enact it.

320. For the suggestion by a knowledgeable commentator that life of the author plus thirty years would be an apt term, see Guinan, *supra* note 15, at 27.

321. *See* H.R. Rep. No. 1476, 94th Cong., 2d Sess. 135 (1976). For an examination of fine point durational inconsistencies between United States law and the Berne Convention, see Nimmer, *supra* note 274, at 224-32. Some of these inconsistencies were resolved with the passage in 1994 of the Uruguay Round Agreements Act, Pub. L. No. 103-465, 108 Stat. 4809 (1994); *see* 17 U.S.C. sec. 104A (1994).

322. A broader process point should be made here about situations where advocates lobby for proposals both as a basis for domestic legislation and international

agreement. International intellectual property treaties generally permit the citizens of a state to claim particular protections abroad only if their own country recognizes those same protections at home. Thus, proponents of expansive intellectual property protection abroad can, by getting other countries to adopt these protections, put heavy pressure on Congress. Only by voting for restrictive rules at home, the argument will go, can we assure that our citizens and companies will be able to compete on a level foreign playing field. This bootstrapping technique clearly has disturbing implications for the value of citizen ability to participate meaningfully in democratic decision making.

323. The EU Harmonization Directive has been subjected to similar criticism. During the deliberative process the Economic and Social Committee expressed serious reservations about the proposed term and suggested that efforts, both within and without the Community, would be better spent in pursuit of a uniform life plus fifty term, which would be less disruptive for most of the Member States and would not create barriers for third countries. The Committee also noted that any transitional provisions necessitated by the life plus fifty choice need not be complex, pointing to the successful experience of Spain when it moved from life plus eighty to life plus sixty in 1987. Opinion on the Proposal for a Council Directive Harmonizing the Term of Protection of Copyright and Certain Related Rights, 1992 O.J. (C 287) 53. Apparently the Committee's concerns received no response as the proposal moved to enactment. The final Council decision, though, was not without dissent, the final tally being 8-3-1. The Luxembourg, Dutch, and Portuguese delegations voted against the Directive, and the Irish delegation abstained. Indeed, the Netherlands offered a blistering dissenting opinion, in which it condemned the process and its result for their exclusive focus on the interests of authors and publishers and their lack of attention to the interests of consumers and users. The opinion noted that on several occasions the Dutch delegation had sought more information and the consideration of alternative approaches in an effort to achieve a resolution which struck a desirable

balance; but this information was never provided nor were other approaches discussed. (Indeed, little discussion at all took place between majority and minority groupings.) The process necessarily affected the quality of the legislation and resulted in a Directive that not only gives "precedence to authors' interests over users' interests but...also undermines legal certainty,...complicates relations with third countries and...seems not to be based on a balanced analysis of the financial and economic advantages and disadvantages involved." *Explanation by the Netherlands Delegation of Vote on the Directive Harmonizing the Term of Protection of Copyright and Certain Related Rights*, in Annex, Council of Ministers Press Release 93-173, Luxembourg, Oct. 29, 1993.

324. Ricketson, *supra* note 26, at 321-23 (Berne minimum neither adopted nor later justified by reference to any clear criterion). *See also* Puri, *supra* note 176, at 12, 13; Dawson, *supra* note 229, at 202-03.

Chapter XI. Conclusion

It is understandable that American authors and publishers--in particular, music and movie producers--advocated a twenty year extension of the copyright term. But the arguments offered in support of the change were, and are, insubstantial. The costs of copyright protection increase significantly as the term lengthens, and a critical analysis of the extension legislation leads to the conclusion that its advantages to most producers are outweighed by the costs to consumers and users of contracting the public domain. An economic or incentive argument, then, does not justify the proposed change. No convincing case has been made that there is a large discrepancy between society's need for the copyright type of incentive and the amount of such incentive being provided under the 1976 Act.[325] And, in any case, the proposition that the extra twenty years will provide an incentive for the creation of new works is dubious at best.[326] Nor are equitable arguments, whether rooted in notions of desert, reward for creation of great works, or increased author longevity, convincing. Moreover, the argument based on the value of uniformity *per se*, while initially attractive, turns out to be of insignificant weight.[327] Furthermore, while the long term effect on the balance of payments via enhancement of foreign revenues is likely to be positive, the effect will be quite slight and its broader economic impact ambiguous; accordingly, this argument does not offer material assistance. Ironically, one of the major economically important copyright sectors, the record industry, will not, in fact, gain additional protection in Europe from its passage. The defects in the Act and the arguments offered on its behalf are magnified by the retroactive application of the change to existing copyrights. This application has virtually nothing to recommend it, and the lack of a persuasive underlying rationale, economic or equitable, for it underlines the weakness of the entire change. Passage of the Term

Extension Act will inflict serious damage on the progress of American culture by diminishing a lively and viable public domain as a basis for the creation of new works and unhindered scholarship.[328]

In the formation of copyright policy the lack of empirical data,[329] the inability to quantify important variables, and the consequent methodological imprecision insure a considerable range of error in reaching conclusions even for the analyst committed to a thorough and balanced examination.[330] While theoretically it may be possible to offer a formula for determination of an optimal length of term,[331] these measurement problems indicate that it is not possible to quantify precisely the number of years required to provide the degree of protection needed to induce resources to flow into authorship and publication.[332] Although acceptance of that imprecision dictates that there is no single, obviously correct term,[333] it is possible to talk meaningfully about more or less protection. The noted limitations on policy formation do not preclude judgment about changes within the system, particularly those that would extend it further. In viewing the congressional process for answering the question of an apt term in the context of the term extension bill, what is depressing is not that, in the end, the arguments for extension are unpersuasive, but that they have almost no substance and yet they are repeated and apparently accepted without question not only by interested spokesmen but by numerous public officials and legislators. This performance underscores the structural bias in the system which gives little attention to diffuse social interests (and facilitates a rush to judgment).

As a matter of policy analysis, the copyright term should be shortened rather than lengthened.[334] Our Berne Convention obligations prevent a significant move in that direction. However, the policy conclusion emphasizes the undesirability of the extension legislation. If a decrease is not feasible, the next best option was to retain the generous life + 50 term,[335] a term which is consistent with that of approximately 90 percent of the member countries of Berne[336] and which accords better than an increased period with the limiting policies expressed in the copyright clause.

Notes

---

325. Though the policy estimates of what is necessary to accomplish the task are inevitably crude, from an economic perspective the purpose of recognition and delineation of property rights in intellectual and artistic works is to equalize private and social net benefits from these activities in order to provide incentives for economic actors to engage in socially constructive behavior. Advocates of term extension have failed to meet the burden of showing that the level of incentive under the 1976 Act was inadequate. They have failed to demonstrate that with an increase we will obtain more intellectual and artistic works or that the value of what we will receive will be greater than the corresponding loss to consumers and the public domain.

326. As we have demonstrated, it is highly unlikely that an extra twenty years of protection added on to the end of a period that is already very long will function as an incentive to any current author to work harder or longer to create works that would not have been otherwise produced. What is sure, though, is that term extension will seriously impede the creative efforts of both current and future authors.

327. In 1976 American authors were frequently protected longer in foreign countries than they and foreign authors were in the United States. For example, by publishing simultaneously in the United States and in a Berne member country such as Canada, American publishers could, via this "back door to Berne", gain protection for life plus fifty years in Berne member countries. This disparity, under which American nationals could take advantage of the broader protections of Berne without bearing the accompanying burdens, gave rise to considerable resentment abroad; and the desire to meet this displeasure was one of the reasons for the congressional decision to move the United States to a term of life plus fifty. *See* H.R. Rep. No. 1476, 94th Cong., 2d Sess. 135 (1976) (difference in copyright duration "has provoked

considerable resentment and some proposals for retaliatory legislation"). Such a concern, though, does not operate with respect to the extension legislation. If the United States had rejected the extension proposal and reaffirmed the life plus fifty term, American authors would not benefit from the European life plus seventy term, there would be no differential in treatment of American works at home and abroad, and accordingly no foreign resentment about disparate treatment.

328. Moreover, as previously noted, Chapter V. *supra*, a general term extension was not necessary to secure for American authors and producers the additional twenty years' benefit abroad under the European Union directive. That objective, if deemed worthy of pursuit, could be accomplished by a decision to apply the life plus seventy term to foreign works while retaining the life plus fifty period of protection for domestic works. That accommodation would guarantee the European benefit to American authors and publishers while relieving American users and consumers of any additional costs for use of domestic works.

329. *See* Hamilton, *supra* note 302, at 657 (absence of empirical information on creativity and reward structure):

> There is much talk in the literature and the cases of the "incentive" nature of copyright law. But there is no factual study that shows how much incentive is enough to further creative activity, or what kinds of incentives work: money, control, or time.

330. *See* Keyes & Brunet, *supra* note 35, at 35 (complexity and magnitude of needed data make it difficult to reach rigorous conclusion about relative costliness of copyright scheme versus regime of no copyright protection); Maskus, *supra* note 43, at 14 (choice of apt protection level complicated by technical and market measurement problems).

331. *See* Landes and Posner, *supra* note 73; Nordhaus, *supra* note 192, at 76-86 (the optimal life of a patent). Even here the formulation must assume a social welfare function to be maximized, and acceptance of that function may well be controversial. *See, e.g., id.* at 76 n.9. *See also* Boudewijn Bouckaert, *What Is Property?*, 13 Harv. J.L. & Pub. Pol'y 775, 812 (1990) (measurement problems make economic analyses about optimal duration unconvincing).

332. Though still complicated, quantification may be more feasible with respect to patents. Inventions are frequently cost-reducing, and the reduction in production cost and enhanced efficiency usually can be calculated. And though it is difficult to gauge the degree of patent protection necessary to induce a given level of intellectual effort, with respect to patents there is no need to quantify consumer satisfaction. *See generally* Viscusi, *supra* note 57, at 833-46.

If one views copyright as a limited grant intended to foster the expressive diversity and creative autonomy needed for democratic governance and not simply as an economic response to market failure, the question of what term would produce optimum support for creative autonomy while still permitting sufficient user access is similarly attended by imprecision. But cruder judgments are possible, and from the perspective of democratic governance any lengthening of duration of protection under the 1976 Act is undesirable and unjustified. *See* Netanel, *supra* note 58, at 368-69.

333. The objectives of encouragement of authorship and of dissemination are inevitably to some extent in tension. The effectiveness of copyright protection in achieving the two aims depends in part on the period of the copyright grant. But that term provision is, of course, part--though a central part--of a larger protective system. And any attempt to fashion a system of rights that gives due consideration to both objectives must steer clear of the notion that there is only a single apt allocation of rights. *See generally* Robinson, *supra* note 62.

334. This conclusion is shared by James Guinan, an independent analyst who composed the study on duration of protection for the Copyright Office as part of the copyright revision process. Guinan concluded that a term of life of the author plus thirty years constitutes the duration of limited time which best promotes the progress of science and the useful arts. *See* Guinan, *supra* note 15, at 27. *See also* Puri, *supra* note 176, at 13, 18-19 (no justification for current lengthy period; term should be dramatically shortened); *House Hearings, supra* note 20, at 393 (statement of Professor J.H. Reichman) (good case for shortening the 75 year term afforded corporate works). For advocacy of a more radical decrease in the term of protection, see Boyle *supra* note 9, at 172 (copyright should subsist for only twenty years). Spain's shift in 1987 from life plus eighty to life plus sixty demonstrates that reduction in copyright periods is actually possible. What is required are transitional provisions to insure that rights in existing works are not diminished.

335. A decision to retain the life + 50 term and not to extend it would hardly send a signal to innovators and creators that their creative efforts are not appreciated by their own government and society.

336. Data from the World Intellectual Property Organization (WIPO) reveal that an overwhelming majority of countries fix the general length of protection at life plus fifty years. *See* Alison Butler, *The Trade-Related Aspects of Intellectual Property Rights: What Is At Stake?*, Fed. Reserve Bank of St. Louis Rev., Nov.-Dec. 1990, at 34, 36 (life + 25--8 countries; life + 50--75 countries; life + 50+--9 countries); World Intellectual Property Organization, Existence, Scope and Form of Generally Internationally Accepted and Applied Standards/Norms for the Protection of Intellectual Property 24-25, GATT Doc. MTN.GNG/NG11/W/24/Rev.1 (Sept. 1988). Since 1990 the number of countries with life + 50 has, of course, increased as more have joined the Berne Convention. *See* M.J. Bowman & D.J. Harris, Multilateral Treaties: Index and Current Status 8-10 (1984); M.J. Bowman & D.J. Harris, Multilateral Treaties 148 (11th Supp. 1995) (current Berne count is 105).

Additionally, the number of countries with terms beyond life + 50 has increased as the European Union countries and some countries connected with the EU, whether by treaty of association or by application for membership, have enacted the life + 70 term.

The rhetoric of international leadership is peppered throughout the debate on the Copyright Term Extension Act. For example, Bruce A. Lehman, Assistant Secretary of Commerce and Commissioner of Patents and Trademarks, testified before a House subcommittee:

> Increasing the copyright term may help to reaffirm the role of the United States as a world leader in copyright protection. By taking the lead, and increasing protection in the United States, we encourage our trading partners to follow our lead and increase the term of protection which will benefit American copyright holders....

House Hearings, supra note 20, at 220.

In a similar vein, Marybeth Peters, the Register of Copyrights asked rhetorically: "[Given] that at some point in the future the standard will be life plus 70... [t]he question is at what point does the United States move to this term?" *Id.* at 197. It is not at all clear, though, how following the lead of the European Union by increasing the American term to match theirs constitutes leadership. And rather than accepting Peters's fatalistic and highly questionable assumption about future standards, the United States would havae been better served by using its international influence to reinforce the prevailing life plus fifty term. The EU Term Directive represents a proposal to the world of a new standard, and that proposal should have been rejected by the United States. Moreover, as previously noted, note 275 *supra*, the simplest way to remedy the alleged discrimination against American copyright owners in Europe and to achieve equal treatment of European and American authors was not by passage of the extension bill here but by having our trade representatives insist on the elimination of Europe's rule of the shorter term and the provision of full national treatment by the European countries.

Bibliography

BOOKS

Alchian, Armen A. & Allen, William R. *University Economics: Elements of Inquiry*, 3d ed., Belmont: Wadsworth Pub. Co., 1972.

Alford, William. *To Steal a Book Is an Elegant Offense: Intellectual Property Law in Chinese Civilization*, Stanford: Stanford University Press, 1995.

Areeda, Phillip & Kaplow, Louis. *Antitrust Analysis: Problems, Text, Cases*, 4th ed., Boston: Little, Brown & Co., 1988.

Beck, Roger L. *Comment: Does Competitive Dissipation Require a Short Patent Life?*, in *Research in Law & Economics*, vol. 8, eds. John Palmer & Richard O. Zerbe, Jr. Greenwich: JAI Press, Inc., 1986.

Becker, Lawrence C. *Property Rights: Philosophic Foundations*, Boston: Routledge, 1977.

Besen, Stanley M. *New Technologies and Intellectual Property: An Economic Analysis*, Santa Monica: Rand Corporation, 1987.

Bentham, Jeremy. *Rationale of Reward*, London: John & H.L. Hunt, 1825.

Bettig, Ronald V. *Copyrighting Culture: The Political Economy of Intellectual Property*, Boulder: Westview Press, 1996.

Birrell, Augustine. *Seven Lectures on the Law and History of Copyright in Books*, London: Cassell & Co., 1899.

Bowman, M.J. & Harris, D.J. *Multilateral Treaties: Index and Current Status*, London: Butterworths, 1984.

Bowman, M.J. & Harris, D.J. *Multilateral Treaties: Index and Current Status*, 11th Supp., London: Butterworths, 1995.

Boyle, James. *Shamans, Software and Spleens*, Cambridge: Harvard University Press, 1997.

246

Braunstein, Yale M., et al. *Economics of Property Rights as Applied to Computer Software and Data Bases*, Rev. ed., New York: New York University, 1977.

Breivik, Gunnar. *Cooperation Against Doping?*, in *Rethinking College Athletics*, eds. Judith Andre & David N. James, Philadelphia: Temple University Press, 1991.

Brennan, Timothy J. *Taxing Home Audio Taping*, Washington: Department of Justice, 1986.

Brewer, John & Staves, Susan. *Introduction*, in *Early Modern Conceptions of Property*, eds. John Brewer & Susan Staves, New York: Routledge, 1996.

Browder, Olin L., Jr., et al. *Basic Property Law*, St. Paul: West Pub. Co., 1966.

Brown, Ralph S. & Denicola, Robert C. *Cases on Copyright, Unfair Competition, and Other Topics Bearing on the Protection of Literary, Musical and Artistic Works*, 7th ed., Westbury: Foundation Press, 1998.

Bugbee, Bruce W. *Genesis of American Patent and Copyright Law*, Washington: Public Affairs Press, 1967.

Cahn, Edmund N. *The Moral Decision: Right and Wrong in the Light of American Law*, Bloomington: Indiana University Press, 1955.

Callan, Benedicte. *Pirates on the High Seas: The United States and Global Intellectual Property Rights*, New York: Council on Foreign Relations, 1998.

Cheung, Steven N.S. *Property Rights and Invention*, in *Research in Law and Economics*, vol. 8, eds. John Palmer & Richard O. Zerbe, Jr., Greenwich: JAI Press, Inc., 1986.

Chin, Judith C. & Grossman, Gene M. *Intellectual Property Rights and North-South Trade*, Cambridge: National Bureau of Economic Research, 1988.

Clark, Bates John, *Essentials of Economic Theory*, New York: The Macmillan Co., 1927.

Cooter, Robert & Ulen, Thomas. *Law and Economics*, Glenview, Illinois: Scott, Foresman, 1988.

Copyright Office. *Copyright Enactments*, Bull. No. 3, 1973.

Cornish, W.R. *Intellectual Property*, in *13 Yearbook Eur. L.*, Oxford: Clarendon Press & New York: Oxford University Press, 1993.

Cowen, Tyler. *In Praise of Commercial Culture*, Cambridge: Harvard University Press, 1998.

Dam, Kenneth W. *Intellectual Property in an Age of Software and Biotechnology*, Chicago: Law School, University of Chicago, 1995.

Dietz, Adolf. *Copyright Law in the European Community*, Alpen aan den Rijn: Sijthoff & Nordhoff [International Publishers], 1978.

Drahos, Peter. *Decentering Communication: The Dark Side of Intellectual Property*, in *Freedom of Communication*, eds. Tom Campbell & Wojciech Sadurski, Brookfield: Dartmouth, 1994.

Drahos, Peter. *A Philosophy of Intellectual Property*, Brookfield: Dartmouth, 1996.

Economic Council of Canada. *Report on Intellectual and Industrial Property*, Ottawa: Information Canada, 1971.

Elliot, Jonathan, ed. *Debates on the Adoption of the Federal Constitution*, vol. 5, Charlottesville: Michie Co., 1974.

Garnett, Kevin et al. *Copinger and Skone James on Copyright*, 13th ed. Supp., London: Sweet & Maxwell, 1994.

Gelatt, Roland. *The Fabulous Phonograph: From Edison to Stereo*, Rev. ed., New York: Appleton-Century, 1965.

Gendreau, Ysolde. *An Intellectual Property Renaissance in European Community Law*, in *International Trade and Intellectual Property: The Search for a Balanced System*, eds. George R. Stewart, et al., Boulder: Westview Press, 1994.

Goldstein, Paul. *Copyright's Highway: From Gutenberg to the Celestial Jukebox*, New York: Hill & Wang, 1994.

Goldstein, Paul. *Copyright Principles, Law & Practice*, vol. 1, New York: Little, Brown & Co., 1989.

Goodman, Dena. *Epistolary Property: Michel de Servan and the Plight of Letters on the Eve of the French Revolution*, in *Early Modern Conceptions of Property*, eds. John Brewer & Susan Staves, New York: Routledge, 1995.

248

Green, Donald P. & Shapiro, Ian. *Pathologies of Rational Choice Theory: A Critique of Applications in Political Science*, New Haven: Yale University Press, 1994.

Grunebaum, James O. *Private Ownership*, New York: Routledge & Kegan Paul, 1987.

Guinan, James J. *Duration of Copyright*, General Revision of the Copyright Law Study No. 3, Washington: Copyright Office, 1957.

Halpern, Sheldon, W., et al. *Copyright: Cases and Materials*, St. Paul: West Pub. Co., 1992.

Hardin, Russell. *Collective Action*, Baltimore: John Hopkins University Press, 1982.

Hartwick, John M. *Aspects of the Economics of Book Publishing*, Kingston, Ontario: Institute for Economic Research, Queen's University, 1984.

Hindley, B.V. *The Economic Theory of Patents, Copyrights, and Registered Industrial Designs*, Ottawa: Economic Council of Canada, 1971.

Hirschman, Albert O. *Shifting Involvements: Private Interest and Public Action*, Princeton: Princeton University Press, 1982.

Horn, Delton T. *DAT: The Complete Guide to Digital Audio Tape*, Blue Ridge Summit, PA: TAB Books, 1991.

Jefferson, Thomas. *The Complete Jefferson*, ed. Saul K. Padover, New York: Duell, Sloan & Pierce, 1943.

Jewkes, John, et al. *The Sources of Invention*, New York: St. Martin's Press, 1959.

Jussawalla, Meheroo. *The Economics of Intellectual Property in a World Without Frontiers*, Westport: Greenwood Publishing Group, Inc., 1992.

Kant, Immanuel. *Of the Injustice of Counterfeiting Books*, in *Essays and Treatises on Moral, Political, and Various Philosophical Subjects*, vol. 1, London: William Richardson, 1798.

Kaplan, Benjamin. *An Unhurried View of Copyright*, New York: Columbia University Press, 1967.

Kasdan, John. *The Economics of Copyright with Applications to Licensing*, New York: Center for Law & Economic Studies, Columbia University, 1986.

Kedourie, Elie. *Engel and Marx: Introductory Lectures*, Cambridge: Blackwell, 1995.

Keeton, W. Page, et al. *Prosser and Keeton on the Law of Torts*, 5th ed., St. Paul: West Pub. Co., 1984.

Kendall, Willmoore. *John Locke and the Doctrine of Majority-Rule*, Champlain: University of Illinois Press, 1941.

Keyes, A.A. & Brunet, C. *Copyright in Canada: Proposals for a Revision of the Law*, Hull, Quebec: Consumer and Corporate Affairs Canada, 1977.

Kohn, Meir G. *Money, Banking, and Financial Markets*, 2d ed., Chicago: Dryden Press, 1993.

Krasilovsky, M. William & Shemel, Sidney. *This Business of Music*, 7th ed., New York: Billboard Books, 1995.

Ladas, Stephen P. *The International Protection of Literary and Artistic Property*, New York: Macmillan, 1938.

Laddie, Hugh, et al. *The Modern Law of Copyright and Designs*, vol. 1, 2d ed., London: Butterworths, 1995.

Lane, Robert E. *The Market Experience*, Cambridge & New York: Cambridge University Press, 1991.

Lasok, Dominik & Lasok, K.P.E. *Law and Institutions of the European Union*, 6th ed., London: Butterworths, 1994.

Laver, Michael. *The Politics of Private Desires*, New York: Penguin, 1981.

Levin, Richard C., et al. *Appropriating the Returns from Industrial Research and Development*, in *Brookings Papers on Economic Activity*, vol. 3, eds. William C. Brainard & George L. Perry, Washington: Brookings Institution, 1987.

Liebowitz, S.J. *Copyright Law, Photocopying, and Price Discrimination*, in *Research in Law and Economics*, vol. 8, eds. John Palmer & Richard O. Zerbe, Jr. Greenwich: JAI Press, 1986.

Locke, John. *The Second Treatise of Civil Government and a Letter Concerning Toleration*, ed. J.W. Gough, Oxford: B. Blackwell, 1948.

250

Macaulay, Thomas Babington. *Miscellanies*, vol. 1, Boston & New York: Houghton Mifflin, 1901.

Macaulay, Thomas Babington. *Speeches, Parliamentary and Miscellaneous*, London: H. Vizetelly; Clarke, Beenton & Co., 1853.

Machlup, Fritz. *Some Economic Aspects of the United States Patent System*, in Ad Hoc Committee on the Role of Patents in Research, National Research Council, *The Role of Patents in Research: Proceedings of a Symposium of the National Academy of Sciences*, Washington: National Academy of Sciences, 1962.

Machlup, Fritz. *An Economic Review of the Patent System*, Study No. 15 for the Subcomm. on Patents, Trademarks, and Copyrights of the Senate Comm. on the Judiciary, 85th Cong., 2d Sess., 1958.

Mackaay, Ejan. *The Economics of Emergent Property Rights on the Internet*, in *The Future of Copyright in a Digital Environment*, ed. P. Bernt Hugenholtz, The Hague & Boston: Kluwer Law International, 1996.

McConnell, Campbell R. & Brue, Stanley L. *Economics: Principles, Problems, and Policies*, 12th ed., New York: McGraw-Hill, 1993.

Mankiw, N. Gregory. *Macroeconomics*, New York: Worth Publishers, 1992.

Maskus, Keith E. *Intellectual Property*, in *Completing the Uruguay Round: A Results-Oriented Approach to the GATT Trade Negotiations*, ed. Jeffrey J. Schott, Washington: Institute for International Economics, 1990.

Mill, John Stuart. *Principles of Political Economy*, ed. Sir William Ashley, London & New York: Longmans, Green, and Co., 1909.

Moon, J. Donald. *Constructing Community: Moral Pluralism and Tragic Conflicts*, Princeton: Princeton University Press, 1993.

Morgan, Charles. *The House of Macmillan (1843-1943)*, New York: The Macmillan Co., 1944.
Munzer, Stephen R. *A Theory of Property*, New York: Cambridge University Press, 1990.

National Research Council, Ad Hoc Committee on the Role of Patents in Research. *The Committee Report*, in *The Role of Patents in Research*, Washington: National Academy of Sciences, 1962.

Nimmer, Melville B. & Nimmer, David. *Nimmer on Copyright*, Albany: M. Bender, 1995.

Nordhaus, William D. *Invention, Growth, and Welfare: A Theoretical Treatment of Technological Change*, Cambridge, M.I.T. Press, 1969.

Nozick, Robert. *Anarchy, State, and Utopia*, New York: Basic Books, 1974.

Olson, Mancur. *The Logic of Collective Action*, Cambridge: Harvard University Press, 1971.

Olson, Mancur. *The Rise and Decline of Nations*, New Haven: Yale University Press, 1982.

Palmer, John P. *Copyright and Computer Software*, in *Research in Law and Economics*, vol. 8, eds. John Palmer & Richard O. Zerbe, Jr. Greenwich: JAI Press, 1986.

Patterson, Lymon R. *Copyright and the Public Interest*, in *Copyright: Current Viewpoints on History, Laws, Legislation*, eds. Allen Kent & Harold Lancour, New York: Bowker, 1972.

Penner, J.E. *The Idea of Property in Law*, Oxford: Clarendon Press & New York: Oxford University Press, 1997.

Penrose, Edith T. *The Economics of the International Patent System*, Baltimore: Johns Hopkins Press, 1951.

Plant, Arnold. *The New Commerce in Ideas and Intellectual Property*, London: University of London, Athlone Press, 1953.

Posner, Richard A. *Economic Analysis of Law*, 5th ed., New York: Aspen Law & Business, 1998.

Posner, Richard A. *Law and Literature: A Misunderstood Relation*, Cambridge: Harvard University Press, 1988.

Price, Monroe E. *Resuscitating a Collaboration with Melville Nimmer: Moral Rights and Beyond*, Occasional Paper #3 in Intellectual Property, New York: Benjamin N. Cardozo School of Law, 1998.

Radin, Margaret J. *Contested Commodities*, Cambridge: Harvard University Press, 1996.

Rand, Ayn. *Patents and Copyrights*, in *Capitalism and the Unknown Ideal*, ed. Ayn Rand, New York: New American Library, 1966.

Rawls, John. *A Theory of Justice*, Cambridge: Belknap Press of Harvard University Press, 1971.

Recording Industry Association of America. *Rewind, Fast Forward*, 1995 Annual Report.

Reeve, Andrew. *Property*, Atlantic Highlands, N.J.: Humanities Press International, 1986.

Ricketson, Sam. *The Berne Convention for the Protection of Literary and Artistic Works: 1886-1986*, London: Centre for Commercial Law Studies, Queen Mary College; Kluwer, 1987.

Ringer, Barbara. *Renewal of Copyright*, General Revision of the Copyright Law Study No. 31, Washington: Copyright Office, 1960.

Robinson, Joan. *The Accumulation of Capital*, London: Macmillan, 1958.

Roemer, John E. *Theories of Distributive Justice*, Cambridge: Harvard University Press, 1996.

Rose, Carol M. *Property and Persuasion: Essays on the History, Theory and Rhetoric of Ownership*, Boulder: Westview Press, 1994.

Royal Commission on Patents, Copyright, Trade Marks and Industrial Design (Canada). *Report on Copyright*, Ottawa: E. Cloutier, 1957.

Samuelson, Paul A. & Nordhaus, William D. *Economics*, 16th ed., New York: McGraw-Hill, 1997.
Saunders, David. *Authorship and Copyright*, New York: Routledge, 1992.

Scherer, F.M. & Ross, David. *Industrial Market Structure and Economic Performance*, 3d ed., Boston: Houghton Mifflin, 1990.

Schmidtz, David. *The Institution of Property*, in *Property Rights*, eds. Ellen F. Paul, et al., Cambridge & New York: Cambridge University Press, 1994.

Schrader, Dorothy. *Proposed U.S. Copyright Term Extension*, Washington: Congressional Research Service, 1995.

Sherwood, Robert M. *Intellectual Property and Economic Development*, Boulder: Westview Press, 1990.

Simmons, A. John. *The Lockean Theory of Rights*, Princeton: Princeton University Press, 1992.

Simmons, A. John. *Original-Acquisition Justifications of Private Property*, in *Property Rights*, eds. Ellen Frankel Paul, et al., Cambridge & New York: Cambridge University Press, 1994.

Skone James, E.P. et al. *Copinger and Skone James on Copyright*, 13th ed., London: Sweet & Maxwell, 1991.

Smith, Douglas A. *Collective Administration of Copyright: An Economic Analysis*, in *Research in Law & Economics*, vol. 8, eds. John Palmer & Richard O. Zerbe, Jr., Greenwich: JAI Press, Inc., 1986.

Sreenivasan, Gopal. *The Limits of Lockean Rights in Property*, New York: Oxford University Press, 1995.

Steiner, Hillel. *An Essay on Rights*, Cambridge: Blackwell, 1994.

Stewart, Stephen. *International Copyright and Neighboring Rights*, 2d ed., Boston: Butterworths, 1989.

Stewart, Susan. *Crimes of Writing: Problems in the Containment of Representation*, New York: Oxford University Press, 1991.

Strowel, Alain. *Droit d'auteur and Copyright: Between History and Nature*, in *Of Authors and Origins*, eds. Brad Sherman & Alain Strowel, Oxford: Clarendon Press & New York: Oxford University Press, 1994.

Swedberg, Richard. *Economics and Sociology: Redefining Their Boundaries: Conversations with Economists and Sociologists*, Princeton: Princeton University Press, 1990.

Thomas, Denis. *Copyright and the Creative Artist*, London: Institute of Economic Affairs, 1967.

Tribe, Laurence H. *American Constitutional Law*, 2d ed., Mineola: Foundation Press, 1988.

UNESCO. *Copyright Laws and Treaties of the World*, Paris: UNESCO & Washington: Bureau of National Affairs, 1956-.

Varian, Hal R. *Intermediate Microeconomics*, 2d ed., New York: W.W. Norton, 1990.

254

Varmer, Borge. *Study No. 13: Works Made for Hire and on Commission*, in *Studies on Copyright*, ed. Copyright Society of the U.S.A., South Hackensack: F.B. Rothman, 1963.

Viscusi, W. Kip, et al. *Economics of Regulation and Antitrust*, 2d ed., Cambridge: M.I.T. Press, 1995.

Von Mises, Ludwig, *Human Action: A Treatise on Economics*, New Haven: Yale University Press, 1949.

Waldron, Jeremy. *The Right to Private Property*, New York: Oxford University Press, 1988.

Watkinson, John. *The Art of Digital Audio*, 2d ed., Boston: Focal Press, 1994.

Wilson, James Q. *The Politics of Regulation*, in *The Politics of Regulation*, ed. James Q. Wilson, New York: Basic Books, 1980.

Woram, John M. *Sound Recording Handbook*, Indianapolis: Howard W. Sams & Co., 1989.

ARTICLES

Adams, John N. & Endenborough, Michael. *The Duration of Copyright in the United Kingdom after the 1995 Regulations*, 11 Eur. Intell. Prop. Rev. 590, 1996.

Adelstein, Richard P. & Peretz, Steven I. *The Competition of Technologies in Markets for Ideas: Copyright and Fair Use in Evolutionary Perspective*, 5 Int'l Rev. L. & Econ. 209, 1985.

Andrews, Edmund L. *Mark-Devoted Germans Gradually Come to Terms with the Euro*, Int'l Herald Tribune, June 22, 1998, at 13.

Aoki, Keith. *(Intellectual) Property and Sovereignty: Notes Toward a Cultural Geography of Authorship*, 48 Stan. L. Rev. 1293, 1996.

Barlow, John P. *The Economy of Ideas: A Framework for Rethinking Patents and Copyrights in the Digital Age (Everything You Know about Intellectual Property is Wrong)*, Wired, March 1994, at 84.

Barnett, Stephen R. & Karjala, Dennis S. *Copyrighted From Now Till Practically Forever*, Washington Post, July 14, 1995, at A21.

Barry, Brian. *You Have To Be Crazy To Believe It*, Times Literary Supplement, Oct. 25, 1996, at 28.

Becker Lawrence C. *Deserving to Own Intellectual Property*, 68 Chi.-Kent L. Rev. 609, 1993.

Bender, Thomas & Sampliner, David. *Poets, Pirates, and the Creation of American Literature*, 29 Int'l Law & Politics 255, 1996-97.

Benko, Robert P. *Intellectual Property Rights and the Uruguay Round*, World Economy, June 1988, at 217.

Blumenthal, Ralph. *A Rights Movement With Song at Its Heart*, N.Y. Times, Feb. 23, 1995, at C13.

Bouckaert, Boudewijn. *What Is Property?*, 13 Harv. J.L. & Pub. Pol'y 775, 1990.

Boyle, James. *A Sense of Belonging*, Times Literary Supplement, July 4, 1997, at 3.

256

Bradshaw, David. *The EC Copyright Directive: Its Main Highlights and Some of its Ramifications for Businesses in the UK Entertainment Industry*, 5 Ent. L. Rev. 171, 1995.

Brennan, Timothy J. *An Economic Look at Taxing Home Audio Taping*, 32 J. Broadcasting & Electronic Media 89, 1988.

Breyer, Stephen. *Copyright: A Rejoinder*, 20 UCLA L. Rev. 75, 1972.

Breyer, Stephen. *The Uneasy Case For Copyright: A Study Of Copyright In Books, Photocopies, And Computer Programs*, 84 Harv. L. Rev. 281, 1970.

Brown, Ralph S. *Eligibility for Copyright Protection: A Search for Principled Standards*, 70 Minn. L. Rev. 579, 1985.

Brown, Jr., Ralph S. *Unification: a Cheerful Requiem for Common Law Copyright*, 24 UCLA L. Rev. 1070, 1977.

Brownlee, Lisa M. *Recent Changes in the Duration of Copyright in the United States and European Union: Procedure and Policy*, 6 Fordham Intell. Prop., Media & Ent. L.J. 579, 1996.

Bryce, Shauna C. *Recent Developments: Life Plus Seventy: The Extension of Copyright Terms in the European Union and Proposed Legislation in the United States*, 37 Harv. Int'l L.J. 525, 1996.

Butler, Alison. *The Trade-Related Aspects of Intellectual Property Rights: What Is At Stake?*, Fed. Reserve Bank of St. Louis Rev., Nov.-Dec. 1990, at 34.

Butler, Henry N. & Macey, Jonathan R. *Health Care Reform: Perspectives From The Economic Theory of Regulation and the Economic Theory of Statutory Interpretation*, 79 Cornell L. Rev. 1434, 1994.

Calabresi, Guido & A. Melamed, Douglas. *Property Rules, Liability Rules, and Inalienability: One View of the Cathedral*, 85 Harv. L. Rev. 1089, 1972.

Cargill, Oscar & Moran, Patrick A. *Copyright Duration v. The Constitution*, 17 Wayne L. Rev. 917, 1971.

Chafee, Jr., Zechariah. *Reflections on the Law of Copyright: I*, 45 Colum. L. Rev. 503, 1945.

Chafee, Jr., Zechariah. *Reflections on the Law of Copyright: II*, 45 Colum. L. Rev. 719, 1945.

Child, James W. *The Moral Foundations of Intangible Property*, 73 The Monist 578, 1990.

Clarification Sought on EU Directive on Copyright Term, J. Proprietary Rts., Dec. 1995, at 33.

Cohen, Julie E. *Reverse Engineering and the Rise of Electronic Vigilantism: Intellectual Property Implications of "Lock-Out" Programs*, 68 S. Cal. L. Rev. 1091, 1995.

Cohen, Saul. *Duration*, 24 UCLA L. Rev. 1180, 1977.

Comment. *Photocopying and Fair Use: An Examination of the Economic Factor in Fair Use*, 26 Emory L.J. 849, 1977.

Cornish, W.R. *Authors in Law*, 58 Mod. L. Rev. 1, 1995.

Cotter, Thomas F. *Pragmatism, Economics and the Droit Moral*, 76 N.C. L. Rev. 1, 1997.

Croskery, Patrick. *Institutional Utilitarianism and Intellectual Property*, 68 Chi.-Kent L. Rev. 631, 1993.

Curtis, Frank. *Protecting Authors in Copyright Transfers: Revision Bill Sec. 203 and the Alternatives*, 72 Colum. L. Rev. 799, 1972.

Debates in British House of Commons on Extension of Copyright Term, 43 J. Copyright Soc'y of USA 198, 1995.

Dam, Kenneth W. *Some Economic Considerations in the Intellectual Property Protection of Software*, 24 J. Leg. Stud. 321, 1995.

Davis, Otto A. & Whinston, Andrew B. *On the Distinction Between Public and Private Goods*, 57 Am. Econ. Rev. 360, 1967.

Dawson, N. *Copyright in the European Union--Plundering the Public Domain*, 45 Northern Ireland L.Q. 193, 1994.

Dawson, John P. *The Self-Serving Intermeddler*, 87 Harv. L. Rev. 1409, 1974.

Demsetz, Harold. *Information and Efficiency: Another Viewpoint*, 12 J. Law & Econ. 1, 1969.

Disputed Harding Love Letters Will Be Locked Up Until 2014, N.Y. Times, Dec. 30, 1971, at 1.

258

Drake, Ervin. *Perpetuating Aid To The Arts*, Billboard, April 4, 1982, at 20.

Dreyfuss Cooper, Rochelle. *A Wiseguy's Approach to Information Products: Muscling Copyright and Patent into a Unitary Theory of Intellectual Property*, 1992 Sup. Ct. Rev. 195.

Dreyfuss, Cooper Rochelle. *The Creative Employee and the Copyright Act of 1976*, 54 U. Chi. L. Rev. 590, 1987.

Dworkin, Gerald. *Authorship of Films and the European Commission Proposals for Harmonising the Term of Copyright*, 5 Eur. Intell. Prop. Rev. 151, 1993.

Easterbrook, Frank H. *Intellectual Property Is Still Property*, 13 Harv. J. L. & Pub. Pol'y 108, 1990.

Easterbrook, Frank H. *Foreword: The Court and the Economic System*, 98 Harv. L. Rev. 4, 1984.

Elhauge, Einer R. *Does Interest Group Theory Justify More Intrusive Judicial Review?*, 101 Yale L.J. 31, 1991.

Elwood, Phil. *Record Archives in Sorry Shape, Magazine Series Laments State of Historic Material*, San Francisco Examiner, July 18, 1997, at D6.

Epping, Jr., Jerome N. *Harmonizing The United States and European Community Copyright Terms: Needed Adjustment or Money for Nothing?*, 65 U. Cin. L. Rev. 183, 1996.

Evans, Luther H. *Copyright and the Public Interest*, 53 Bull. N.Y. Pub. Libr. 3, 1949.

Fialka, John J. *Songwriters' Heirs Mourn Copyright Loss*, Wall St. J., Oct. 30, 1997, at B1.

Finkelstein, Herman. *The Copyright Law--A Reappraisal*, 104 U. Pa. L. Rev. 1025, 1956.

Fisher, William W. III. *Reconstructing the Fair Use Doctrine*, 101 Harv. L. Rev. 1659, 1988.

Fraser, Caroline. *Mrs. Eddy Builds Her Empire*, N.Y. Rev. Books, July 11, 1996, at 53.

Garrow, David. *Stifling the Work of Dr. Martin Luther King*, N.Y. Post, Jan. 29, 1997, at 23.

Geller, Paul Edward. *New Dynamics in International Copyright*, 16 Colum.-VLA J.L. & Arts 461, 1992.

Gendreau, Ysolde. *Copyright Harmonisation in the European Union and in North America*, 10 Eur. Intell. Prop. Rev. 488, 1995.

Gerstenblith, Patty. *Architect as Artist: Artists' Rights and Historic Preservation*, 12 Cardozo Arts & Ent. L.J. 431, 1994.

Gilbert, Richard & Shapiro, Carl. *Optimal Patent Length and Breadth*, 21 RAND J. Econ. 106, 1990.

Ginsburg, Jane C. *Reforms and Innovations Regarding Authors' and Performers' Rights in France: Commentary on the Law of July 3, 1985*, 10 Colum.-VLA J.L. & Arts 83, 1985.

Gold, Sylviane. *Theater: The Beckett Brouhaha*, Wall St. J., Dec. 28, 1984, at A10.

Goldstein, Paul. *Copyright and Its Substitutes*, 1997 Wis. L. Rev. 865.

Goldstein, Paul. *The Competitive Mandate: From Sears to Lear*, 59 Calif. L. Rev. 873, 1971.

Gordon, Wendy J. & Postbrief, Sam. *On Commodifying Intangibles*, 10 Yale J.L. & Human. 135, 1998.

Gordon, Wendy J. *A Property Right in Self-Expression: Equality and Individualism in the Natural Law of Intellectual Property*, 102 Yale L. J. 1533, 1993.

Gordon, Wendy J. *Assertive Modesty: An Economics of Intangibles*, 94 Colum. L. Rev. 2579, 1994.

Gordon, Wendy J. *Asymmetric Market Failure and Prisoner's Dilemma in Intellectual Property*, 17 U. Dayton L. Rev. 853, 1992.
Gordon, Wendy J. *On Owning Information: Intellectual Property and the Restitutionary Impulse*, 78 Va. L. Rev. 149, 1992.

Gorman, Robert A. *Intellectual Property: The Rights of Faculty as Creators and Users*, Academe, May-June 1998, at 14.

260

Gorman, Robert A. *Comments on a Manifesto Concerning the Legal Protection of Computer Programs*, 5 Alb. L.J. Sci. & Tech. 277, 1996.

Graubart, Jeffrey L. *Music Industry's Rights Battles Not Over*, Billboard, Nov. 4, 1995, at 8.

Grossberg, David. *Extending Copyright Term Isn't Enough*, Billboard, Oct. 12, 1996, at 10.

Gumerman, Amy. *Unfair Use: Copyright Decision Cramps Writers' Style*, Wall St. J., April 10, 1990, at A22.

Haden-Guest, Anthony. *Picasso Pic Has Heirs Seeing Red!*, The New Yorker, Aug. 21 & 28, 1995, at 53.

Hakkio, Craig S. *The U.S. Current Account: The Other Deficit*, Federal Reserve Bank of Kansas City Economic Review, Third Quarter 1995, at 11.

Hamilton, Marci A. *Copyright Duration Extension and the Dark Heart of Copyright*, 14 Cardozo Arts & Ent. L.J. 655, 1996.

Hansmann, Henry & Santilli, Marina. *Authors' and Artists' Moral Rights: A Comparative Legal and Economic Analysis*, 26 J. Legal Stud. 95, 1997.

Hattenstone, Simon. *Keep Open the Routes to the Past*, The Times, Nov. 5, 1991, at 14.

Hearing Held On Possible Extension Of Copyright Term, 46 Pat. Trademark & Copyright J. (BNA), at 467, Sept. 30, 1993.

Heller, Michael A. & Eisenberg, Rebecca S. *Can Patents Deter Innovation? The Anticommons in Biomedical Research*, 280 Science 698, 1998.

Hettinger, Edwin C. *Justifying Intellectual Property*, 18 Phil. & Pub. Aff. 31, 1989.

Heymann, Philip. *The Problem of Coordination: Bargaining and Rules*, 86 Harv. L. Rev. 797, 1973.

Hirshleifer, Jack. *The Private and Social Value of Information and the Reward to Inventive Activity*, 61 Am. Econ. Rev. 561, 1971.

Holland, Bill. *Music Biz Bills Await Action--WIPO Treaties' Ratification at Stake*, Billboard, Sept. 19, 1998, at 8.

Holland, Bill. *Upgrading Labels' Vaults No Easy Archival Task*, Billboard, July 19, 1997, at A1.

Holroyd, Michael & Jobson, Sandra. *Copyrights and Wrongs: D.H. Lawrence*, Times Literary Supplement, Sept. 3, 1982, at 943.

Holroyd, Michael. *How Do We Block The Drain? The Problems of Locating and Retaining Literary Papers*, Times Literary Supplement, June 23, 1995, at 24.

Hudon, Edward G. *The Copyright Period: Weighing Personal Against Public Interest*, 49 A.B.A.J. 759, 1963.

Hughes, Justin. *The Philosophy of Intellectual Property*, 77 Geo. L.J. 287, 1988.

Hurt, Robert M. & Schuchman, Robert M. *The Economic Rationale of Copyright*, 56 Am. Econ. Rev. 421, 1966.

Jaszi, Peter A. *Goodbye to All That--A Reluctant (and Perhaps Premature) Adieu to a Constitutionally-Grounded Discourse of Public Interest in Copyright Law*, 29 Vand. J. Transnat'l L. 595, 1996.

Jaszi, Peter. *Toward a Theory of Copyright: The Metamorphoses of "Authorship"* 1991 Duke L.J. 455.

Jaszi, Peter. *When Works Collide: Derivative Motion Pictures, Underlying Rights, and the Public Interest*, 28 UCLA L. Rev. 715, 1981.

Kaplan, Benjamin. *Impact of Proposed Copyright Legislation: The Businessman, The Government and the Public*, 8 Idea Conference No. 154, 1964.

Kaplan, David A. *The End of History?*, Newsweek, Dec. 25, 1989, at 80.

Kase, Francis J. *Copyright in Czechoslovakia--The New Copyright Statute of 1965*, 14 Bull. C. Soc'y 28, 1966.

Kastenmeier, Robert W. & Remington, Michael J. *The Semiconductor Chip Protection Act of 1984: A Swamp or Firm Ground?*, 70 Minn. L. Rev. 417, 1985.

Kinsley, Michael. *The Thinker*, The New Republic, August 14, 1995, at 36 (book review of *To Renew America* by Newt Gingrich).

Kitch, Edmund W. *The Nature and Function of the Patent System*, 20 J.L. & Econ. 265, 1978.

262

Klemperer, Paul. *How Broad Should the Scope of Patent Protection Be?*, 21 RAND J. Econ. 113, 1990.

Kozinski, Alex. *Mickey & Me*, 11 U. Miami Ent. & Sports L. Rev. 465, 1994.

Lacey, Linda J. *Of Bread and Roses and Copyrights*, 1989 Duke L.J. 1532.

Landes, William M. & Posner, Richard A. *An Economic Analysis of Copyright Law*, 18 J. Legal Stud. 325, 1989.

Landes, William M. *Copyright Protection of Letters, Diaries, and Other Unpublished Works: An Economic Approach*, 21 J. Legal Stud. 79, 1992.

Lange, David. *At Play in the Fields of the Word: Copyright and the Construction of Authorship in the Post-Literate Millennium*, L. & Contemp. Probs., Spring 1992, at 139.

Latham, Paul L. *Copyright Duration*, 50 A.B.A.J. 958 (1964).

Lavigne, Joseph A. *For Limited Times? Making Rich Kids Richer Via the Copyright Term Extension Act of 1996*, 73 U. Detroit L. Rev. 311, 1996.

LeFevre, Karen Burke. *The Tell-Tale "Heart": Determining "Fair" Use of Unpublished Texts*, L. & Contemp. Probs., Spring 1992, at 153.

Lehmann, Michael. *Property and Intellectual Property--Property Rights as Restrictions on Competition in Furtherance of Competition*, 20 Int'l Rev. Indus. Prop. & Copyright L. 1, 1989.

Lemley, Mark A. *Romantic Authorship and the Rhetoric of Property*, 75 Texas L. Rev. 873, 1997.
Lemley, Mark A. *The Economics of Improvement in Intellectual Property Law*, 75 Texas L. Rev. 989, 1997.

Leontief, Wassily. *On Assignment of Patent Rights on Inventions Made Under Government Research Contracts*, 77 Harv. L. Rev. 492, 1964.

Les Benedict, Michael. *Historians and the Continuing Controversy over Fair Use of Unpublished Manuscript Materials*, 91 Am. Hist. Rev. 859, 1986.

Leval, Pierre N. *Toward A Fair Use Standard*, 103 Harv. L. Rev. 1105, 1990.

Litman, Jessica. *Copyright As Myth*, 53 U. Pitt. L. Rev. 235, 1991.

Litman, Jessica. *Copyright, Compromise, and Legislative History*, 72 Cornell L. Rev. 857, 1987.

Litman, Jessica. *Copyright and Information Policy*, L. & Contemp. Probs., Spring 1992, at 185.

Litman, Jessica. *Copyright Noncompliance (Or Why We Can't "Just Say Yes" To Licensing*, 29 Int'l L. & Pol. 237, 1996-97.

Litman, Jessica. *Copyright Legislation and Technological Change*, 68 Or. L. Rev. 275, 1989.

Litman, Jessica. *The Exclusive Right To Read*, 13 Cardozo Arts & Ent. L. J. 29, 1994.

Lunney, Jr., Glynn S. *Reexamining Copyright's Incentives-Access Paradigm*, 49 Vand. L. Rev. 483, 1996.

Machlup, Fritz & Penrose, Edith. *The Patent Controversy in the Nineteenth Century*, 10 J. Econ. Hist. 1, 1950.

Mackaay, Ejan. *Economic Incentives in Markets for Information and Innovation*, 13 Harv. J.L. & Pub. Pol'y 867, 1990.

Maskus, Keith E. *Intellectual Property Rights and the Uruguay Round*, Federal Reserve Bank of Kansas City Economic Review, First Quarter 1993, at 11.

Masouye, Claude. *Les Prolongations de Guerre*, 3 Revue Internationale Du Droit D'Auteur (RIDA) 49 (1953) (Part I), 4 RIDA 80 (1954) (Part II), 9 RIDA 82 (1956) (Part III), 14 RIDA 109 (1957) (Part IV), 20 RIDA 59 (1958) (Part V), 1953-58.

McCain, Roger A. *Information as Property and as a Public Good: Perspectives from the Economic Theory of Property Rights*, 58 Libr. Q. 265, 1988.

McGill, Meredith L. *The Matter of the Text: Commerce, Print Culture, and the Authority of the State in American Copyright Law*, 9 Am. Literary Hist. 21, 1997.

McKuin, Joel L. *Home Audio Taping of Copyrighted Works and The Audio Home Recording Act of 1992: A Critical Analysis*, 16 Hastings Comm. & Ent. L.J. 311, 1994.

Meiners, Roger E. & Staaf, Robert J. *Patents, Copyrights, and Trademarks: Property or Monopoly?*, 13 Harv. J.L. & Pub. Pol'y 911, 1990.

Michelman, Frank. *Property, Utility, and Fairness: Comments on the Ethical Foundations of "Just Compensation" Law*, 80 Harv. L. Rev. 1165, 1967.

Miller, Arthur. *Extending Copyrights Preserves U.S. Culture*, Billboard, January 14, 1995, at 4, *reprinted in* 141 Cong. Rec. S3394 (daily ed.) March 2, 1995.

Mills, Mary L. *New Technology and the Limitations of Copyright Law: An Argument for Finding Alternatives to Copyright Legislation in an Era of Rapid Technological Change*, 65 Chi-Kent L. Rev. 307, 1989.

Moore, Adam D. *A Lockean Theory of Intellectual Property*, 21 Hamline L. Rev. 65, 1997.

Morrison, Richard. *New Rights for all the Wrong Reasons*, The Times, Feb. 18, 1995, at 5.

Mount, Ferdinand. *Soil Science*, Times Literary Supplement, March 7, 1997, at 13.

Nance, Dale A. *Foreword: Owning Ideas*, 13 Harv. J.L. & Pub. Pol'y 757, 1990.

Nash, Nathaniel C. *Europeans Agree on New Currency*, N.Y. Times, Dec. 16, 1995, at 1.

National Treatment Under Berne Is Subject Of House Panel Hearing, 46 Pat. Trademark & Copyright J. (BNA), at 116, June 3, 1993.

Netanel, Weinstock Neil. *Copyright and a Democratic Civil Society*, 106 Yale L.J. 283, 1996.

Newman, Jon O. *Copyright Law and the Protection of Privacy*, 12 Colum.-VLA J.L. & Arts 459, 1988.

Newman, Jon O. *Not The End of History: The Second Circuit Struggles With Fair Use*, 37 J. Copyright Soc'y 1, 1989.

Nimmer, David. *Nation, Duration, Violation, Harmonization: An International Copyright Proposal for the United States*, L. & Contemp. Probs., Spring 1992, at 211.

Nimmer, David. *U.S. Should Extend Copyright Terms*, Billboard, April 16, 1994, at 8.

Nimmer, Melville B. *Does Copyright Abridge the First Amendment Guarantees of Free Speech and Press?*, 17 UCLA L. Rev. 1180, 1970.

Niskanen, William A. *Why Our Democracy Doesn't Work*, The Public Interest, Summer 1994, at 88.

Nordemann, Wilhelm. *The Term of Protection for Works by U.S.-American Authors in Germany*, 44 J. Copyright Soc'y of USA 1, 1996.

Note. *Copyright Protection, Privacy Rights, and the Fair Use Doctrine: The Post-Salinger Decade Reconsidered*, 72 N.Y.U. L. Rev. 1376, 1997.

O'Hare, Michael. *Copyright and the Protection of Economic Rights*, 6 J. Cultural Econ. 33, 1982.

O'Hare, Michael. *Copyright: When Is Monopoly Efficient?*, 4 J. Pol'y Analysis & Mgmt. 407, 1985.

Olson, Thomas P. *The Iron Law of Consensus: Congressional Responses to Proposed Copyright Reforms Since the 1909 Act*, 36 J. Copyright Soc'y U.S.A. 109, 1989.

Paine, Lynn Sharp. *Trade Secrets and the Justification of Intellectual Property: A Comment on Hettinger*, 20 Phil. & Pub. Aff. 247, 1991.

Palmer, Tom G. *Artists Don't Deserve Special Rights*, Wall St. J., March 8, 1988, at 34.

Palmer, Tom G. *Intellectual Property: A Non-Posnerian Law and Economics Approach*, 12 Hamline L. Rev. 261, 1989.

Parrinder, Patrick. *The Dead Hand of European Copyright*, 15 Eur. Intell. Prop. Rev. 391, 1993.

Parrinder, Patrick. *Who Killed Clause 29?*, Times Literary Supplement, Feb. 9, 1996, at 16.

Passell, Peter. *Economic Scene: America's Trade Gap Is (1) a Disaster (2) a Sign of Success*, N.Y. Times, April 17, 1997, at D2.

Patently Outdated: Changes in the Way Drugs Are Invented Are Making Patents Unworkable, The Economist, July 18, 1987, at 17.

Patry, William F. *Copyright and the Legislative Process: A Personal Perspective*, 14 Cardozo Arts & Ent. L.J. 139, 1996.

Patry, William F. *The Copyright Term Extension Act of 1995: Or How Publishers Managed To Steal the Bread from Authors*, 14 Cardozo Arts & Ent. L.J. 661, 1996.

Patry, William. *The Failure of the American Copyright System: Protecting the Idle Rich*, 72 Notre Dame L. Rev. 907, 1997.

Patterson, L. Ray & Birch, Jr., Stanley F. *Copyright and Free Speech Rights*, 4 J. Intell. Prop. 1, 1996.

Patterson L. Ray. *Copyright and "The Exclusive Right" of Authors*, 1 J. Intell. Prop. L. 1, 1993.

Person, Jr., James E. *Plath's "Bell Jar" Firmly Sealed*, The Virginian-Pilot & The Ledger-Star, May 22, 1994, at C3.

Pethig, Rudiger. *Copyright and Copying Costs: A New Price-Theoretic Approach*, 144 J. Institutional & Theoretical Economics 462, 1988.

Phillips, Jeremy. *The Diminishing Domain*, 8 Eur. Intell. Prop. Rev. 429, 1996.

Plant, Arnold. *The Economic Aspects of Copyright in Books*, 1 Economica 167, (new series) 1934.

Posner, Richard A. *When Is Parody Fair Use?*, 21 J. Legal Stud. 67, 1992.

Puri, Kanwal. *The Term of Copyright Protection--Is It Too Long in the Wake of New Technologies?*, 12 Eur. Intell. Prop. Rev. 12, 1990.

Rapp, Richard T. & Rozek, Richard P. *Benefits and Costs of Intellectual Property Protection in Developing Countries*, 24 J. World Trade 75, 1990.

Reese, R. Anthony. *Reflections on the Intellectual Commons: Two Perspectives on Copyright Duration and Reversion*, 47 Stan. L. Rev. 707, 1995.

Reichman, J.H. *The Duration of Copyright and the Limits of Cultural Policy*, 14 Cardozo Arts & Ent. L. J. 625, 1996.

Reichman, J.H. *Universal Minimum Standards of Intellectual Property Protection Under the TRIPS Component of the WTO Agreement*, 25 Int'l Law. 345, 1995.

Ricketson, Sam. *The Copyright Term*, 23 Int'l Rev. Indus. Prop. & Copyright L. 753, 1992.

Rose, Lance. *The Emperor's Clothes Still Fit Just Fine Or, Copyright Is Dead. Long Live Copyright!*, Wired, Feb. 1995, at 103.

Ruping, Karl. *Copyright and an Integrated European Market: Conflicts with Free Movement of Goods, Competition Law, and National Discrimination*, 11 Temple Int'l & Comp. L.J. 1, 1997.

Samuelson, Paul. *The Pure Theory of Public Expenditure*, 36 Rev. of Econ. & Stat. 387, 1954.

Saperstein, Lanier. *Copyrights, Criminal Sanctions and Economic Rents: Applying the Rent Seeking Model to the Criminal Law Formulation Process*, J. Crim. L. & Criminology 1470, 1997.

Sarraute, Raymond. *Current Theory on the Moral Right of Authors and Artists Under French Law*, 16 Am. J. Comp. L. 465, 1968.

Schelling, Thomas. *On the Ecology of Micromotives*, The Public Interest, Fall 1971, at 61.

Scherer, F.M. *Nordhaus' Theory of Optimal Patent Life: A Geometric Reinterpretation*, 62 Am. Econ. Rev. 422, 1972.

Schlesinger, Jr., Arthur. *The Judges of History Rule*, Wall St. J., Oct. 26, 1989, at A16.
Schonning, Peter. *The New Copyright Act in Denmark*, 27 Int'l Rev. Indus. Prop. & Copyright L. 470, 1996.

Singer, Max. *The Vitality of Mythical Numbers*, The Public Interest, Spring 1971, at 3.

Smith, Douglas A. *Recent Proposals for Copyright Revision: An Evaluation*, 14 Canadian Pub. Pol'y 175, 1988.

Stallman, Richard. *Reevaluating Copyright: The Public Must Prevail*, 75 Or. L. Rev. 291, 1996.

Stolberg, Sheryl Gay. *U.S. Life Expectancy Hits New High*, N.Y. Times, Sept. 12, 1997, at A14.

Sterk, Stewart E. *Rhetoric and Reality in Copyright Law*, 94 Mich. L. Rev. 1197, 1996.

Sutherland, John. *The Great Copyright Disaster*, London Rev. of Books, Jan. 12, 1995, at 3.

Tai, Linda W. *Music Piracy in the Pacific Rim: Applying a Regional Approach Towards the Enforcement Problem of International Conventions*, 16 Loy. L.A. Ent. L.J. 159, 1995.

Thompson, Kristin. *Report of the Ad Hoc Committee of the Society for Cinema Studies, "Fair Usage Publication of Film Stills"*, Cinema Journal, Winter 1993, at 3.

Trickey, Mike. *Russia; 'Pirates' Profit Selling Cut-rate Movies, CDs*, The Ottawa Citizen, July 24, 1995, at A6.

Tufte, David. *Communications: Why Is the U.S. Current Account Deficit So Large?*, 63 S. Econ.J. 515, 1996.

Tyerman, Barry W. *The Economic Rationale for Copyright Protection for Published Books: A Reply to Professor Breyer*, 18 UCLA L. Rev. 1100, 1971.

Tyler, Tom R. *Compliance With Intellectual Property Laws: A Psychological Perspective*, 29 Int'l L. & Pol. 219, 1996-97.

Tyson, Laura D. *Trade Deficits Won't Ruin Us, N.Y.* Times, Nov. 24, 1997, at A23.

Vaver, David. *Some Agnostic Observations on Intellectual Property*, 6 Intell. Prop. J. 125, 1991.

Verstrynge, Jean-Francois. *The Spring 1993 Horace S. Manges Lecture--The European Commission's Direction on Copyright and Neighboring Rights: Toward the Regime of the Twenty-First Century*, 17 Colum.-VLA J.L. & Arts 187, 1993.

von Lewinski, Silke. *EC Proposal for a Council Directive Harmonizing the Term of Protection of Copyright and Certain Related Rights*, 23 Int'l Rev. Indus. Prop. & Copyright L. 785, 1992.

Waldron, Jeremy. *From Authors to Copiers: Individual Rights and Social Values in Intellectual Property*, 68 Chi.-Kent L. Rev. 841, 1993.

Wanat, Daniel E. *Fair Use and the 1992 Amendment to Section 107 of the 1976 Copyright Act: Its History and an Analysis of Its Effect*, 1 Vill. Sports & Ent. L.F. 47, 1994.

Justin Watts, *New Labour, Privatisation and Nurturing Talent*, 8 Ent. L. Rev. 279, 1997.

Weinreb, Lloyd L. *Copyright For Functional Expression*, 111 Harv. L. Rev. 1149, 1998.

Weinreb, Lloyd L. *Fair's Fair: A Comment on the Fair Use Doctrine*, 103 Harv. L. Rev. 1137, 1990.

Wilson, John S. *Time Remembered--Blues*, Jazz and Swing, N.Y. Times, Nov. 28, 1971, sec. 2, at 32.

Yen, Alfred C. *Restoring the Natural Law: Copyright as Labor and Possession*, 51 Ohio St. L.J. 517, 1990.

Yen, Alfred C. *The Interdisciplinary Future of Copyright Theory*, 10 Cardozo Arts & Entertainment L.J. 423, 1992.

Yen, Alfred C. *The Legacy of Feist: Consequences of the Weak Connection Between Copyright and the Economics of Public Goods*, 52 Ohio St. L.J. 1343, 1991.

Zeitlin, Steve. *Strangling Culture with a Copyright Law*, N.Y. Times, April 25, 1998, at A15.

MISCELLANEOUS

Agreement Between the German Reich and the United States of America, 27 Stat. 1021, Jan. 15, 1892.

American Law Institute. *Restatement of the Law Second, Contracts*, St Paul: American Law Institute Publishers, 1981.

American Law Institute. *Restatement of the Law Second, Torts*, Philadelphia: American Law Institute Publishers, 1977.

American Law Institute. *Restatement of the Law Third, Unfair Competition*, St. Paul: American Law Institute Pubishers, 1995.

Berne Convention for the Protection of Literary and Artistic Works (Paris Revision) 1971.

Comment of Copyright Law Professors on Copyright Office Term of Protection Study, Oct. 27, 1993.

Comments of the National Music Publishers' Association, Inc. (NMPA), *In the Matter of Duration of Copyright Term of Protection*, Docket No. RM 93-8, Copyright Office, September 22, 1993.

Copyright Law Revision, Report of the Register of Copyrights on the General Revision of the U.S. Copyright Law, 87th Cong., 1st Sess. (House Judiciary Comm. Print) 1961.

Copyright Law Revision, Part 2, Discussion and Comments on Report of the Register of Copyrights on the General Revision of the U.S. Copyright Law, 88th Cong., 1st Sess. (Comm. Print) 1963.

Council of Economic Advisors, *Economic Indicators Online via GPO Access*, May, 1997, Washington: U.S. G.P.O.

Explanation by the Netherlands Delegation of Vote on the Directive Harmonizing the Term of Protection of Copyright and Certain Related Rights, in Annex, Council of Ministers Press Release 93-173, Luxembourg, Oct. 29, 1993.

Fair Use and Unpublished Works: Joint Hearing on S. 2370 and H.R. 4263 Before the Subcomm. on Patents, Copyrights and Trademarks of the Senate Comm. on the Judiciary and the Subcomm. on Courts, Intellectual Property, and the Administration of Justice of the House Comm. on the Judiciary, 101st Cong., 2d Sess., 1990.

Ginsburg, Jane, *Surveying the Borders of Copyright*, Address at the WIPO Worldwide Symposium on the Future of Copyright and Neighboring Rights 5-9, June 1-3, 1994.

Hearings on S.1006, Copyright Law Revision--CATV, Before the Subcomm. on Patents, Trademarks, and Copyrights of the Senate Comm. on the Judiciary, 89th Cong., 2d Sess., 1966.

Hearings on H.R. 4347, H.R. 5680, H.R. 6831, H.R. 6835 Before Subcomm. No. 3 of the House Comm. on the Judiciary, 89th Cong., 1st Sess., pt. 3, 1965.

Hearings on H.R. 989 Before the Subcomm. on Courts and Intellectual Property of the House Judiciary Comm., 104th Cong., 1st Sess., 1996.

Home Recording of Copyrighted Works: Hearings on H.R. 4783, H.R. 4794, H.R. 4808, H.R. 5250, H.R. 5488, and H.R.5705 Before the Subcomm. on Courts, Civil Liberties, and the Administration of Justice of the House Comm. on the Judiciary, 97th Cong., 2d Sess., 1982.

International Monetary Fund. *Balance of Payments Statistics Yearbook*, pt. 1, 1966.

Joint Comments of the Coalition of Creators and Copyright Owners, *In the Matter of Duration of Copyright Term of Protection*, Docket No. RM 93-8, Copyright Office, September 22, 1993.

National Center for Health Statistics, Monthly Vital Statistics Report, Vol. 43, No. 13, October 23, 1995.

Prohibiting Piracy of Sound Recordings: Hearings on S. 646 & H.R. 6927 Before Subcomm. No. 3 of the House Comm. on the Judiciary, 92d Cong., 1st Sess., 1971.

Statement of Copyright and Intellectual Property Law Professors in Opposition to H.R. 604 and S. 505 "The Copyright Term Extension Act of 1997", June 16, 1997.

Statement of Sen. Orrin G. Hatch Before The U.S. Senate, The Introduction of the Copyright Term Extension Act Of 1995, March 1, 1995.

The Audio Home Recording Act of 1991, Hearing on S. 1623 Before the Subcomm. on Patents, Copyrights, and Trademarks of the Senate Judiciary Comm., 102nd Cong., 1st Sess., 1991.

The Copyright Term Extension Act of 1995: Hearing on S. 483 Before the Senate Judiciary Comm., 104th Cong., 1st Sess., 1997.

Treaties Establishing the European Communities, Luxembourg: Office for Official Publications of the European Communities, 1987.

Universal Copyright Convention (Paris Revision) 1971.

U.S. Congress, Office of Technology Assessment. *Copyright and Home Copying: Technology Challenges the Law*, 1989.

INDEX

transaction cost, 45, 59, 85, 197

U

UNESCO, Copyright Laws &
Treaties of the World, 92, 117

V

Viscusi, Wikip, 44, 240

W

Waldron, Jeremy, 24, 42, 102, 130
Wanat, Daniel I., 124
Weinreb, Lloyd, L., 27, 32, 33, 44,
46, 53, 112, 115, 120, 149, 150,
151, 157, 163, 221

West German Copyright Law of
1965, 89
Wheaton v. Peters, 149
White v. Samsung Electronics
America, Inc., 84
World Intellectual Property
Organization, 241
Wright v. Warner Books, Inc, 126

Y

Yen, Alfred C., 33, 54, 103, 143,
155, 160

Z

Zeitlin, Steve, 84, 122